BLACK
SHEEP

Other novels by Donna Scuvotti
Just Jonathan
Deadly Vendetta

BLACK SHEEP

DONNA SCUVOTTI

Copyrighted Material

Black Sheep

Copyright © 2025 by Donna Scuvotti.
All Rights Reserved.

No part of this publication may be reproduced, stored in a retrieval system or transmitted, in any form or by any means—electronic, mechanical, photocopying, recording, or otherwise—without prior written permission from the publisher, except for the inclusion of brief quotations in a review. For information about this title or to order other books and/or electronic media, contact the publisher:

Donna Scuvotti
www.donnascuvottiauthor.com
info@donnascuvottiauthor.com

ISBNs:
978-1-7371576-6-3 (Hardcover)
978-1-7371576-7-0 (Softcover)
978-1-7371576-8-7 (eBook)

Printed in the United States of America

Cover and Interior design: 1106 Design

To Julian and Maisie
My light. My love. My joy.

CONTENTS

ACKNOWLEDGMENTS	xi
PROLOGUE — Luke	xv
CHAPTER 1 — The Truth	1
CHAPTER 2 — The Change	14
CHAPTER 3 — The Birthday	20
CHAPTER 4 — The Affair	30
CHAPTER 5 — The Nest Egg	39
CHAPTER 6 — The Smile	45
CHAPTER 7 — The Contract	51
CHAPTER 8 — The Moment	60
CHAPTER 9 — The Gift	66
CHAPTER 10 — The Fight	74
CHAPTER 11 — The Aftermath	80
CHAPTER 12 — The Intervention	89

CHAPTER 13 — The Goodbye	94
CHAPTER 14 — The Miracle	100
CHAPTER 15 — The Stalker	111
CHAPTER 16 — The Acclimation	118
CHAPTER 17 — The Talk	127
CHAPTER 18 — The New Beginning	142
CHAPTER 19 — The Heartbreak	151
CHAPTER 20 — The Meltdown	162
CHAPTER 21 — The Bright Idea	166
CHAPTER 22 — The Wild Ride	173
CHAPTER 23 — The Near Miss	178
CHAPTER 24 — The Test	183
CHAPTER 25 — The Plan	197
CHAPTER 26 — The Friend	208
CHAPTER 27 — The Mayhem	221
CHAPTER 28 — The Therapy	228
CHAPTER 29 — The Decision	235
CHAPTER 30 — The Separation	240
CHAPTER 31 — The List	245
CHAPTER 32 — The Meeting	255
CHAPTER 33 — The Struggle	263
CHAPTER 34 — The Visit	268
CHAPTER 35 — The Shelter	277

CONTENTS

CHAPTER 36 — The Brush with Death	285
CHAPTER 37 — The Letter	298
CHAPTER 38 — The Accident	306
CHAPTER 39 — The Move	315
CHAPTER 40 — The Cabin	321
CHAPTER 41 — The Illusion	332
CHAPTER 42 — The Scream	338
CHAPTER 43 — The Forest	345
CHAPTER 44 — The Discovery	353
CHAPTER 45 — The Adventure	358
EPILOGUE	363
ABOUT THE AUTHOR	367
REQUEST FOR REVIEWS	369

ACKNOWLEDGMENTS

Writing has become a fulfilling passion for me. It allows my imagination to go places I can only imagine and often leads me down paths that even scare me at times. Writing *Black Sheep* has been a completely different experience for me because it's not my normal genre. Which leads me to ask the question, " Do I have a normal genre? And what does normal even mean?"

One thing I do know is I wouldn't want to embark on this amazing journey without some wonderful people in my corner.

First and foremost my husband of twenty-seven years, Tony. Being married to a book worm like myself, one would think he loves to read too. Nope. He doesn't so his support doesn't come from bouncing ideas off of, having him read my manuscript to see if it flows the way I want or if there are evident plot holes. His support comes in the form of his adoration for me and my craft. Always the first one to tell me how proud he is of me or that I'm amazing gives me the ambition to continue. Thanks for that. I love you and can't imagine doing life with anyone but you.

I have met some incredible authors in the Instagram writing community that have become more than just an invisible person behind a post. I am honored to call them my friends and their knowledge and support are immeasurable.

First and foremost, Diane Chattaway. What would I have done without you? You took your time, away from writing your own fabulous books, to read mine when it was in the raw. Having read my other two books, you knew and loved Luke already, which helped you immerse yourself into his life offering helpful and necessary critiques. Thank you from the bottom of my heart, my friend, for always being a text away.

There probably wouldn't be a *Black Sheep* if it wasn't for my British bestie, Helen Aitchison. It was because of your suggestion that Luke needed his own book, that I wrote this. You also took your valuable time to beta read and do a developmental edit for the first two-thirds of my manuscript. Your 'show, don't tell' suggestions made me dig deep and expand on what was already there. Thank you for sharing my heart.

To my other author friends, Susan Smith, Emersyn Park and Jo Delancey. Thank you for your input when Black Sheep was in its early stages. Your friendship is a joy to me.

My Instagram bookstagrammers are some of my biggest supporters. I'm also thrilled to call them friends now too. You know who you are, you wonderful humans! Thank you for reading, reviewing and posting about my books. I appreciate you more than you know. I couldn't do it without you.

Thanks Mom for reading and loving my story. You've always been an inspiration to me and your undying mother's love is like no other. Dad, I hope I've made you proud. I regret you passed before

ACKNOWLEDGMENTS

having read my books but I'm positive you're looking down from above with love in your heart.

My kids, Jason and Ali and grandchildren Julian and Maisie I love you all to Pluto and back.

I chose 1106 Design once again to bring my manuscript to life. Thanks Michele, Ronda, Frank and the gang for once again bringing your A-game. Your professionalism and expertise is the best around.

Last but most definitely not least, you guys, my readers. I could have never in my wildest dreams imagined I would have people that love what I put out. Your reviews, comments and letters make this all worthwhile. Now that my imagination has been woken up, there's no stopping me now so get ready for more adventures and jumping down rabbit holes in the future.

PROLOGUE

LUKE

Age is a funny thing. I'd been finding myself in a reflective mood more times than not lately. Sometimes it was great, but, other times, it stirred up memories I would have rather kept buried in the deep, dark recesses of my mind, where old phone numbers and passwords lived. Recently, while playing bingo and shootin' the shit at the local senior center, I was nonchalantly asked one naive, simple question that opened a floodgate of memories. I had worked years and endured countless hours of therapy to come to terms with some of these memories. Now, I was lost in a sea of emotions I wasn't prepared to deal with ever again.

"Luke, you seem like such an interesting man, with a colorful backstory. Would you care to elaborate?" my pal Blaine casually inquired. *"No,"* I wanted to scream from the rafters, as I stood stroking my beard, but, instead, I graciously declined, playing down the notion that I'd had anything but a colorful past. Unbeknownst to them, the damage had already been done, as a reel of my life started playing in my mind in slow motion, with no way to stop it.

Lately, I have also found myself a little bored—in kind of a melancholy mood. I wasn't accustomed to feeling this way, up until now. Age was catching up with me, making me move a little slower and think twice before I tackled the chores I had done just last week. I'd always heard that age is an issue of mind over matter: *If you don't mind, it doesn't matter.* But I was starting to mind, not prepared for all that it was bestowing upon me. Looking into the mirror these days, often left me with sadness. The eyes that stared back at me weren't my own—they belonged to someone much wiser and older. In my mind's eye, I was a young, vibrant soldier, ready to take on the world, but my body, sadly, has retired to a rocking chair. The wrinkles and scars that have earned their place on my body served as reminders of a life lived. But my time hasn't always been happy. Anything but, in fact.

I stood gazing out at the forest that outlined my ten acres of property in my own little peaceful corner of the world. The town of Mount Sierra, Oregon, had been home for more years than I could remember. I loved everything about this little paradise I called home, with its breathtaking views of the majestic mountains and the canopy of branches the forest offered. The air was clean as I took a deep breath, reaching down to pet my trusty right-hand golden retriever therapy dog, Ginger. I stood, realizing that the inevitable was knocking on my door. I wasn't ready. Would I ever be ready?

Through the years, I had built a good life for myself—a life I can look back on and be proud of. Proud of the husband I once was. Proud of kicking alcoholism to the curb once and for all. Proud of having served my country. Proud of my pure heart. Proud of my

PROLOGUE ... LUKE

relationship with my son Jonathan and his beautiful family. And now that the doors of hell had been opened, the shadows behind them made me realize I was proud of the obstacles in my childhood I had overcome, thanks to my best friend, my beloved golden retriever, Marmalade. My childhood still gnawed at my heart, leaving me misty and confused. Why did it have to be that way, and why was it? An explanation had never been offered, and, as a child, I was too frightened to ask for one. All I had were vivid memories that were hard to revisit but cathartic all the same.

Needing to bury my wretched memories once and for all, so I could live the rest of my life free of what has haunted me for decades, I decided to write them down, starting from when I was twelve and reflecting back throughout a lifetime of obstacles, heartache, and stone-cold determination. Revisiting the years in all their heart-crushing detail was something I needed to do to free myself of the evil that still haunted me—the evil that was my childhood.

CHAPTER 1

THE TRUTH
TWELVE YEARS OLD

The clouds were threatening—ominous and dark, mimicking my mood. The funk I was in was all-consuming, leaving me on the brink of the unthinkable. I really *did* want to live—but not like this, my days filled with constant ridicule and belittling. It had destroyed the small bits of self-worth I had once felt—on a good day, anyway. This was not one of those. In fact, I couldn't remember when the last time was that I'd had a good day, to be honest. These kinds of thoughts were typical when I was twelve.

This was all too much for a twelve-year-old to be consumed with. Wasn't childhood supposed to be filled with adventures, fun, and laughter? I was pretty sure I wasn't the norm. I rolled over in my bed, wrapping the down comforter around me and covering my head, imagining that this is what a coffin would feel like. It was dark and suffocating. I reached out to wrap my arms around Marmalade, my trusty sidekick golden retriever. Her fur was wet as my tears soaked her; she nudged me, offering a paw and warm lick across my mouth. Sometimes I thought that she was the only thing keeping me alive.

Maybe if I hadn't seen the darkness blowing my way, I could have begun to form a semblance of a plan—a plan to see the good again and stop wallowing in the self-pity that depleted me. It would have to be a well-thought-out plan, one that I would need help and support with. That was going to be a problem, though—a big problem because I was what you would call a loner, introvert, outcast. Not a great place to be or a great time to be me.

"Come on, Luke. It's time for school. You don't want to be late again just because you're lazy," my mom, Jane, yelled from the kitchen in a high-pitched screech. The tea kettle whistled simultaneously, competing for the loudest, most-irritating sound. She won. Was I imagining the hatred in her voice? I'd always read that a mother's love was unconditional, but I didn't feel like mine even *liked* me. Seriously—I'd felt like this for years. Most of my life, actually. My mom tolerated me, at best, and I'd had enough. I had wanted to ask her how she felt for years, but every time I opened my mouth, the words couldn't find their way out.

I knew better than to ignore her, so I shuffled into the kitchen. As I looked around, I was surrounded by the exact opposite of what I was feeling. It was painted in a bright, cheery yellow, with valances embroidered with sunflowers hanging over the windows that looked into the spacious backyard. Sunflowers were my mom's favorite flower, and, every chance she got to incorporate them into her surroundings, she did. In the middle of the room stood a big,

CHAPTER 1 ... THE TRUTH

round knotty-pine table with six chairs tucked in neatly around it. Sunflower placemats were sitting on the table in front of each chair, adding cheer to the room. The room cried *cozy*, but I never felt comfortable sitting through family dinners. I felt like I didn't belong or wasn't wanted. Or both, actually.

Not knowing what had come over me, I threw caution to the wind on that cold, dreary winter day, and, before I lost my nerve, I blurted out, "Mom, why don't you like me?" I had my head down, not wanting to make eye contact as she plopped an old moldy orange wrapped in a dirty paper towel down in front of me. I wasn't sure if she would even give me the time of day. Nor was I sure I wanted to hear the answer, so when she responded, I was shocked and caught off guard.

She put her coffee cup in the sink, turning to look my way as she rubbed her bloodshot, weary eyes. My mom normally was pretty, with dimples that played at the corners of her mouth when she smiled. She wasn't short, like my dad, but not tall, like me, either, but on this particular day she looked haggard and hunched over, like she was pained by something she chose not to share.

A look of abhorrence danced across her face as she nonchalantly said, "Oh, Luke—enough with the pity party. I like you just fine—I just don't love you."

And there it was. What I suspected to be true for years. I sat dumbfounded as I watched her turn her back to me as she waltzed out of the room, whistling "Happy Days Are Here Again," with not a care in the world that she had crushed my soul.

As I struggled not to cry, I went to my room, avoiding my brothers. My room was my sanctuary and about the only place in the house that I felt comfortable. When we moved to this house, my brothers got to pick the rooms they wanted, and I was given the leftover one, which I was surprisingly OK with because it was the one I would have chosen anyway. It was upstairs at the end of the hall, overlooking the front yard and the street we lived on. There was a huge willow tree, under which Marmalade and I spent many a day. It was simple, with sparse furniture but a totally comfy trundle bed. I had painted the room myself, and the walls were a dismal black, which always gave the room a gloomy look. It matched my mood perfectly. But the best part was that it was all mine and a chance to get away from my brothers and dad.

My brothers and I hadn't always been at odds, but, for as long as I can remember, they'd had it out for me. When I was younger, it used to bother me. I spent countless hours trying to figure out if it was something I had done that caused them to treat me like this. But no matter how hard I thought, nothing came to me. I was a firm believer in learning by example, and years of witnessing my parents treat me like shit made them think it was the norm.

I even point-blank asked them one day, and their response reaffirmed my thoughts all along. We were uncharacteristically playing a game of catch in the backyard when I blurted out, "Hey guys, why can't we do this more often? After all, we are brothers and should have each other's backs, right?" They both looked at each other and burst out laughing, mumbling under their breath, "Fat chance, loser. Why should we like you when mom and dad don't?" Just what I suspected all along. My parents had tainted their opinion of me and ruined the chance of us having any type of relationship. What I didn't know was why my parents felt the way they did—a mystery that went unsolved.

CHAPTER 1 ... THE TRUTH

I was supposed to be going to school, but, instead, I climbed under my comforter, snuggled close to Marmalade, and made myself a promise. From that day on, I made it my mission to be the best person I could be. Thinking of getting married and having kids of my own was too daunting to consider, but I also made a promise to myself that, if I was lucky enough to have a family to call my own, I would give them the world.

I hated when she called me "Luke." If I told her once, I told her a million times I preferred "Lucas." That was my given name, after all, and that was my wish—which is, of course, precisely why she refused. It hadn't always been like this; I never told her the real reason, and she, unfortunately, never asked. That would involve caring. The kids at school had started calling me "Luke Puke" in their singsong mocking tone. They would form a circle around me, linking arms and making it impossible for me to escape. I cringed and looked for the closest escape route, but they were relentless. More times than not, I was reduced to tears as I picked my underwear out of my butt cheeks after enduring my twice-daily wedgie. What hurt the worst was my brothers leading the group with their smirks of contempt.

School that year was a nightmare, at best. The ironic thing about it was that I loved to learn. The topic didn't matter—I was all ears. And I was smart, always the teacher's pet, but that ultimately worked against me. Why is it that the older I got, the more relentless and mean the other students got? I was actually a teacher's dream, eager to participate until I heard the other students in their whispered tones mocking me. Mocking the way I dressed, how tall I was, calling me a kiss-ass—it didn't matter. All that mattered to them was that they got a laugh at my expense. That's when I stopped participating and instead spent my time concocting a plan to get even. Now that I look back on it, that's when it all began—my downward spiral and my first visit down the rabbit hole. A rabbit hole that swallowed me whole, refusing to spit me out.

I lived in a small town named Piedmont, in Vermont. It sat smack dab in the middle of the state, with nothing to offer but wide-open acres of land. In the summer, miles of wispy grass and beautiful wildflowers in every color of the spectrum would dot the landscape and could be seen for as far as your eyes could focus. The sun would frequently shine high in the sky, while wispy clouds floated to an imaginary tune. I came to love how the sun warmed my damaged, broken-down soul. It often gave me hope that something good was around the next corner, and that love and acceptance were not just figments of my imagination but a reality waiting to embrace me.

I would spend hours on hours outside, with Marmalade always by my side. Riding my skateboard that I had built from scratch—doing odd jobs for the neighbors to buy the wheels and ball bearings, was my favorite pastime. I had asked for a skateboard for Christmas the previous year, not thinking there was a chance in hell I would get one—and I was right. My parents had refused. That's all I had on my list. One measly item. Sadly, I had come to expect rejection from them, no matter what it entailed. It really didn't matter what the circumstances were; I was always denied pleasure. I got smart, though, and tried some reverse psychology on them, hoping that if I acted like I *didn't* want something, they would get it for me. It didn't work, and I was left disappointed once again.

What I found almost unbearable was pretending that it didn't hurt. Even though years of broken promises had left me calloused

CHAPTER 1 ... THE TRUTH

and broken, I still had feelings I couldn't turn off. On Christmas morning, as the snow covered the ground and stuck in the branches of the trees, my brothers were surrounded with gifts of all shapes and sizes, meticulously wrapped in green-and-red-plaid paper and finished off with beautiful tartan bows. I, on the other hand, had *two* if I was lucky, usually thrown in an old used paper bag. Inside there was never anything I wanted. It was usually clothes from The Salvation Army thrift shop, which sat on Main Street in the middle of the town square. I had long ago learned to play my parents' game and act grateful with a smile spread across my face, when, inside, my plan to someday leave and never look back was getting closer to becoming a reality. I was more determined than ever not to give them the satisfaction they got from singling me out and crushing my spirit.

Whereas the summers were delightful, the winters were totally opposite, with a frozen tundra that made me shiver just thinking about it. Where the fields were covered with wispy grass and wildflowers in the summer, they were submerged in freezing cold snow in the winter months. The days were dark and dreary, making my depression almost unmanageable. I would spend hours thinking about how I would be better off six feet under—that way, I wouldn't be such a burden to my parents.

They clearly didn't love me. For a *fact*, I knew my mom didn't, judging by the words that came out of her smug, condescending mouth. I had a sneaking suspicion my dad felt the same way. They tolerated me on their generous days. Then, on other days, I was brushed aside as if I were an unwanted crumb that had fallen from my burnt toast at breakfast.

One night, my parents thought I had gone to sleep, but I hadn't. I tiptoed down the stairs, taking extra-special care not to step on the squeaky stair my dad had promised to fix months ago. I sat on the stairs, listening to them talk shit about me—their own flesh and blood.

How could they?

Why would they?

I sat, traumatized, as I heard my dad first. He sounded angry, like something had seriously pissed him off. Bad. "Is it just me, or is Luke more of a pain in the ass these days than normal? I can barely stand to look at him. He's some kind of freak, being so tall and out of proportion. And I won't even get into his withdrawn, irritating personality. It's clear he doesn't belong here. I really think we would be better off without that black sheep."

I suppressed a gasp as I sat listening but not believing what I was hearing. I watched as my mom looked at him with a blank stare, mulling over what to say before blurting out, "You would have been proud of me today. I told him I didn't love him. I could tell it hurt him." He reached over, telling her "Good job" and giving her a high five.

A pained expression flashed across her face as her brow furrowed. She began to speak more softly this time as she said, "Er, um, really, Peter—a *black sheep*?"

Did I detect a tear in the corner of her eye as her shoulders slumped, making me think she genuinely gave two shits. But how could she when she had just admitted that she knew I had been hurt by her own admission of not loving her own flesh and blood?

"Don't you think that's a little harsh? I think he's going through his awkward phase. You know all kids…" She wasn't even allowed

CHAPTER 1 ... THE TRUTH

to finish her sentence, as I watched in horror as my dad grabbed her by the throat and started yelling in her face.

"Yes, Jane, a *black sheep*. You heard me loud and clear. Now what are we going to do about it? And don't you dare protect him—or else!"

Or else what? I thought. I was more than a little eager to know the answer but far too scared to ask, so I shrank a little more inside myself, fearing what life had in store for me next.

He released his grip, storming out of the room, knocking over his chair on his way. My mom was left sitting on her chair, dumbfounded, rubbing her neck, with tears spilling out of her eyes and landing on the floor by her side.

What had I just witnessed? Did he threaten my mom? It made me sad. Actually, *worse* than sad. Not just sad, but *angry*. And confused. That's when the demons came knocking on my door, trying to consume my brain and take over my life. I had to fight hard to keep them at bay—especially this particular night, when I heard my dad say their life would be better off without me and called me a black sheep! As tears wracked my body, I made my way back to my room to process what I had just heard. No matter which way I looked at it, it wasn't good. I was actually scared of my own dad and how he treated my mom and me. I would try to fly under the radar, and, when I was old enough, I would leave and never look back. Nobody wants to stay where they're unwanted.

Unfortunately, the winters lasted longer than the summers, and I found myself having to adjust accordingly. I learned to ski, but I was too clumsy to get the knack of it. Even though I loved the wind whipping against my face as I barreled down the mountain, my mom made me give it up after I'd had one too many run-ins with trees and suffered broken bones as a consequence. I was foolish enough to think she didn't want to see me in pain, until I heard her mumble under her breath that I was costing them too much money. So much for a mother's love. I tried my hand at ice hockey, but after getting into too many fights, I was asked to quit the team. I found this so ironic because the old saying "I went to a fight and a hockey game broke out" was accurate on all counts.

At school, I excelled at dodgeball. I had finally found my niche, and I was relentless! I soon learned that I could take out my frustrations on my unfortunate opponents. Since I was already five feet ten inches tall at twelve years old, I towered over my classmates, which gave me the upper hand—one I used to my advantage. It was the only time I felt wanted, because everyone wanted me on their team. It was guaranteed that, if I was on your team, you would win. Every single time, we kicked ass and took names. The number of black eyes and bruised bodies multiplied while I took great pleasure in honing my skills. I was crazed when I got out there. It didn't help much in the making-friends category, but, quite frankly, I didn't care. I was learning to enjoy my time in solitude. Having friends was overrated unless you were lucky enough to have that one *special* friend, like I did.

She was the one great friend I could tell my secrets to. She *got me* because we were kindred spirits. She, too, was a victim of a lonely, solitary life. Hers was even a sadder story than mine because she was a product of the foster-care system. It was a broken system back in the 1980s, and, sadly, it still has many unsolved problems to this day. Her name was Ivy, and I worshiped the ground she walked on. I guess you could call her my lifeline. Partially because she also meandered through life, searching not only for answers but also for love. The ultimate prize would be acceptance. She was

CHAPTER 1 ... THE TRUTH

a bit of a tomboy, with short-cropped hair, the color of copper; she had hacked off herself. Her eyes were a beautiful cornflower blue when they weren't bloodshot and cloudy from tears of despair. She was as skinny as a toothpick but not by choice. I would sneak her food just so she could survive.

"Hey, Lucas—you want to hear something funny?" She didn't stop for me to answer as she continued on, "The one good thing in my life—besides you, of course—is my name. It describes me to a "t." I wish I was just like it and could climb over walls and escape. Escape my life and all the crappy people who pretend like they care, but we all know they're interested only in the money they can make by taking me in." I wanted to argue with her, but, unfortunately, I had to agree with her. I felt awful for her and told her that, when I was old enough and had a life of my own, in her honor, I was going to take in foster kids and give them the world. I certainly hope I'm given the opportunity to make a child's life complete by being that someone who actually cared. That made her laugh, and we did a pinky swear. When I wasn't doing chores in the neighborhood, you could bet I'd be with her and Marmalade. She loved Marm almost as much as I did. And I was happy to share her because she brought Ivy some much-needed joy.

We spent all our waking hours talking about a life we wished we had, until one day she was gone. Not a note. Not a goodbye. Nothing. I was distraught for weeks, even though I knew she didn't do it on purpose. That's how the foster-care system worked. When one family didn't want you anymore, they threw you out like trash. I often thought about her and wished upon the brightest stars at night that she had landed somewhere that saw her for the exceptional person she was.

When I wasn't in school, I took up ice fishing. It was a solitary hobby, and that's precisely why I liked it. I could sit for hours upon hours, chilling my bones, while my teeth chattered nonstop, waiting for that nibble at the end of my makeshift pole. Before she was sent away, Ivy would sometimes join me. We would sit shoulder to shoulder, lost in our own thoughts. True friendship to me was feeling comfortable in silence. We both weren't what you would call conversationalists, partially because nothing good ever happened in our lives to talk about, so silence it was.

I would save every single penny from the many chores I performed in my neighborhood so that I could get money to buy bait. By process of elimination, I found that the fish preferred live worms. So, live worms they got. And lots of them. It really never mattered to me if I caught anything, because, if I was lucky enough to, I threw them right back in to join their friends. I hated the thought of eating anything I'd seen alive at one point. It was the exact opposite of why most people fished, but I wasn't like most people.

In fact, I was unique in every way. My name is Lucas Travers, and I'm a twelve-year-old lonely, lost soul. It hasn't always been to this point, where I feel alone and lost in the world. But, come to think of it, it's been a common thread in my life since my brothers decided to join the family. I was ecstatic to have siblings to play with. At first, anyway. Thinking back, it all changed when they started developing personalities that were the exact opposite of my own. I swear they came out of the womb magnetic and more than a little bit mischievous.

All my earliest—and happiest, for that matter—recollections involving my childhood were with animals of any type. I couldn't get enough of them—their unconditional love and eager-to-please

CHAPTER 1 ... THE TRUTH

attitude wrapped in the fluffiest fur. I credit my past animals with keeping me sane and alive. Totally out of character, my parents got a dog when I was about six. That's how Marmalade came to be. She was a deep-red golden retriever—and my world. I loved that dog with all my whole soul but pretended like I didn't give two shits, because if they saw the joy I received from her, they would take her to the pound to get euthanized. I would bury my face in her fur for hours and spend all my time telling her my thoughts and dreams. Dreams that would take me far away from here, living a popular life where everyone liked me and, most importantly cared about me. Cared that I had clean clothes to wear and that I didn't go to bed hungry.

It's not like my family was poor, because we were far from it. My dad sold insurance and was quite successful. My mom opted to be a full-time stay-at-home mom so she could dote on her family. What a joke *that* was, at least from my perspective. Everyone else was well taken care of, but, unfortunately, I was not included in the mix. If you asked my mom, she would tell a different tale. Just goes to show you no one ever really knows what goes on behind closed doors.

So, the abuse continued. Physical abuse, no, but the emotional abuse was all-consuming and detrimental to my development. Years later, in therapy, I would learn how my formative years had been marred by my near-intolerance of my so-called parents.

CHAPTER 2

THE CHANGE
FOUR YEARS OLD

Not everyone remembers their childhood as vividly as I do. It kinda reminds me of that saying "You remember one negative comment before you remember a dozen good ones," but I was the opposite. I attribute it to the fact that it was the only time in my childhood that I felt love. I was a chubby little kid with blond curls that sat, with a mind of their own, atop my head. Right out of the womb, I was not the norm. Well off the "charts" that were used by the pediatrician to measure normal development. I had been huge at birth, weighing in at a whopping ten pounds three ounces, and twenty-two inches long. My mom affectionately recalled stories of how I was *the most beautiful, cherub-like baby. Slept through the night from the get-go. Never cried much and smiled and laughed nonstop.* I can't recall how many times she told the story about how the pediatrician kidded that I was up crawling around minutes after my birth.

CHAPTER 2 ... THE CHANGE

My parents were ecstatic to become parents. All was right in the world from my perspective. I had two parents who adored me and worshiped the ground I walked on. The country was recovering from the Vietnam war and losing over fifty-eight thousand servicemen. It was a mixed bag of emotions—mourning the loss of innocent lives or rejoicing over the fact that the travesty of a war had finally come to an end, after twenty years of conflict. My dad had been fortunate enough to avoid the draft due to a congenital medical abnormality. Although it didn't affect his everyday life, it was enough to keep him out of harm's way. And, for that, I was eternally grateful.

He would often wrap me in a warm blanket straight out of the dryer, perch me on his lap, snuggling me firmly in his muscular arms and sing soothing lullabies into my ear. His singing voice was gentle and melodic, and, more times than not, sent me into a deep sleep, dreaming of puppies and kittens. I was obsessed with animals. My favorite play dates were those to the zoo, where I would stand transfixed on any animal I had the privilege of watching. I begged relentlessly for a pet of my own but was told I needed to be older, as they would be my responsibility. I had something to look forward to, and I prayed every day to get older.

My days were filled with undivided attention from my mom—play groups, trips to the library and the toy store. Family vacations that involved road trips to kid-friendly attractions. I quickly learned road trips equaled candy. And lots of it. I developed a sweet tooth that would carry on into my adulthood. Old habits are hard to break, and anything containing peanut butter always took the top spot on my favorites list. That and chocolate. Was there anything better?

I fondly remember piling into the old bright-red T-bird with the soft top down and hitting the open road. My mom was always sitting shotgun with a colorful scarf tied around her head, so that her hair didn't end up in a tumbleweed of knots, as the wind swirled around, embracing me in happiness. My mom had long, wavy blond hair that reminded me of a horse's mane but shone like diamonds when the sun hit it just so. Her eyes were the color of the ocean, and her smile was intoxicating and, to me, the best sight in the world. The smell of my dad's aftershave, like the forest, with its damp ground and pine needles mixed with intrigue, wafted through the air, permeating my nostrils. We would sing at the top of our lungs anything from Led Zeppelin to Simon and Garfunkel and everything in between. My dad, who was never one to be the life of the party, joined in, oftentimes belting out the wrong lyrics. But all that really mattered was that we were having fun and making memories as our perfect little family. Looking back at this bit of nostalgia, I am again reminded that that was the foundation of my love for music and the open road. Both still hold a place in my shattered heart, fighting each other to remember the good times before everything came tumbling down like a house of cards.

I was extremely smart for my age. At least that's what I would hear my mom brag to her friends about. "You aren't going to believe what Lucas did today! He read a book from cover to cover, pronouncing all the words correctly," she bragged, with a smile plastered across her pretty face. She would beam with pride, leaving out the part that it was a basic animals-and-colors childhood-teaching book. I didn't care. I took it all in and basked in the love. All was right with the world until the day my brothers made their abrupt entrance into the world.

I would sit for hours wrapped in my mom's arms, with my head lying on her belly, talking to my brothers, as she rubbed my back and

CHAPTER 2 ... THE CHANGE

played with my curls. I was as excited as my parents to welcome them into the world. I never gave it a second thought that they would take my parents' love away from me and make my life a living nightmare. Instead, the thoughts that danced in my imagination was to have two brothers to play with. Build sandcastles on our yearly trip to the beach, play endless hours of catch, and share secrets under the pillow forts we created. Boy, was I in for a rude awakening.

The day they made an appearance was the happiest day of my life up to that point. My dreams of having someone to share my days with were becoming a reality. It was early one spring morning. The birds were chirping as they perched on a limb in the plum tree that sat outside my bedroom window. The tree was still barren from the harsh winter weather but showed signs of coming back to life, as its pink blossoms bloomed and smelled like the perfume my mom wore.

"Lucas. Wake up, sweetie," my mom cooed in my ear as she rubbed my back with her warm hand. "Daddy and I are off to the hospital!" I managed to open an eye and saw her beaming with pride. It was time, and I couldn't have been happier. I jumped up, scrambling to throw my clothes on so I could go with her. She laughed and said, "Don't be silly—you have to stay here with Grandma, but I promise, when I return you'll have the best present of them all." I reluctantly let her leave, wishing I could have her by my side forever.

I wasn't a fan of my Grandma, and I can tell you, she felt the same way. She always acted like she couldn't be bothered with me and smelled like rotten eggs and mothballs. It wasn't a good combination. No matter what I said, she waved me away with a flick of her wrist and a *tsk, tsk, tsk* under her stinky breath. Even though she was small in stature, she made up for it in the weight department, giving the appearance of a beach ball. With thick, unkempt eyebrows, resembling caterpillars, over beady, intense eyes, she sneered as thick creases formed on her forehead. She scared me a little. Actually, she scared me a lot, so I spent my time entertaining myself when she was near. It suited me just fine, because I enjoyed my company.

I remember like it was yesterday, the moment my life was supposed to change for the better but instead took an abrupt turn and headed south faster than I could say "boo." I was sitting in my room, gazing out the window at my favorite tree, thinking about asking my dad to build me a treehouse. I could see it now, spending days playing ball with my brothers and at night playing checkers in the treehouse as fireflies buzzed around and lit up the night sky.

And then my brothers came home, and they were nothing like I pictured. They couldn't play. In fact, all they did was cry, sleep, poop, and take away my attention. It started out slow at first, but, as the days passed, I was quickly becoming neglected. The attention that had been showered on me had now been rerouted to them, and every time I tried to talk to my mom, all she would say was, "Lucas, do you have to be so needy? Can't you see I'm tired? Tired of you and your constant nagging!" I didn't know it was even possible that my life could turn on a dime like this, but it was etched in my mind forever.

Shhhhh, shhhhh, shhhhh became her favorite word, so I withdrew further into my shell. I loved going to preschool not only because I loved learning but mostly because I got attention. I wasn't told to go away or to shut up. It soon became the highlight of my days—until my mom forgot to pick me up one day. I wasn't a crybaby or a mama's boy, but, as I sat waiting, with my red backpack with my name proudly embroidered in blue, strapped over my shoulders, tears streamed down my face. They wouldn't stop as numerous calls

CHAPTER 2 ... THE CHANGE

to my parents remained unanswered. My teacher, Ms. Hawthorne, graciously volunteered to take me home, reassuring me it was an oversight. But even she couldn't deny the truth when no apology was offered by my mom when she opened the door with a crying baby on each hip. That's when I knew my life was never going to be the same, because she was more wrapped up in my brothers' lives to care about mine.

As I was starting to see a pattern developing before my very eyes, I reached out to my dad. He loved football. Anything to do with football. Watching it, playing it, reading about it, betting on it, you name it. I would climb on the couch and snuggle next to him, trying desperately to stay awake. I felt safe and secure while Howard Cosell and Frank Gifford lulled me to sleep. But even these times started to change as time wore on.

This was to be the beginning of the end for me, as my life started a downward spiral of neglect and despair. It only gained in momentum as, day after long day, I was thrust into a world of my own.

CHAPTER 3

THE BIRTHDAY
SIX YEARS OLD

I rolled over on my cot, gripping my Big Bird blanket in my hand, pulling it up to cover my chilled arms. I stretched and audibly yawned. "Ms. Richardson, can we have fifteen minutes added to our nap time today?" I pleaded, wiping the sleep from my eyes. All of my classmates were waking up eagerly, waiting for their graham-crackers-and-milk snacks. But not me. I was tired, as usual. Sleeping at home was almost impossible. At least quiet, restful sleeping. My brothers, Christopher and Brian, at age two, were hell on wheels. It seems like they never slept and were screaming the most high-pitched squeal one could ever imagine. I always equated the sound to a wild bear caught in a trap. Even with all the racket they created, my mom and dad thought they could do no wrong and I could do no right.

CHAPTER 3 ... THE BIRTHDAY

From getting chastised for making my bed with a wrinkle in the blanket to sitting politely with my hands folded in my lap at the dinner table instead of helping serve. "Lucas why do you always sit there like you deserve to be waited on hand and foot? Get up and earn your keep!" my dad grumbled while shooting daggers at me with his beady little eyes.

Kindergarten was my lifeline. I found acceptance, patience, friendship, and understanding within those four walls. If I could have lived there, I would gladly have moved in and never looked back. I loved everything about it. The smells of paint and glue, mixed with Ms. Richardson's vanilla-jasmine perfume, was intoxicating. I always welcomed the snacks because, quite honestly, it was hit-or-miss for me getting fed at home. Sometimes they remembered, and, when they did, it was an afterthought and consisted of leftover scrapings from their plates. Many a night, I'd put myself to bed with a grumbling tummy. I had already learned that asking for food was a no-no, as it was greeted with a snarl and a time-out.

My own cubbyhole in my classroom was a highlight for me—something I could call my very own. It had my name written in block letters in the color of my choosing. I chose yellow because it reminded me of sunshine. Sunshine warmed me and gave me hope that better days were on the horizon. I would eagerly stuff my empty backpack in my cubby. I was so proud of my red backpack with my name embroidered in navy blue, mostly because I had picked it out with my mom, when she still cared about me. It was frayed and tattered now, but it was mine and a reminder of a life long gone. I would gleefully stuff my art and projects in it at the end of the day, eager to share them with my mom when I got home.

"Mom, look what I drew for you today," I would cheerfully say, pulling my picture with brightly colored hearts and flowers out of my bag. She would turn and grab it angrily from my dirty hand, rip it up, and throw it in the trash with the coffee grounds and spoiled food, saying it was where it belonged. I longed to have her hang one of my pictures on the refrigerator next to the god-awful scribbles my brothers had made, but it never happened. I never stopped dreaming or wishing that someday I would be given the coveted spot for all to see and admire.

The excitement I often felt when coming home and showing my projects to my mom soon turned to dread. Coming home to anything other than chaos at the end of a perfect day at school became wishful thinking. Once I walked through the door, all hell broke loose. I got blamed for everything bad my brothers did. And trust me, bad things were *all* they did. One day, they decided to paint the walls with their own poop. It was disgusting, and I tried to get them to stop, but they continued, laughing uncontrollably. I ran to get my Mom, screaming as I ran down the hallway. "*Mom, come quick. Christopher and Brian are making a huge, gross mess!*"

"What now, Luke? What are you blaming them for now?" she would reply, always taking their side. That incident was worse than most because she made *me* clean it up *with a toothbrush* while they watched, gloating and snickering, eating fresh-baked sugar cookies.

I was beyond disgusted as I dipped the toothbrush in the bucket of soapy water. I wanted in the worst way to throw the soapy water over their heads, but I knew I would get in trouble, so I powered through, on the verge of throwing up. It took me hours to clean up their mess, and I missed my cartoons that afternoon only to have my mom criticize me for not doing a good job.

CHAPTER 3 ... THE BIRTHDAY

"Lucas, if you had been watching your brothers, like you should have been, this wouldn't have happened in the first place—so this is your punishment: start over, and do it right!"

I wanted to cry, but I was determined to not show how upset I was.

One day as I was lying under the big willow tree in the front yard, making out images in the cloud formations that floated overhead, I saw a football-shaped cloud. I immediately had a lightbulb moment, running into the house, searching high and low for my dad. It was clear that my mom was too busy for me with the twins, but maybe if I reached out to my dad, things could get better at home.

"Dad, where are you? Let's go outside and throw the football around. I learned some new moves today at recess," I excitedly yelled.

Sadly, he wasn't home, but it wasn't going to stop me from trying to connect with him later. I smiled to myself thinking about all the fun we would have.

As I look back, I try to remember why my teachers didn't try to intervene. Come to my defense and save me. It had to have been painfully obvious that something was askew at home. Or was it? Maybe it was in my head because I was living it. Day in and day out. I often came to school in the same clothes I'd worn the day before. They were often dirty and definitely tattered. I myself wasn't the cleanest and oftentimes wondered where the horrible smell that followed me around was coming from. I was always ravenous and devoured my after-nap snack.

I do remember a Back-to-School Night when my mom and I, sans dad, showed up so late that Ms. Richardson was locking the classroom door. She looked at me, covered in filth. I witnessed a moment of sadness wash across her face and a tear form in the corner of her beautiful gold-flecked brown eyes. And then her eyes moved to my mom, looking clean and put-together. I saw in her eyes the questions she was thinking, but, before she could speak, my mom started rambling a bunch of made-up lies.

"My sincere apologies for arriving so late. Lucas was so busy having a good time making mud pies with his brothers that I lost track of time. We were so late already, I didn't have time to clean him up. I know you understand how boys can be!"

I was surprised her nose didn't grow. A myriad of emotions played across Ms. Richardson's face; she wanted to believe my mom, but an inchworm of doubt was slowly digging its way deeper into her heart. My mom could have won an Oscar for her performance that night, while looking at my schoolwork. She *ooohhed* and *aaahhed* at my paintings and complimented me on my writing of the alphabet. I even got a hug out of it—all for show.

The minute we were back in the car, my mom flipped a switch. It was back to how embarrassed she was of me and how dare I put her in a position that she had to concoct a lie at the last minute. And then the unthinkable occurred…she threatened me.

"Lucas, if you think for a second that you can go to school and tell Ms. Richardson—or anyone else, for that matter—about what goes on behind closed doors, you'd best think twice. You think your life is bad now? You haven't seen anything yet!" For a second, I thought she was kidding, but when I looked at her face, her eyes spoke differently. Her mouth was set in a hard grimace, making wrinkles appear out of nowhere. And her eyes were black as the night sky, filled with rage. I knew right then and there that I'd better keep my mouth shut, or my life would somehow go from bad to worse.

The next day at school, Ms. Richardson pulled me aside at the end of nap time. She looked so serious that I immediately thought

CHAPTER 3 ... THE BIRTHDAY

I was in trouble and started to shake. She took my hand in hers, placing a chocolate bar inside it, and wrapped me in a warm hug.

"Lucas, I'm worried about you. Last night when you were at Back-to-School Night, I felt like something was going on between you and your mom and life at home isn't the way she portrays it to be. Is there something you would like to share with me?"

As I looked into her eyes, I witnessed genuine concern. This was my chance to spill the beans, but when I opened my mouth to let it all out, I heard my mom's threat loud and clear, so I clammed up. I tried my best to offer a convincing smile and told Ms. Richardson that I was perfectly fine and very much loved. I hated lying to her, but it was either that or suffer the wrath of my parents.

It wasn't all doom and gloom that year, though. My parents unexpectedly offered to take us all on a road trip to the local animal shelter. I was so excited that I almost peed my pants. As we pulled up in front of the drab brown building, all I could hear was barking loud enough to pierce my eardrums. But I didn't care. I was the first one out of the car, skipping with anticipation, a smile spread from ear to ear across my elated face.

"Yippee, yippee, yippee! We're going to get a dog! You better get ready, little doggies, because I'm going to smother you with kisses and love you forever!" I couldn't contain my joy, and I was surprised to see my mom looking on with a smile and twinkle in her eyes as she watched my excitement.

We walked down aisles upon aisles of separate cages lined up side by side. Each one housed an assortment of dogs. Small ones. Big ones. Brown ones. White, black, and red ones. All clamoring at the chain link for a much-needed pet. I remember wanting them all, but after an hour, my parents made us choose.

Miracles do happen, because we were all in agreement for the first time ever. We chose a dark-red golden retriever whose name was "Marmalade," and she was perfect. Perfect in every way. On the way home, she curled up in my lap and instantly fell asleep. From that second on, I was positive we would be the best of friends. I wasn't sure what had changed my parents' mind about getting a dog that day, but I wasn't about to question the best thing that had ever happened to me.

I made friends that year, too. Things were looking up for me lately. I reveled in the foreign concept of being liked. And listened to. Jason and Ali were my best friends, because we all loved to play on the monkey bars and make messes with paste. We were the three musketeers and were inseparable during school hours. My time with them let me be a kid and forget about my troubles at home. The places we put paste! We had to sit in the corner because of it. I'm laughing right now as I remember it. It tasted interesting, too, especially to a six-year-old who was always hungry. Funny how I still crave that taste.

What I also found funny—not *ha-ha* funny, but in an odd, strange way—was how the mind is so selective on the memories it chooses to remember. Why did the bad times snuff out the good times like a candle that had been lit to light the dark night sky? The only reason I can come up with is that, sadly, the good times were few and far between, and all the heinous acts of abuse I suffered on a daily basis exponentially outnumbered any joy I had.

I woke the morning of my seventh birthday with determination to make it a day to remember. Marmalade stretched and let out a roar that would have rivaled a lion as she yawned. The sun was hidden behind a cloud, trying to peek through and light

CHAPTER 3 ... THE BIRTHDAY

up the day but failing miserably. I can't help thinking about the irony of this now. It explained me to a *t*. I wanted in the worst way to celebrate with my school friends, and my mom had sent out invitations. I barely got a wink of sleep the night before in anticipation. I dug through my dresser drawers, pulling out holey pants and ragged t-shirts searching for something party worthy. I finally settled on a bright-yellow shirt that was stained and tight but semi-clean. I scrubbed myself in the tub from top to bottom without being told to and ran downstairs with the biggest smile on my face and in my heart—and Marmalade trailing close behind.

Expecting to smell the sweetness of a cake in the oven, I was greeted with silence. Where was everybody? "Mom? Dad? Anyone?" I yelled at the top of my lungs. Nothing. My party was set to start in three hours, so I thought that my dad must have been out back, playing with my brothers, and my mom at the store, picking up last-minute decorations. I had opted for a dinosaur party. I loved everything about them. A tyrannosaurus was my favorite, because he was considered to be one of the fiercest animals of all time. He lived the life I wished I could live, so I lived vicariously through them, often pretending I was a force to be reckoned with.

I made my way out back and still couldn't see anyone. I was starting to feel anxiety taking hold. Had they left me alone to fend for myself? On my special day of all days? I was what anyone would consider an old soul and older than my seven years, but the fact remains I was still a child. A child who was quickly starting to lose control. I had learned about policemen and how they were your friends in school, so I contemplated calling them. *And tell them what, exactly?* I thought. I instead decided to sit on the couch and wait. I was positive that they would return any minute, because even that was out of character for them.

Looking longingly at the mahogany leather couch, I threw caution to the wind and curled up, making sure I removed my shoes. I wasn't positive what my punishment would be if I was caught lying on it, since it was considered off limits, but I remember not caring at that moment. Wrapping myself in a wool scratchy blanket balled up in the corner of the sofa, around my chilled arms, I rocked myself back and forth, trying to soothe my mind and lull myself into a false sense of security. I was spiraling out of control. I wish I had thought to bring Marmalade back in from her morning potty break. But as I lay alone, I waited and waited, but no one ever came. I eventually fell into a fitful sleep.

"Ouch!" I screamed, as my hair was firmly grasped in my dad's big, callused hand. I was in the air as my legs dangled, frantically trying to connect with the ground. Pee was running down my leg and pooling on the floor under me. My mom stood with her arms crossed over her chest, as a look of total disgust spread across her face. My brothers were peeking around the corner, laughing like they had been caught in the middle of a cartoon and they were the main characters. Me, I was panicked and wondering what I had done to deserve this injustice. Once again, I was being punished. For what I didn't even know. Existing, I guess.

"Lucas, what the fuck do you think you're doing? I should throw you out with the trash where you belong, you good-for-nothing little bastard!"

A barrage of cuss words I had never heard before came tumbling out of my dad's mouth, mixed with spittle that connected with my face. His face was redder than I had ever seen, with veins protruding

CHAPTER 3 ... THE BIRTHDAY

on his forehead and neck. Rage had taken over, and I was on the receiving end. My parents had never been physically abusive to me until now. As I look back now on that nightmare of a day, I am still mystified by what had my parents in such a livid state. All I really remember was that it was a soul-crushing day and a shitshow of a birthday.

No party. No presents. No cake. And, actually, no invitations. My miserable excuse for a mom had lied to me again.

CHAPTER 4

THE AFFAIR
JANE

I hated myself. Hated myself more than I thought was possible. Abusing my own child was never on my radar, but here I am, doing exactly that and not knowing how to stop. Shame on me. But yet, I continue. A child I had desperately wanted and adored. I have to play the game now, because I'm in too deep to turn back. If only things could have been different—but, regrettably, my life is a total mess, and I have no one to blame but myself.

I've gone beyond trying to fathom what I've become. Yeah, I look normal on the outside, but the inside is a decaying, rotten shell of what used to be a decent human. Full of life and promise without a care in the world. And all it took was one weak moment that changed the trajectory of my life forever.

Working late was something I did often, so this particular night wasn't out of the ordinary. A snow squall with gusty winds

CHAPTER 4 ... THE AFFAIR

had made the roads nearly undrivable, like most winter nights in Vermont. Stubbornness was a strong trait of mine, so, donning my down parka, mittens with the little gray kittens embroidered on them, and a hat, I made my way out the front door of my six-story office building that housed the law firm I worked for. I wasn't going to let a storm stop me. All I really wanted was a cup of tea, a fire, a good book to read, cozy in my sweats, curled up on the sofa, surrounded by dogs. That wasn't too much to ask after putting in a twelve-hour day, was it?

As I fought through the snow, it licked at my face, freezing my nose hairs and stinging my eyes, causing tears to stream down, leaving a trail of smudged black mascara parading down my face. Maneuvering myself into my car, I chuckled to myself while I moved the seat back to make room for me and my coat. It had so much fluff I could easily be mistaken for someone fifty pounds heavier than my trim frame. After removing my mitten, I inserted the key in the ignition and turned it, waiting for the engine to come to life, but nothing. Again I tried. Again nothing. Pounding my fist on the steering wheel, I screamed out of frustration. Dislodging my body from behind the steering wheel, I made my way back to work.

Stanford, Bridges and Howe had been my home away from home for the last three years, where, I was proud to say, I was a legal secretary for one of the partners, Gregory Stanford. I loved my job and was told I was excellent at it. Although my job was important to me because I needed the money, I loved the compliments I got for a job well done. I was showered with gifts and flowers, wooed with expensive dinners. Innocent, young, and naive, I didn't see all the attention as flirting. Looking back at it now, many years later, I don't know how I could have been so gullible, but I was. And now I pay the price day in and day out for my indiscretions that night.

Mr. Stanford was tall, handsome, charismatic, and irresistible. Unlike my husband of two years, he appreciated me. Suffice to say I was flattered and fell for his charm hook, line, and sinker. "Ms. Travers, I'm so glad you're back. You shouldn't be driving in that mess out there. Please let me warm you up," he offered with open arms. And I eagerly agreed. Looking into his dreamy chocolate-brown eyes, I melted. That was the exact moment common sense was overtaken by lust, and there was no turning back. As butterflies did somersaults in my belly, I began traveling down a road of no return. What a fool I was to think that he really cared about me. I knew he was married, but then again, so was I.

The excitement of the affair was like a drug, giving me a high like no other. Clandestine meetings in hotels off the beaten path, where I was treated like royalty and satisfied beyond my wildest dreams. And, trust me: I had some very vivid, wild, satiating dreams that left me in a puddle of sweat. Soon, I wanted more: a commitment, so I wasn't left feeling like a dirty whore. It was more than he was willing to give. I spent my days at work dreaming of a life as Mrs. Stanford instead of doing my work. Nothing good came out of that, and I soon found myself the subject of office gossip. Whispered voices, judgmental stares, and unanimously venomous notes randomly placed under my windshield wipers.

Did I need to seek medical help, join a cult, read self-help books to breathe an inkling of reality into my head, which had now taken up residency in the clouds? Part of me knew it couldn't/wouldn't continue, but that same part was quickly dismissed and locked away in the drawer with doubts and broken dreams. I was enjoying my

CHAPTER 4 ... THE AFFAIR

forbidden pleasure a little too much, so when Mr. Stanford came waltzing into my office looking like a Greek god, I broke out in a cold sweat. He would have had to be blind and deaf to not have caught wind of the gossip that was now circulating around the office at lightning speed.

"Ms. Travers, can I please have a word with you in my office?" he nonchalantly whispered, as I tried desperately to read between the lines and not overthink the situation. But it's easier said than done, because "overthinking" was my middle name, and I often said that if I didn't overthink, I wouldn't think at all. I reluctantly followed him with my head bowed, trying to will myself to another dimension. Was I imagining eyes from fellow employees burrowing into my soul as I took the walk of shame into his office, feeling my face flush twenty shades of red?

Clenching his jaw, trying to look calm and in control, he was anything but. Perspiration had begun to glisten on his forehead, and he nervously chewed on the inside of his cheek while picking at a hangnail on the corner of his sexy masculine thumb. His eyes were bloodshot but still the sexiest eyes I had ever had the pleasure of gazing into.

"First of all, let me tell you that I think you're a wonderful person and have been a great asset to our firm, but..."

Why did there always have to be a "but"? Couldn't he have just left it dangling there that I was a wonderful person? I had read that, whenever a tough conversation was to be had, to always start out with compliments to make the bad news seem less severe. Dreading what I knew in my heart was coming next, he grabbed my hands. Clasping them and rubbing his thumb slowly and sensually back and forth over my skin sent a chill through me.

"...but I, er, I'm not sure how to tell you this."

I looked into his eyes with the sexiest look I could muster up and said, "Then don't."

He laughed, and I melted.

"Although I won't deny the chemistry between us, I was out of line and shouldn't have led you on. This can never be what you want it to be, and, unfortunately, tongues have begun to wag, and it's just not acceptable. This is a respectable business, and I take full responsibility for acting anything but respectable. Not only has your work ethic slipped, but your head spends more time in the clouds than in your work. Please accept my apologies, but I'm going to have to let you go."

He pulled me into an awkward hug and whispered, "I honestly wish things could have been different" in my ear before releasing me, leaving me with mixed signals. Ultimately, it didn't matter how I felt or what I thought—I was the hired help, after all. I left with my tail tucked firmly between my butt cheeks, broken-hearted with a box full of my personal belongings, a severance check, and a note thanking me for my time there. Although I vaguely understood, I couldn't help the feelings of bitterness that consumed me.

Looking back at that night of the snowstorm, when I innocently fell into his arms, it ended up being the start of our affair and the one that ruined me as a person. I was left hollow, ashamed, unemployed, and pregnant.

My pregnancy progressed, and I never told Mr. Stanford he had impregnated me. Nor did I tell my husband, Peter, about the affair, although I had a sneaking suspicion that he had a sixth sense—something had been going on, with all the late nights I had worked. I spent my days talking to my angel growing in my belly, loving

CHAPTER 4 ... THE AFFAIR

that I would always have a part of Mr. Stanford to love. I couldn't help but suppress a giggle thinking back at why I called him "Mr. Stanford." It had been a running joke between us, telling him he was my dom. And so it stuck, an inside joke between two lovers.

Mum was the word; some things were better left unsaid. I worked on my marriage, concentrating on rebuilding the love we once shared, leaving the past behind me buried under a mountain of troubles I'd swept under the rug. Vowing to stay faithful, I spent my days decorating the nursery in a zoo theme. Appliquéd giraffes, elephants, and lions having a picnic under a vibrant-green big willow tree with the sun peeking through a collection of fluffy white clouds high in the sky adorned one wall, while the others were painted in muted yellows.

My pregnancy was anything but easy, but I was a champion and powered through, determined not to complain. The guilt of my past indiscretions weighed heavily on my mind, constantly at battle with my moral compass. I had fleeting moments in which I thought that I wouldn't be able to love my child knowing what I'd done. As for keeping secrets buried ten feet under, I was skeptical my life would ever be normal again. I was consumed with guilt, so I was relieved when, on the night of May 1, 1972, I went into labor, and, thirty-six hours later, my first son was born.

He was perfect. Weighing in at whopping ten pounds three ounces, he was a chubby, wrinkled spitting image of his dad. I gasped the first time my eyes gazed into his, wondering how long my secret could stay hidden. I started to hyperventilate, hoping and praying I wasn't as transparent as I felt. I vowed to myself once again that I would take my secret to my grave, but, unfortunately, it wasn't that simple.

Lucas' first years of life filled me with joy. I loved being a mother, and I flourished in the role. Doting on him was everything I could have imagined it would be and more, but, as the days ticked by, he reminded me so much of his father. Every feature in his perfect little face was like staring straight at Mr. Stanford, taunting me, ready to blow my secret out into the open. I lived in constant fear that my charade would be up, and I would have to divulge my indiscretions, leaving me and Lucas vulnerable, potentially without a home, having to fend for ourselves. I was slowly but surely losing my mind as Lucas thrived without a care in the world.

Lucas was a little genius. He walked and talked sooner than "the norm." His personality started emerging, and he was charismatic, just like his dad. His mannerisms—oddly enough, since he had never met his real father—were exactly the same and nothing like Peter's. And even when he started talking, he had the slight rasp to his little voice that I had found so irresistible in Mr. Stanford. I knew it was only a matter of days before I would be on the hot seat, because Peter was a lot of things, but blind wasn't one of them. I bided my time and dreaded the day until the inevitable erupted.

Sitting in the playroom, listening to Lucas recite his ABCs, I jumped a foot in the air as I heard a loud bang, and heavy footsteps vibrated the walls. Peter burst through the door, screaming at the top of his lungs, and I froze, knowing my day of reckoning was upon me. He kicked the chair I had been previously sitting on, sending it flying through the air, missing Lucas' head by a mere couple of inches.

"Jane, you two-timing, lying bitch! Is there something you would like to tell me?" Peter shouted at me as a look of contempt covered his face. He was so pissed that, at that moment, I feared for my life.

CHAPTER 4 ... THE AFFAIR

I had witnessed his temper flare numerous times over the years, resulting in holes punched in walls and broken furniture, but he had never laid a hand on me, although he had come close with a raised fist poised in the air, before stopping himself and walking away. I knew by the look in his eye that he would not be walking away this time. Not without answers, anyway. I had been thinking day in and day out about what I would confess and decided that honesty was the best approach, followed by remorse and my undying love for Peter. I just needed to be convincing. Honesty was something I wasn't sure I could pull off.

So, I spilled it. I spilled it all—well, most of it. I blamed Mr. Stanford for taking advantage of me. I knew in my heart that wasn't the case, but if I told Peter how I had fallen in love with my boss, I would be thrown out on my ear. I couldn't allow myself to contemplate what fate would be bestowed upon poor, innocent Lucas. I tossed the whole honesty thing out the window and played to my audience. He was beyond furious, accusing me of cheating and playing off Lucas as his own. As furious as he was, I was every bit as scared. I broke down and crumbled to the ground, holding my face in my trembling hands, as sobs consumed my body.

"Peter, please forgive me. I don't know what came over me. I had a weak moment, and I'm ashamed of the way I acted. I love you and only you." Begging for forgiveness, I lied and told him I was embarrassed by my impulsiveness. For a split second, I contemplated telling Peter I had been raped, but I knew that would send him into a rage like no other. Fearful for my life and for Lucas' I told him I would do anything to make it right.

I wasn't proud of my lies, but I needed to try and save what little I had left of a not-so-perfect marriage. He not only scared me—he petrified me. Numerous times throughout our marriage, he had been on the receiving end of a bar fight gone wrong. He showed no remorse and held a grudge forever. Needless to say, I wasn't willing to put myself or my son in harm's way. As I looked up at him through swollen eyes, he was glaring at Lucas, with hatred oozing out of every pore.

I yelled, "Peter! Stop!" watching him raise his fist to strike him. I threw myself on top of Lucas, taking the brunt of his punch. I heard my jaw crack, and excruciating pain shot through my face. No apology was offered. Instead, he pushed me aside, spitting in Lucas's face. "You bastard, I will never love you!" he shouted as he stormed out of the room, slamming the door on his way out. That was the beginning of the end.

My twins had been born just days before that frightful confrontation. They looked like Peter, only making it more obvious that Lucas didn't resemble either of us. Putting two and two together, he snapped. Plain and simple, he lost his shit, demanding I turn my back on my firstborn. Never dreaming it would come to this, I sat trembling, trying to sort through the mess I was in, all the while praying my jaw wasn't broken.

CHAPTER 5

THE NEST EGG
SEVEN TO TEN YEARS OLD

Trying to describe my life in the years that followed was almost impossible. At least impossible without an anxiety attack forming and taking hold. I would say I *existed*. Barely. The day of my seventh birthday still haunts me for many reasons. I was never given a reason for the abuse I endured that day. I hardly thought lying on a couch that was off-limits—treating me like a dog—was reason enough for the abuse, but anything was possible in my parents' warped, demented minds. The only thing positive that came out of that day was that it was the last day I was ever abused. Physically, anyway. The mental anguish continued on a daily basis.

I continued to excel in school. It was my happy place. I still loved to learn, and I also still loved helping my teachers out. I know they suspected things were amiss at home, but they stayed in their own lane. My parents were a lot of things, but they weren't dumb. They made sure everything appeared to be hunky-dory to an outsider looking in. One big happy family, loving life. If only an outsider could see what was going on behind closed doors. I'm positive that's why the physical abuse stopped. That would raise red flags and elicit questions they didn't want to answer. I was reminded on a daily basis to keep my mouth shut, or I wouldn't be allowed to speak again. I feared for my life, so I kept quiet and slowly withdrew into a shell, where I could protect myself.

Becoming an expert at coexisting was something I'm very proud of. I had to dig deep as a child and grow up quickly. I didn't learn to walk on eggshells; instead, I walked on land mines, not knowing when the next grenade would explode, covering me in shrapnel, struggling to survive. The key word here is *survive*, and I did. I actually learned a lot about many things a child that age should never be bothered with.

You know the old adage "What doesn't kill you makes you stronger"? I was living proof, because, with all the duress I was under, I began to look to the future. I dreamt of the day Marmalade and I could run like the wind and leave Vermont and my parents in our dust. Every single chance I got, I would spend my time in the library, combing through articles on life in other places, self-help books, and books on survival under the worst of circumstances. It gave me a glimmer of hope and something to hang on to when I was hanging by the slimmest of threads.

I had my eye on the Pacific Northwest for a couple of reasons. It was on the west coast, which made it as far away from Vermont as I could get, which appealed to me for obvious reasons. Being on the coast attracted me because I loved the way the ocean made me

CHAPTER 5 ... THE NEST EGG

feel. I hadn't been there for a long time, but we used to go when I was younger, and the time there had left a lasting impression on me. The waves crashing against the shore, washing all my troubles away, sounded like a little slice of heaven to me. The promise of a brighter future gave me reason to survive.

When I wasn't at the library, I was looking for chores I could perform in my neighborhood. Anything to get me out of the house and give me the opportunity to make some extra money for my future gave me the purpose I was needing. My mom never asked where I was when I came home at the end of the day sweaty and grimy. And, for once, I was grateful for small favors.

We had moved to a different part of the city at the beginning of my fourth-grade year of elementary school. It was bittersweet for me. I hated leaving my old school behind. But I loved leaving the house that held so many bad memories. Call it paranoia, but I somehow thought my parents put the house up for sale to spite me. They knew how much I loved my teachers and school; so, uprooting me, forcing me to start all over, was a punishment of sorts.

Saying goodbye to my favorite teachers and friends I had made was one of the low points of my childhood. I felt safe with them. Although I never divulged what was happening at home, I felt like they knew. Maybe not to the full extent, but I could tell by the way the teachers coddled me: they saw a broken, beaten soul struggling to survive. They would often bring snacks for me when they witnessed me drooling over everyone else's lunch in the cafeteria. They awarded me Star Student of the Week more times than any other student, making a big deal of it, like I was the most important kid in the world. I was being celebrated just for being me, and it made me glow with pride.

BLACK SHEEP

When the day came to start a new life in the new neighborhood, I cried. I walked into my old classroom and was instantly greeted with a huge, colorful banner wishing me farewell. There were balloons of every color and size and a chocolate sheet cake decorated with little basketballs. Big tears welled up in my eyes, threatening to spill down my cheeks. My teachers even got misty eyed as they wrapped me in bear hugs and showered me with going-away gifts.

"Lucas, we are going to miss you so much. You always are such a bright light and a joy to have around," they all chimed in at the same time. Then they broke out in song, and my fellow students joined in. It was obvious they had practiced, which made it even more extra-special. I felt loved and secure there, like I hadn't felt in years at home. I could still hear the tune playing in my head decades later.

The house we moved into was a sprawling, drab-gray colonial-style home with a red-brick façade, shutters, and a gabled roof. I guess it was pretty enough, but it smelled weird. I had a hard time pinpointing the smell but finally landed on farts and dirty feet. An old, rancid odor that permeated the walls and seeped out of the olive-green shag carpet. I tried not to think about what was potentially living in there. It was apparent, for some strange reason, that I was the only one who noticed it. My mom seemed to be on cloud nine as she puttered around with a goofy smile, humming to herself. For a brief moment in time, I hoped that these new beginnings would be a good thing and that she would turn over a new leaf, remembering how much she used to love me. I was mistaken.

My dad must have really upped his game at work, because our new neighborhood was more upscale than our last one, which was both positive and negative for me. There were more chores that my neighbors needed done, and they paid significantly better, but the people were

CHAPTER 5 ... THE NEST EGG

more uptight and kept to themselves. More times than not, when I stood on their vast verandas, ringing their doorbell, I could see a curtain pull back with questioning eyes and a sourpuss look on their tired faces. The majority of the time, they ignored me and never gave me a chance to offer my spiel. On the off-chance I was lucky enough to have someone physically answer, I had memorized all the chores I could do and the prices I was asking, always open to negotiations, of course.

I was relentless, like a pirate in search of buried treasure, always exploring new ways to make money. Saving every penny, I purchased a secondhand lawn mower and edger, which opened a whole new slew of customers. Soon I found the more money people made, the lazier they got, hiring out everything to be done for them and I was *A-OK* with that. More money for me and a chance at a better life grew closer as each day passed.

Surprisingly, not one person ever asked my age. Despite being malnourished the majority of the time, I had continued to grow by leaps and bounds, towering over everyone my age. Not only was I goliath in stature, but having to grow up quickly matured me, too. So, I passed for a teenager and spent every waking moment that hot, sticky summer working my tail off, while my brothers spent their days living the life of Riley. One would have thought jealousy would churn through my veins like hot lava, but I was over caring about them and their cushy life.

My main concern now was finding the perfect hiding place for my cash that kept multiplying faster than I ever thought possible. I came home unexpectedly early one afternoon, and I caught those little weasels going through my stuff. Wringing their scrawny little necks flashed through my mind, and a satisfied smile played on my lips, but my parents' threats ran on repeat through my head. All that would come out of it was another punishment for me, while they got off scot free, as usual. No thanks.

Pretending like I didn't care, I plastered a toothy smile on my face and said, "Hey, guys. What's ya lookin' for? Something I can help you with?" They didn't even have the decency to try to look surprised, guilty, like they were caught with their pants down, or remorseful. That spoke volumes of their lack of character, only convincing me more than ever to keep my nose to the grindstone and get the hell out of Dodge the first chance I got.

Up until this latest fiasco, I had kept my cash in a fake rock that was hollow, allowing access through the bottom. I had purchased it at the secondhand store one day when I was looking for gardening tools. Keeping it in my closet didn't seem a viable option anymore, now that I had caught the little troublemakers red-handed, so I set my alarm for the middle of the night and crept outside to dig a hole and bury it.

The air felt cool against my skin, a sharp contrast from the scorching sun of the daylight hours. Owls hooted in the distance, while the bullfrogs' croaking broke through the silence of the night. I hadn't bothered with shoes, and the grass was moist between my toes, making me forget why I was there. Instead of finding the perfect hiding spot, I ran around, loving the feeling of freedom and nature uniting. For a couple of minutes, I was a kid, enjoying the simple pleasures life had to offer.

Coming to my senses, I spotted an area covered over by some ivy along the fence line, and I commenced to dig a hole round enough and deep enough to securely hide my treasure. After my covert operation, I tiptoed back up the stairs, climbed in bed, snuggling Marm by my side. Life wasn't so bad after all.

CHAPTER 6

THE SMILE
TEN TO TWELVE YEARS OLD

It must have been the new neighborhood and the keeping up with Joneses persona that triggered something in my mom's warped, demented brain. I came home one day—and lo and behold!— a stack of new, clean clothes were sitting perfectly folded and stacked on the end of my bed with a note that read…

To Lucas

Love,

Mom

I caught myself with my mouth hanging open, not believing my eyes. I inspected them, expecting there to be a catch. Perhaps a hidden listening device? What can I say? I was paranoid. And skeptical. I couldn't remember the last time she had done anything nice for me.

Running through the house, checking in each room, I found my mom staring out the living-room window in a trance-like state. I followed her gaze, expecting there to be a puppy or something interesting happening out there, but there was nothing out of the ordinary. She had a faraway look in her eye, as a smile played on her lips. She wrapped her arms around herself in a hug, rocking back and forth, humming "What a Wonderful World" softly under her breath. It's as if she was remembering something from her past. Something that made her happy. I'm not sure what got into me that day, but I grew a pair and got brave.

"Mom, you look like you're lost in some kind of glorious memory. What are you thinking about?"

An actual smile appeared as she spoke. "Oh, Lucas—if I could only share, but it's nothing that would interest you."

"Let me be the judge of that, Mom," I pleaded. And then my brothers came in punching and yelling at each other, followed by my dad scowling at us both—and the moment was lost, never to happen again. I never got a chance to thank her for my new clothes.

I held that smile in a special place in my heart. In that moment, she was on the verge of telling me something. Something big. Something meaningful, but I'll never know. When my life got close to unbearable, I pulled that smile out of my heart and dreamt about what a mother's love would feel like. Back when I was four, she would always go on about me, how I was her everything, until something changed, sending my life into the depths of hell. I spent countless hours wondering what I had done wrong. Was it something I said? Was it something I did? I would give anything to go back in time to right my wrongs, given the chance.

CHAPTER 6 ... THE SMILE

Some unknown force told me to keep my mouth shut about the clothes and the note. I tucked the note under my mattress for safekeeping. I was prepared to say I bought them for myself, but no one ever asked. I had gone back to being invisible in a family that shared a mutual love for one another, except me. I was the outcast, the black sheep that could have been thrown out with the trash and no one would shed a tear. Except me.

Oddly enough, I was learning to live with the rejection, but to say it didn't bother me anymore would be a lie. I had become an expert at brushing it off and acting like it hadn't crushed me, though. It was my way of living—mind over matter. Letting it consume me and allowing myself to wallow in the deep, dark hole where I lived would be giving up and giving in. I was determined not to let them win. So, I continued to work my ass off. Day in and day out, I mowed lawns and planted flowers. I even got a paper route. It was the best decision I made, partly because Marm got to run like the wind next to me and partly because, when I rode, I wasn't thinking about life at home, as I rode my secondhand red Sting-Ray bike I had purchased for myself. It made me feel in control of my life. In control of my own destiny. And—mostly—in control of my future.

Unfortunately, the summer came to a close, and I was thrust back into school, come fall. I had been dreading it in the worst way. For a couple of reasons, actually. One was because I was going to be the new kid on the block. All eyes would be on me, putting me in the spotlight—and I despised being the center of attention. I had continued to grow despite my lack of nutrition at home. Every now and again, my mom would leave goodies in my room. No note, but I knew they could only be from her, a secret shared between us.

I was a loner and awkward on a good day, not really interested in making friends. Looking back on those sad days for me, I blame my parents. As a child, you need support, guidance, love, and understanding to become a well-rounded, likable child. Obviously, I wasn't given any of those things, so I turned into someone who got ridiculed on a daily basis.

To be away from Marm all day long was torture for me. I knew my mom had seen how inseparable we were, and I often feared I would come home and Marm would be gone. It was the sort of punishment that would inflict the most pain on me, and I lived in constant fear. Marm and I were the best of friends, never leaving each other's side. She was the best friend I needed in the days I had nobody. Nobody to tell my secrets to or my aspirations for the future. I'd always believed dogs have a sixth sense; she saw the broken heart and crushed spirit that lived within me, and she was there to offer her undying love. Whoever said dogs are a man's best friend had nailed it.

My school had been built on the outskirts of town, much too far away to walk or ride my bike. This left only one mode of transportation feasible—my parents. Actually, it was my mom, because my dad had flat-out refused to take me, always leaving for work at the crack of dawn, not to return home until the sun had set for the day. I was okay with that because being around him made me uncomfortable and squeamish. There was something about him that I couldn't pinpoint, but it was clear as the day was long he didn't like me. He avoided me like the plague, and, on the rare times we did come face to face, he turned away, mumbling something under his breath. Before long, we had a mutual disgust for each other.

CHAPTER 6 ... THE SMILE

In the morning. Christopher and Brian constantly caused a whirlwind of chaos, making us late more times than not. Always too late to call shotgun, I would have to sit in the back of our Oldsmobile Cutlass with one of my two brothers. We were anything but close, and they spent their days trying to make me miserable. Most days, they succeeded.

Ridiculing me was common, but, on one particular day, it was painstakingly unbearable, and I began to cry. As the tears welled up in my eyes, I tried to shut him out, along with my tears. Shut out the jabbing and kicking while calling me a stinky loser, but I'd had enough. I knew better than to fight back, so I sat there wrapping my arms tightly around myself, looking straight ahead, *willing* the tears to stop. That's when I saw my mom looking at me through the rearview mirror. A look of compassion flashed through her eyes, and she silently mouthed, "I'm sorry," and then it was gone. She then chimed in and sided with my brothers, telling me to not be a cry-baby and act my age.

Had I conjured up that scene later in years because I wanted so badly to believe that she had cared? It's so real to me now, but it could be years of wanting to believe I deserved to be loved in a world that offered me only hate and pain.

Days turned into months, and sunshine turned into gray, overcast skies as winter was upon us. Managing to get through school without getting into a fight called for a celebration on my part. Whereas, when I was younger, I had hidden within myself when I got upset. But, as I got older, my hormones had shown up to the game. The more they increased, the less tolerant I became. It was a new me— one that I hadn't gotten accustomed to yet. I wasn't sure I liked me with an edge. At first, anyway, but as time wore painstakingly on, I learned to embrace it while mostly keeping it under wraps. I managed to muddle through my days at school, searching for a way to fit in.

Winter lasted an eternity, and my lawn-upkeep business changed into shoveling snow for my neighbors. For the most part, though, my chores came to a screeching halt, leaving me more hours to withdraw. Learning and doing well in school continued to be a bright spot for me. It was a small accomplishment I did for myself, since home life was still dismal at best. Knowing that an education and hard work would be my ticket to a better life, I excelled in school, devouring book after book, learning and escaping my reality. I spent hours dreaming about my future. Life with me, myself, and Marmalade, living off the land.

CHAPTER 7
THE CONTRACT
JANE

What the hell had I agreed to? It's a pity I couldn't have seen into the future when I signed Peter's contract nine years ago, but you know what they say: hindsight is twenty-twenty. I'm trapped and miserable, buried under the rubble that is my life. Every morning I wake up, put my mask on, the mask I wear when I'm pretending to be someone I'm not. Someone who gives a damn.

I've considered seeing a shrink—someone who could potentially offer me a lifeline and help me justify what I've done. But with all their psychological superpowers, I'm afraid the opposite will happen. Instead, I'd be dissected with my morals in question *as well as* my sanity. I wouldn't blame them; I myself often question my sanity. Am I a freak, with no moral compass? No compassion? I'm reasonably sure many would answer with an astounding "Yes," and I'm not prepared to hear the brutal truth.

Or worse, scared for my safety, they would get the police involved. So I toss the idea aside hoping and praying that I can somehow get through another day. Peter and I had always been polar opposites. Nothing in common at all, even when it came to our taste in music. Where I preferred listening to the likes of Bread and Cat Stevens, his jam was heavy metal, clear down to the air guitar. As I strain my memory to remember what attracted me to him, it all seems hazy. Is my subconscious trying to protect me somehow, or had I settled and never actually felt an attraction?

Thinking back, I'm sure I must have been in love with the idea of being in love. Seeing everyone around me settling down and starting a family made me envious, and that's never a good place to be. It's also never a good idea to settle, and that's precisely what I did. I settled, pure and simple, and, now, I was stuck. It's not as if I hated him—more like I hated what he had become. There were times in our relationship that were actually fun but never *I worship the ground you walk on* kind of love. The love that takes your breath away and leaves you weak in the knees. Nope, never that kind of love. More like a means to an end.

Strolling late into class at my university, I tried to make myself invisible so I wouldn't disrupt the lecture on Medieval History that had started ten minutes prior. I ducked down and silently maneuvered myself into the desk placing my heavy book bag on the floor by my feet. Taking a deep breath, trying to ground myself, I looked up and saw a guy staring at me. He had a smirk and was giggling under his breath while flashing me a thumbs-up. I had been caught, and I couldn't help suppress a giggle of my own, drawing the unwanted glare of our professor. Needless to say, I was mortified.

CHAPTER 7 ... THE CONTRACT

Packing up my bag after class, I felt a presence standing over me. I looked up to see the same guy, smiling, with his hand outstretched. "Hi, let me formally introduce myself. I'm Peter and would love to get to know you," he enthusiastically said. He certainly wasn't much to look at, with his pointy nose that served as a perch for his thick horn-rimmed glasses. He looked to be about my age but had started the unfortunate process of balding, leaving behind spots that shone through in the afternoon sun. He was a pipsqueak of a guy, standing barely five feet two inches, but there was something about him that I found mesmerizing. So, on the spur of the moment, I made what would be a life-changing decision, throwing caution to the wind and agreed. Oh, if I could turn the clock back, I would—in a nanosecond—but, instead, I hold out a teeny sliver of hope that things will change.

Intellect had always been a turn-on for me, so, when we met for coffee at the student union, I was pleasantly surprised to find him well-spoken. After hours and copious amounts of coffee, I discovered I was smitten with the meaningless trivia that flowed out of his endearing lips. His quick wit and observations on current affairs and the government kept me entertained and wanting more. Somehow, I overlooked the lack of a filter and ignored the short fuse of a temper that I saw flare up over trivial things. Young and naive, I jumped in feet first. Now, I'm trying to claw myself out of the hell I call my life.

Our courtship was a whirlwind. Concerts, road trips, book signings, and dinner under the stars had become my life, and I was all in. In love with my new life and not being lonely anymore monopolized my thoughts. Not once did I listen to the voice in the back of my head screaming at me to walk away. One night, after throwing back a pint or two of the local beer on tap, Peter dropped a bombshell and professed his love. Then he dropped to one knee, sloppily asking for my hand in marriage before he turned and vomited. It was anything but romantic, but it had a certain flair to it that spoke of who he was. Outlandish dreams for my future felt possible in that moment, and I agreed while being two sheets to the wind.

We eloped on one beautiful spring day. The sun was high in the sky, and a breeze blew any doubts I may have had far away. Birds happily chirped, and everything was right with my little world. Married life was everything I always wanted it to be—until it wasn't. Peter began staying out late, only to return home reeking of marijuana. I quickly learned asking about his whereabouts set a mean streak in motion that scared the crap out of me, so I stayed; I'm not sure why. This was my chance to walk away and never look back, but he was always apologetic, vowing his undying love. Believing our vows meant something to us both, I gave him another chance.

Days became weeks, and weeks turned into years, but nothing really changed between us. Plans derailed as quickly as they were formed, leaving me an emotionally fragmented mess playing pretend. And that's when I fell in love with Mr. Stanford, and when I found out what love really was. I never intended it to happen, but life with Peter was far from perfect. In all actuality, it bordered on awful. But I stayed and lived an idealistic life of happiness away from home. There was a cacophony of voices ever present in my ears, telling me what I was doing was wrong, yet I was unable to stop myself.

Day in and day out I dreamed of life with Mr. Stanford. A life filled with operas where I could don luxurious evening gowns, emerald green to match my eyes. Picnics in the park, being fed chocolate dipped strawberries while sipping on champagne. He was

CHAPTER 7 ... THE CONTRACT

everything and more of what I was desperately missing in my life with Peter, and I fell hard. Straight out of a fairy tale with him as my Prince Charming. Even though I knew fairy tales weren't real, I continued to skip down the yellow brick road, living in a fantasyland.

When my world crumbled—the day Mr. Stanford ended things with me—I was distraught. I left my dream job with my head bowed, ashamed it had come to this, knowing I had no one to blame but myself. And nowhere to go but back to Peter, hoping and praying he'd be none the wiser. And it might have worked had I not been pregnant.

The pregnancy brought us closer again. We were both on cloud nine, ecstatic that we would finally become a little family. I knew in my heart my baby wasn't Peter's, dying a little inside every day waiting and hoping the other shoe wouldn't drop. Four years passed quickly and drama-free for the most part. I wasn't stupid and knew what buttons of Peter's not to push, which was not an easy chore. He was a volcano waiting to erupt, burying me deep under ash, trying to breathe. I didn't care as much what happened to me, but I did care what happened to Lucas, so I played by Peter's rules and acted the part of the doting wife.

Lucas was pure joy. I loved him more than life itself, unable to stop smothering him in kisses and wrapping him in my arms while inhaling his intoxicating scent. Peter even showed a sensitive side I hadn't seen in the past. We were happy until the twins came into the picture. I can't pinpoint the exact time when everything took a drastic turn that led to the destruction of our family, but I could feel it building.

Poor innocent Lucas couldn't help that he looked and acted like Mr. Stanford.

Because it left me with physical and emotional scars, I'll never forget the dreaded day Mount Peter erupted. Accusations flew, doors slammed, walls were punched, and hatred was spewed. We never recovered. Although I tried for Lucas' sake, there was no coming back from this. Not for Lucas, anyway. He may as well have been the devil himself, the way Peter treated him. All you had to do was glance at Lucas to know he wasn't Peter's biological child, but the world came crashing down when I admitted my infidelities. It was like throwing fuel on a burning flame, impossible to extinguish.

I hid in my room, with the boys, holding my breath as I heard tires screech out of the driveway, knocking over our mailbox and taking out the flowers that adorned our park strip, leaving deep grooves of tire imprints in the pristine green grass. I needed to think, but the twins wouldn't stop crying. They sensed the tension in the house and that I was a bundle of frayed nerves on the verge of a nervous breakdown. I knew in my heart that we had come too far to repair what had transpired, but I never in my wildest dreams could have predicted what would happen next.

Peter came home hours later, stinking drunk, looking like he had been caught in a cat fight and lost. Blood was caked around his mouth, while a trickle dripped from his nose. His clothes were ripped and filthy, but he still had his arrogant, pompous attitude when he handed me a contract he had drawn up. On the front, in bold capital letters, it said...

NONNEGOTIABLE

"Take it or leave it, but if you don't, you only have yourself to blame. Good luck living with the consequences. They are not only brutal but deadly," he sneered while detestation radiated from his squinty little eyes. As I read it, word for word, my hands shook.

CHAPTER 7 ... THE CONTRACT

As hard as I tried to contain my emotions, I couldn't. The very last thing I wanted was to give Peter the satisfaction of knowing he had me right where he wanted me. Tears streamed down my cheeks, and I choked back the sobs consuming my body. He stood silent, glaring at me while I contemplated my choices. I came up empty and ultimately did what I felt was my only choice to let myself and Lucas live. Even though Peter didn't hold a gun to my head that day, the threat was just as persuasive, so I signed it, knowing my life would never be the same.

It was ludicrous. And barbaric. I would shower him and the twins with affection, giving the impression we were one big happy family. And I was allowed to stay as long as I pretended Lucas didn't exist. I wasn't allowed to love, support, or nurture him in any way—because Peter had threatened to kill Lucas and me. It wasn't actually a threat, but more like a promise. One I knew deep down to my toes he was capable of, so I allowed my heart to break to save my son.

Finding it unbearable most days, I decided to test the waters and give Lucas a tad bit of hope. I had managed to set aside a little money every payday without Peter becoming suspicious. It was enough that I went on a shopping spree for Lucas. I couldn't contain the joy in my heart when I picked out brand-new clothes, envisioning his excitement when he saw them neatly folded on the end of his bed. It broke my heart day in and day out seeing him in tattered secondhand clothes, when his brothers were dressed to the nines. He had such a pure heart and never complained. I could see the sadness in his eyes as his spirit got crushed a little more every day.

I got really brave one day and gave him a smile through the rearview mirror, silently saying, *I'm sorry*. I hoped he understood, but he looked perplexed, turning to look over his shoulder, like I was talking to someone else. I was putting my and Lucas' lives in danger, because if Peter ever found out I was starting to give Lucas the tiniest bit of hope and attention, it would backfire on me big time. The twins were an extension of Peter and a direct pipeline, making it more difficult to let my true feelings show.

My biggest accomplishment to this day is convincing Peter to let the kids have a dog. I knew a dog for Lucas would be the best thing to happen to him, since I was not allowed to be a mom to him. He needed to feel the love of another living, breathing creature, and what better way than to have a dog to cuddle with? It was one of the happiest days of my life, watching Lucas' eyes light up and to see the bond they formed. They were inseparable, and my heart did a happy dance every time I saw them together.

I spent hours dreaming about what my life would have been like to shower my Lucas with the love he deserved. I tried to concoct plans where I could get Lucas secret messages, but Peter was always lurking, raising his finger to his throat with a slashing movement. Was I that transparent?

One would have thought I would pack up the boys and hightail it out of this torture chamber—and I thought about it often, especially when I saw the toll it was taking on Lucas. I couldn't figure it out myself, until one night I was flipping through the channels on television and landed on PBS, where a documentary on Stockholm Syndrome was playing. I watched in horror as my life was playing out in front of me. OMG, it was me and Peter as my captor. It all made sense, and, in a weird way, it helped me come to terms with the what and the why my life remained in the sorry state it was. I hope that I can somehow break away, but it doesn't look hopeful

CHAPTER 7 ... THE CONTRACT

for me. What I do know is that, every chance I get, I will continue to send the slightest of messages to my firstborn.

The worst part is that Lucas may never know. He may never know how much I loved him. How much I admired him. Or what heartache I endured daily so he could live to see adulthood and finally escape the life of abuse I was forced to dish out daily.

CHAPTER 8

THE MOMENT
THIRTEEN YEARS OLD

Whew! I thought my hormones were bad when I turned twelve, but that was nothing like what's happening to me now. I'm confused about why my body is changing so much. My voice is getting deeper, and I'm growing hair in places I never thought imaginable. And we won't even discuss my thoughts about girls. I needed guidance and answers ASAP. Not knowing what came over me one day, I approached my mom as she was sitting on the patio, staring off into space, as she often did. I hesitated, trying to read her mood before I approached her. She was humming to herself again, when a smile slowly spread across her face. I was hoping this meant she was in a good mood, but if I were a betting man, I'd probably lose my shirt.

Diving in before I lost my nerve, with sweaty palms, I softly tapped her on the shoulder as my heartbeat vibrated in my eardrums.

CHAPTER 8 ... THE MOMENT

It seriously was a crapshoot on what would happen next, and the odds weren't in my favor of anything favorable. A waft of her perfume filtered through the air as I caught a whiff of vanilla and jasmine. It was intoxicating. She turned at my touch and looked terrified when she saw it was me standing there. Looking around frantically, she whispered, "Lucas, what are you doing here? And what do you want?" She hadn't called me "Lucas" in years. I stood with my mouth hanging open, unable to find words.

"Well? Cat got your tongue?" she said softly, as she reached out and grabbed my hand. Her hand was soft and warm to the touch. I almost peed my pants on the spot, I was so excited. Someone who has done nothing but make my life miserable was showing me a tender moment.

"Mom, I er, I, er, I want to ask you something." I managed to utter. I'd never had a stutter before, but I was so caught up in the moment that I was at a loss for words.

She raised her eyebrows as if to say, *Well, what's stopping you?* as she hysterically looked to and fro. A noticeable twitch I had never seen before involuntarily appeared in the corner of her mouth as sweat beaded on her brow. I thought for a split second she was having a stroke, when, out of nowhere, my dad appeared. She dropped my hand like a hot potato, and the moment was broken. She sprinted to the house, leaving me in the garden wondering what I had just witnessed as my dad chased after her, shouting for her to stop.

I was in an utter state of confusion but also on a high of all highs. Maybe my mom didn't hate me after all, like she had said just last year. If I remember correctly, she never really said she hated me, just that she didn't love me. Was there really a difference? I liked to think so and held on to the possibility that she could change her feelings.

I spent the better part of the day holed up in my room with my face buried in Marmalade's fur, trying to come to terms with my feelings and going over numerous scenarios, but not one made sense. I must have drifted off to sleep, because I was awoken by a loud, tumultuous *Bang!* The wall in my bedroom shook, and then I heard screaming. My dad was yelling, but I couldn't make out what he was saying. I cautiously tiptoed down the stairs and peered around the corner, making sure I held my breath. My dad was livid, standing over my mom as she sat shaking in a kitchen chair. He had his face inches from her face, which was now covered in his spit. Fragmented words filtered through my ears, but I could make out not even one cohesive sentence. I heard *hate, warned, last chance* and *sorry* mumbled as he slapped her across the face.

I gasped involuntarily and ran up to my room, taking three stairs at a time. Locking the door behind me, I pressed my ear against the door, straining to hear, but all I got in return was the barely audible sound of my mom weeping as my dad slammed the door and peeled out of the driveway, tires shrieking. I peered through my dusty metal mini-blinds just in time to see my dad plow into garbage cans lined up on the pristine sidewalk. Milk cartons and other garbage catapulted into the air, and then I lost sight of him peeling around the corner.

I was torn about what to do. I was pissed, scared, and confused. My mom definitely was not my biggest fan, and I was reasonably certain I would be the last person she would confide in, so I wrapped myself in my warm down comforter, rested my head on Marm's back, and prayed. I had never prayed before and wasn't even sure there was a God, but I was willing to take my chances, because desperate times called for desperate measures. I fell asleep with my hands clasped together, dreaming of better days.

CHAPTER 8 ... THE MOMENT

The morning rolled around too soon. As I looked through the branches of my favorite plum tree, I saw ominous gray clouds threatening to rain. The weather matched my mood perfectly. If Marmalade didn't have to pee and eat, I may have spent the day in my room. I wasn't a fan of confrontation, and not knowing what to say to my mom made matters worse. The air was stale and musty smelling, leaving me to question if it was vomit or blood that permeated the air. Bounding down the stairs, I had decided I would take my mom's lead. If she wanted to offer an explanation, then by all means, I was all ears, but she was nowhere to be seen.

After feeding Marm her favorite kibble, I waltzed, with more exuberance than I was feeling, into the backyard, to find my brothers sitting on the patio huddled together, erecting a bug fort with popsicle sticks. They had collected roly-polies, worms, and a couple of earwigs for good measure, decorating the outside with some dandelions they had picked from the yard. I was equal parts amazed and surprised that they were doing something nice instead of pouring salt on snails just to watch them bubble up and die. Maybe there was a sliver of hope, after all.

Talking to them was not on my list of top one hundred favorite things, but I needed answers. "Do you know where Mom is?" I questioned, trying not to sound as panicked as I was feeling. They continued to work on their fort, ignoring me. "Excuse me, guys. Seriously—have you seen mom?" I repeated with more urgency.

They both looked up, irritated that I had the audacity to bother them. They were identical twins and not only looked exactly the same, with sandy blond hair cut in a surfer style, but both of them also had the same foul personality toward me. Looking me up and down like I had two heads and was purple with pink polka dots, they answered simultaneously. "Yeah, she said she would be in her room all day and didn't want to be bothered. And then she mumbled something ridiculous like we were supposed to listen to you because you were in charge!" They broke out in laughter that had them rolling on the ground.

I failed to see any humor in the subject, but you would have thought they were reading a joke book, they were laughing so hard. I walked away shaking my head, knowing that getting any more answers out of those two would be impossible. They were in their little demented world, and I wasn't a welcome guest. It was clear they despised me as much as I did them, and my earlier thoughts about there might be a sliver of hope for them were quickly abandoned.

Wanting to honor my mom's wishes for being left alone had me at odds with how I wanted to handle things. It puzzled me that I cared so much, when 99 percent of the time, she treated me like I had the plague and the other one percent like I was horseshit. But I did care. A lot. At that moment, I remembered one of my teachers telling me that I had a heart of gold, and this made me feel warm inside. It was a feeling I didn't have often unless I was wrapped around Marm's body.

I tiptoed up the stairs like I was on some sort of clandestine mission. In a strange way, I kinda was. A mission to make sure she was all right, without bothering her or letting my dad see me. I looked out the hall window and heaved a sigh of relief when my dad's red Mustang wasn't parked in the driveway in its normal spot. With the coast clear, I listened at her door. I could hear faint sobs and the sound of her nose being blown. And then I heard her talking to someone. Or was it to herself? I raised my fist to knock, but, at the last second, I changed my mind. I couldn't help but feel

CHAPTER 8 ... THE MOMENT

like I was eavesdropping where I wasn't wanted, so I walked away, more confused than ever about what had transpired the night prior.

The day turned into night, and a horrendous rainstorm started, with lightning illuminating the sky, imitating the mood that hung over the house and sucking any good air out that had been left behind. The only positive was that my dad had stayed away. Wanting to make my mom proud for leaving me in charge, which still baffled my mind, I made the twins dinner and tidied up. They even thanked me, which was a miracle all by itself.

Nothing ever came of that fretful night. My dad finally returned home days later, in just as much of a glum mood that he was in when he left. I had a looming feeling that our paths were on a collision course that would change my life, but it never happened. Not yet, anyway. Life returned back to its "normal" existence, and my mom never uttered a word. Whatever happened that night and in the days to follow had turned her back into her sour, surly self. I kept hidden away either in my room, doing chores, or spending time in the library to keep from suffering her wrath. I was back to being public enemy number one.

CHAPTER 9
THE GIFT
FOURTEEN TO FIFTEEN YEARS OLD

Everything had returned to the status quo after that wicked night when I was thirteen. Oftentimes I reflected back on the tender touch my mom gave me when she held my hand in hers. It all seemed like a dream now, because she'd shown no signs of caring about me since then. A total one-eighty in fact. She glared at me during family dinners, spoke to me only if it was necessary, and avoided me at all costs. I was confused to say the least but once again accepted it as my not-so-new normal.

School was school. I didn't hate it, but I didn't love it, either. I still loved learning and excelled in class, but I was sick of being the brunt of everyone's jokes. I had been given a new nickname that was degrading. Everyone called me "the jolly green giant" because I was taller than anyone else in the whole school. I even towered

CHAPTER 9 ... THE GIFT

above the majority of the teachers. Growing was one of the things I had mastered, and I didn't see it changing anytime soon.

Whereas my hair had been blond with curls when I was younger, it had darkened a bit through the years and became what I call frizzy corkscrews. Humidity was not my friend. I wasn't ugly by any stretch of the imagination; some, well most, would say *handsome*, so I wasn't sure why everyone always made fun of me. Maybe because word had spread, thanks to my two evil brothers, that I was like the red-headed stepchild of the family and an easy target. When the other kids weren't ridiculing me, they looked at me with pity. I wasn't sure which was worse.

There were highlights, though. I was now in high school, which meant I didn't have to bump into my brothers. Our town wasn't huge, so we had two schools—one that took you from kindergarten through eighth grade, and the other one was high school. It was a true testament to my pathetic life that I would consider this a highlight. But any amount of time I could be away from my two nemeses was a welcome relief for me.

Settling into a routine of sorts at school, I kept my head down, avoiding eye contact of any type, and studied. I wasn't much for any extracurricular activities, until I got a wild hair one day and tried out for the track team. I was so damn proud of myself when I made the team—the coach actually said that he was *happy* to have me on-board. That was a foreign concept to me. Someone happy to have me around?

Where I was awkward and uncoordinated a couple years back, I had learned to use my size to my advantage and grew into myself. I was quick and limber from years of manual labor, which helped me stand out. Even though I was part of the track team, it was largely an individual sport, which appealed to me. I was socially inept and uncomfortable around others, so when I met a fellow team member, named Theo, I wasn't sure how to act. I'd had friends in the past, but my friendships never lasted. Either they disappeared like my friend Ivy when I was twelve, or we drifted apart, with different interests. This was different. He was different.

I was sitting on a bench, bent over, tying my shoes before track practice was set to start. The day was like any other spring day in Piedmont. The sun was peeking around a sky full of the puffiest cloud formations. I loved cloud formations and often lay with Marm, staring at the sky, making out imaginary images. What made today different was how my day had started out. I was still in seventh heaven hours later from my earlier interaction with my mom.

I was in the kitchen, packing up my backpack with my school textbooks, when, out of nowhere, she appeared like an angelic vision. "Lucas, do you have a moment to talk?" she breathlessly said while scanning the room for my dad or brothers. I wanted to yell, *"Are you kidding me? Of course, I have a minute. I have a whole lifetime,"* but instead I nonchalantly stopped what I was doing and said, "Sure, Mom. What's up?" I could tell she was nervous because she was fidgeting with the hem of her sunflower apron, picking at an imaginary thread while clearing her throat. She reached out and daintily took my hand in hers. Her hand felt as soft as Marm's fur. I felt something being transferred and pressed hard into the palm of my hand.

As she released my hand, I opened it to see she had placed into it a neatly folded one-hundred dollar bill. "I want you to know how proud I am of you for making the track team. I noticed how worn your running shoes are, and I wanted you to be able to buy a new pair.

CHAPTER 9 ... THE GIFT

A gift from me to you, so please don't tell your father or brothers." As she mentioned my dad and brothers, she looked spooked. And then she did the unthinkable. She reached up on her tiptoes and gently planted a kiss on my cheek, before abruptly waltzing out of the room, leaving me bewildered and taken by surprise—but happier than I'd been in years.

A deep voice brought me to the present out of my memory. "Excuse me, but is this where we meet for the Highland High track team?" I looked up to see a tan, short, gangly guy with a buzz cut so blond it almost looked transparent, smiling down at me. He extended his hand to shake mine and introduced himself as Theo Baldwin. "Please to meet you, Theo. I'm Lucas—Lucas Travers—and to answer your question, yes, we meet here after school Monday through Friday for practice. Are you a long-distance runner, too?" I inquired, eager to know more about this stranger with the infectious smile.

Turns out he wasn't a long-distance runner but instead took on field events, specializing in the long jump. He was different from anyone I had ever met. Where I was tall, he was short. Where I was quiet, he never stopped talking. Where I was an introvert, he was an extrovert. And the list went on and on. I had to admit the old adage *Opposites Attract* was spot on. Theo and his family had just moved from California, so he was what I called a clean slate. He hadn't been caught up in the unsavory comments and relentless jibes that had become my everyday life. We became inseparable.

After practice, I would run home, collect Marm, and spend the afternoon hanging out at his house. My bank account was taking a hit because I was putting my chores on the back burner, but I had never felt so happy and accepted. What I found most refreshing was that I was never judged or questioned about my past. His parents loved me and welcomed me with open arms. It was the most foreign concept to me that someone would take time out of their day to care about mine. There were bottomless snacks, home-cooked dinners, and sleepovers under the stars. I never knew what I had been missing out on, and I soaked it all in like a six-foot-four-inch sponge.

Theo's parents went to not only his events, but they also came to mine, cheering me on from the bleachers. I had finally found acceptance and love after years of the exact opposite. They even went so far as to take me and Marm on vacation to Cape Cod, where we road-tripped and spent endless hours splashing in the ocean. I swear the smile never left my face or my heart until we had to return, and I was greeted with not-so-open arms. I was a bit surprised to realize I didn't care in the least. I had found what I had been missing.

Spring was in full swing, and rain was more common than sunshine. I had breezed through my classes, eager to meet up with Theo at practice, but he didn't show. The next day, no Theo. By the end of the week, there was still no sign of him, so Marm and I went over to his house. The moment I rounded the corner, I got a feeling in the pit of my stomach knowing in my heart something bad had happened. Building up my courage to walk up the steps to his veranda, I broke out in a sweat. Time stood still as I transfixed on the old oak tree in his front yard blowing in the stiff breeze as bees pollinated the colorful flowers that lined the front of his house. I couldn't bring myself to knock on his door, but I didn't have to, because a grandmotherly woman with gray hair wrapped tightly in a bun at the base of her neck appeared out of nowhere.

"May I help you, son?" she questioned with a warm, tender smile but a furrowed brow. Her eyes were rimmed red and weepy. Noticeable bags had formed on her wrinkled face, and a sadness lay

CHAPTER 9 ... THE GIFT

under the surface. I was afraid to ask the question I already knew the answer to, but I blurted out, "Is Theo home? Can you tell him Lucas is here, please?"

In what seemed like an eternity but was only seconds, she explained she was Theo's grandma and motioned for me to sit on the step next to her. Taking my hands in her own, she let out the biggest sigh I had ever heard. I looked at her hands, wrinkled and aged with brown spots; I saw a life lived and loved. As we sat in silence, a tear ran down her cheek and landed on my thumb, telling me all I really needed to know.

"Son, it pains me beyond words to tell you this, but a trip that Theo, my son, and daughter-in-law had been looking forward to over the past weekend has ended in tragedy for all, as their car hydroplaned out of control, plummeting down a ravine before catching on fire. No one survived." I gasped as she placed her arm tightly around my shoulders and pulled me into a much-needed hug.

Distraught didn't begin to explain how I felt. Why did God hate me so much, taking away anything good in my life? I don't remember walking home, but when I looked up, I was crossing the street to my house. It was dark, and raindrops had begun to fall, mixing with the tears flowing nonstop down my cheeks. Marm was by my side, looking up at me and mirroring the sadness I was feeling.

We managed to make it to my room without seeing anyone. Not that anyone would care, but I wasn't in any mood to explain my tears. My days and nights blended into each other; I emerged from my room only to take care of Marm's needs. I refused to go to school, spending my days in my room, living in a zombie-like state, mourning the only family that had ever loved me. Anyone would have had to be blind not to see it: I was unhinged. After a week of trying to come to terms with the tragedy, I poked my head out of my bedroom to see if the coast was clear.

Right outside my door, there was a tray with a blueberry-banana smoothie and peanut butter toast and jam. I looked up and down the hallway, but it was empty. Not a sound could be heard throughout the house. Looking at the grandfather clock at the end of the hallway, I saw it was 9 a.m. My brothers should have been in school, and God knows where my wicked mom was. Probably out shopping for a new broom to ride off into the sunset on. I wasn't sure how long the snack had been sitting outside my door, but the smoothie was still cold, with condensation dripping down the side of the glass.

Not realizing how famished I was, I drank it without even giving a second thought there could be poison mixed in. I felt pretty confident I was safe in that department. If they wanted me dead, I would have died years ago. Besides, if I wasn't around, who else would they torture? I accidentally kicked the tray with my toe, and the plate shifted, revealing a note written on my mom's personal stationery. I would know it anywhere. Not only did it have her initials—JT—at the top in calligraphy, but it also had tiny sunflowers, all around the borders. My breath caught for a second as a lump formed in my throat. I lifted it up to read with shaking hands. In her writing, it said, "I'm sorry for what you're going through. Wish I could help. Mom."

What the hell was this? I thought out loud. Now she's going to act like she gives a shit, but when I see her, she'll turn her back to me, mumbling under her breath some kind of derogatory comment. These random, mixed emotions were playing with my sanity. I tucked the note, along with the other one, under my mattress for safekeeping.

CHAPTER 9 ... THE GIFT

Even though I knew she didn't love me, it gave me a small, wee bit of hope that she had some compassion in her black heart.

I finally returned to school and track. Track was therapeutic, and I ran like I was being chased, but, in all actuality, I was running from reality and my painful realization that I was all alone in the world once again. Facing the cold, hard truth was a slap in my face but the experiences with Theo and his parents had taught me never to let my guard down again or put my love and trust in anyone else ever again. I was becoming too calloused for my own liking, but when life shits on you every corner you turn, that's what happens.

The irony of the whole debacle that was my life made me realize the years of abuse had worked in my favor, for once, because I learned to count on myself only. It made me more self-sufficient and determined to succeed. I laughed at the thought of thanking my parents for hating and abusing me all my life. I was more dedicated than ever to overcome any obstacle that dared to get in my path.

CHAPTER 10

THE FIGHT
SIXTEEN YEARS OLD

By the time I turned sixteen, I was all of six-feet-six-inches of pure muscle. I maintained my running ritual, finding it not only therapeutic but a great healing tonic for my heart. I needed a release from the pressures I felt at home. With age comes maturity, and with maturity comes intuitiveness. I couldn't help notice the sharp contrast between my dad and myself. Not just in our personalities but especially in our looks. Where I was exceptionally tall, he was on the short side. On the rare moments we were even in the same room, I dwarfed him. I could tell it irritated him even if he didn't say anything. Sometimes actions speak louder than words, and his silence spoke volumes.

School was in full swing, and my sophomore year was no different than any other year. Except for me, academically. I had made the honor roll and been given an award at the school assembly. God, I

CHAPTER 10 ... THE FIGHT

was proud of myself! Of course, nobody from my so-called family showed up to support me, but I would have fallen over in a dead faint if they had. Long ago, I decided I didn't need them. Or, I should say, I didn't *need them the way they were*. If we had been one big happy, supportive, loving family like Theo's had been, then that would be a different story. Them not showing up then would have caused me alarm, sending my head spinning, thinking the worst had happened. But, instead, I held my head high, thanked the principal for my award, and beamed with pride inside. I was one step closer to a career and a life far away from here.

Oftentimes I lay in bed mulling over a life away and on my own. The only thing I knew for sure was that I *didn't* want to be an insurance salesman like my dad. I wanted nothing whatsoever to do with him, and *following in his footsteps* was never an option. The law interested me. I had a very strong pull toward seeing justice done on all fronts. It was a powerful job, but it would take a great deal of money for schooling—money I didn't have or could get my hands on. I could apply for a scholarship, but my grades, although good, weren't consistently genius level.

A lightbulb clicked on in my brain recently when a recruiter from the Army had come and spoken at an assembly for Career Day. It offered a variety of benefits I was interested in. First and foremost, it offered me an opportunity to get away from this hell- hole. Secondly, I could travel the world. Third, I would be taught a trade, and, lastly, but needing repeating, that I would be offered an opportunity away from my dismal existence in the middle of nowhere. I filed the information away to revisit as the day grew closer.

In the meantime, I signed up, as an elective, to attend shop classes, otherwise known as "career and technical education." I loved to work with my hands and figured why not tackle these classes for free? They offered carpentry, electrical, masonry, welding, and woodworking. Besides a career as an attorney, the only other thing that appealed to me was working with my hands. It came naturally to me to fix things or build things—two jobs on totally opposite ends of the spectrum but equally as rewarding.

As I continued to meander through life and the lazy days of summer, they were anything but lazy for me. Marm was getting old, and thoughts of life without my constant companion were too painful to fathom. Whereas she would always accompany me on my daily runs and all my lawn jobs in the neighborhood, I left her behind now, curled up under a soft blanket on my bed. I would rush through my jobs, eager to return home to her and smother her with kisses and special treats. She was my everything. In a world that had dealt me a bad hand, she was my royal flush.

One exceptionally hot summer day, I came home, dripping in sweat, after my daily chores, to find a note posted on my bedroom door. Instead of on my mom's stationery, it had been scribbled on a stained paper towel that looked as if it had been rescued from the trash before coffee grounds got ahold of it. *What now?* was all I could think before reading that my dad had beckoned me, demanding I find him ASAP. I was in no mood for any of his bullshit accusations. Giving Marm an extra pet for luck, I ran down the stairs in search of his royal highness.

Dread started coursing through my veins. I had no reason to think anything good was going to come out of this summoning. He hadn't given me anything but dirty looks and snide remarks since the twins had entered the picture. I searched the whole house, but he was nowhere to be found. I was positive this was part of his plan.

CHAPTER 10 ... THE FIGHT

He wanted me to sweat bullets and have my stomach turn inside out with the thought of our impending confrontation. After a solid half hour of searching and researching every room and closet, I broke down and found my mom tediously folding clothes in the laundry room.

"Mom, do you have any idea where Dad is? I've searched everywhere three different times," I said, while anticipation held me captive.

Not thinking she would care or even answer me, I was mistaken. Her eyes bugged out, as panic spread across her face. "Wh, wh, what?" she managed to eke out. After telling her he had left me a note, she literally broke out in a sweat and had to brace herself against the wash sink. My spidey senses were on high alert. This was not a normal response for anyone, not even my wack job of a mom. She was acting terrified, so I took advantage of a weak moment and pried. "Mom, why are you acting so distraught? You look like you're on the verge of losing your shit. Has dad abused you? Are you scared of him?"

I watched her for signs—anything different than what I was already witnessing. An eye twitch? Absent-mindedly picking at an invisible thread? Shifty eye placement? Not knowing what I'd do if I saw anything, I certainly was not expecting to see all three! I was livid. Right then and there, I wanted to hunt down that sorry excuse for a human, knowing full well that, if I found him, I would clam up. If I had to be brutally honest with myself, I would have to admit that he scared the bejesus out of me. The last thing I wanted was my mom to suffer because of my disrespect.

"Please, mom. Talk to me. What has he done? Tell me," I begged. She looked confused and petrified. I saw the wheels churning in her brain as a myriad of emotions played across her face. It confused me why I cared. I shouldn't, because God knows she'd done nothing to deserve my respect or sympathy. But my heart hurt for what I saw in front of me—a broken, beaten-down shell of a human with a mean streak that would rival the world's worst.

Before I could think, I folded her into my arms, stroking her hair and whispering that it would be OK. She stood rigid against my embrace, but I heard her sigh and felt the tension relax and leave her body. Silence spoke volumes between us as we stood blocking out the world; no words needed to be spoken. A tender moment between mother and son until a thwack reverberated through the room. We both jumped, turning to see my dad as angry as a hornet. His mouth was set in a grimace causing his lip to literally curl with disgust. Before I could speak, he was on me faster than a lightning bolt, shoving me and screaming obscenities.

"What the hell do you think you're doing, Luke? Get your filthy, disgusting hands off of her!"

Caught off guard, I stumbled, causing my mom to fall hard against the sink and land on the ground. I bent to help her up, and he slapped my hand away, yelling, "As for you, Jane, get out of my sight before you won't be able to!" My mom scrambled, crawling as fast as she could to get away from him. I wanted to run after her, but he blocked the doorway and stared me down. I'd never seen him so vexed. His face was flushed, and throbbing veins pulsed in his neck as he balled his fingers into fists. But as mad as he was, I was madder. At that very second, I got lost in the moment, not being able to distinguish any sense of what was right and wrong, only seeing red, as I cold-cocked him into oblivion. He didn't have a chance, and I couldn't have cared less.

CHAPTER 10 ... THE FIGHT

The series of events that followed were a blur, and I snapped out of my trance only when sirens blared in front of our house. Unfortunately, the joke was on me, and my dad got the last laugh as the police came and took me away. It was my first brush with the law, but I had a strange feeling it wouldn't be my last.

CHAPTER 11

THE AFTERMATH
SEVENTEEN YEARS OLD

Have you ever acted in the moment, letting anger—instead of reason—take over? That day back in August of last year had changed me. Come to find out the courts don't look too kindly on aggravated assault, even if it was provoked. I soon found out that an attempt to willfully cause or recklessly cause serious bodily injury to a family member will land you in jail, minor or not. So that's where I went. To cool my jets. In hindsight, it probably was the best place for me at the time, because I was wound tight, ready to explode. Now I had a blemish on my record, a dent in my funds to the tune of $500, and a strong desire to stay far away from my dad, aka Satan.

My night behind bars was anything but a pleasant experience. I was treated like a second-class citizen, stashed in a holding cell with five other men at different levels of sobriety. It stunk like barf and what I suspected an old honky-tonk bar would smell like. I tried my

CHAPTER 11 ... THE AFTERMATH

best to get comfortable on the wooden bench that had seen better days, but all I succeeded in doing was getting a nasty splinter wedged in the palm of my hand. I kept my head down and pretended like I didn't hear the others when they asked me questions. And prayed for morning to come as I counted off the minutes.

"Lucas Travers—it's time to follow me," an angry-looking deputy sheriff growled as he opened the metal door, leading me to freedom. "There is some paperwork to sign at the front desk, and then you're free to leave with your mom." I wanted to scream, *"Yippee—it's my mom!"* but I kept my mouth shut and my eyes down. I was so relieved that she was the one who had come to get me. I probably would have chosen time behind bars over getting in the car with my dad. As I rounded the corner, I saw my mom sitting uncomfortably against the dark-wood-paneled wall in metal chairs. She looked haggard and sad—really sad, as she caught sight of me. Her hair had been thrown up into a messy top knot, and black streaks of mascara were flowing like lava down her cheeks. She was wearing a pair of jeans and an old green sweatshirt with the words *Bookmarks Are For Quitters* printed on the front, which made me second-guess if I ever really knew who she was. I had never seen her read a book—even *once*—in my life. She stood and extended her hand to me, mouthing, *I'm sorry.* Did she really mean it?

She had parked her car in the parking structure across the street. I felt like I was taking my walk of shame as she remained silent; I had no inkling of what was going through her head. As we walked, time stood still. I waited for her to expand on the *I'm sorry* comment, but all that followed was a cold shoulder. She fumbled with the keys, trying to insert them into the ignition, but her hands were shaking.

In a weird way, I was hoping I was the reason behind her attitude and not something my dad had done to her.

I glanced her way, and she was staring at me, looking disconsolate. "Luke—what on Earth were you thinking? Are you out of your mind—disrespecting your father like that? I really don't know what's in store for you now, because there's only so much I can do to help you." The look of compassion I'd witnessed just moments earlier had been erased from her face and replaced with repulsion. I would give anything to know what had made her change her attitude toward me—out of nowhere. It was almost like an unforeseen pull from the universe had gotten ahold of her mind.

I fired a barrage of questions, not waiting for answers. I was just hoping this would be the day she could shed some much-needed light on what the hell was going on between her and my dad and between me and her. "Mom, please let me explain. First of all, why are you taking his side? He threatened you and pushed me. Was I supposed to stand by and let matters escalate until someone got seriously hurt? I'm not a child anymore, and I can stand up for myself—and you if you would just let me. Please tell me what is going on!"

I felt defeated as I stared at her, feeling like I might burst if I didn't get to the bottom of things. I begged, hoping she would finally come clean. I reached across the seat and put her hand in mine, hoping to console her, but she yanked it away with no explanation. "Mom, please talk to me." I wasn't above groveling; I batted my eyes in a futile attempt to convince her to open up to me. I begged again, adding a cherry on top, but all was for naught. All I got was more silence until we pulled up into the driveway.

She turned the car off and let out an exasperated sigh. "Drop it, Luke, for both of our sakes. That's all I'm going to say on the

CHAPTER 11 ... THE AFTERMATH

matter. Now go inside and apologize to your dad—and pretend like our conversation never took place." And, with that, she huffed off, slamming the door behind her, causing the windows to rattle.

I was back to being "Luke" again, instead of "Lucas," so I knew I was once again on her shit list.

I wasn't sure who I was anymore. But one thing I did know for certain was that I would not be apologizing to my dad. Not today—or any other day, for that matter. Just one night behind bars had enlightened me. What parent would allow their minor child to be carted off to jail to rot away for a night? A coward, that's who, and that's exactly what my dad was. I also knew, with one hundred percent certainty, that I was beyond frustrated with my life and the situation at home. I knew in my heart something was wrong, but my hands were tied, so to speak. My mom refused to talk about the fears that were written all over her face. My dad, well, he was an asshole.

Turns out hitting him that day wasn't the best decision I've ever made. In fact, it ranks right up there with the worst day of my life, but, given the circumstances, I'd do it all over again. Thinking it was one of the worst days of my life was saying something, since I've had nothing but awful days. The only day I can think of getting worse is the day I will have to say goodbye to my Marmalade.

Being able to take care of myself was something I had learned to do at an early age, or I wouldn't be alive today. Proud to admit I was not only alive but living life to its fullest. Except for a temper that had appeared out of nowhere that day. I was unable to shake the feeling of rage that came over me when I so much as caught sight of my dad. I wanted to strangle his measly little neck. And I was afraid that, given the opportunity, I might succumb to my desires. Whereas before, I was driven by survival, I was now driven by rage.

It didn't take much to distance myself from everyone at home because I was hardly the life of the party around my house. The tender moment my mom and I had shared at the police station was long forgotten. If at all possible, she was meaner and more distant than ever. I knew if I was ever going to leave in one piece and make a life for myself, I had to make it my mission not to give a damn and turn down any offer to join in any family festivities—or else, a life behind bars was in my immediate future. It was the easiest thing I ever had to do, because, if I had ever been invited anywhere to start with, it had been an afterthought, like throwing a scrap to a caged animal. I was bound and determined not to let the evil musings in my head come to fruition so I busied myself with the most mundane chores to occupy my time. At first.

My nest egg was growing by leaps and bounds. So much so that I had to dig another hole for my cash, this time putting it in a wooden box I had crafted in shop class. I had originally designed it with my mom in mind, but she was back to giving me the cold shoulder. It was more than a shoulder though, her whole body acted like she was repulsed at the looks of me, giving me a wide berth if we were to ever be in the same area of the house. Even though I no longer needed her to survive like I had when I was young, it hurt me to my core the way she ignored me. "Self-sufficient" should have been my middle name, because I was a champ at it.

Not sure how my brothers had made it into high school that year, but they had, by the skin of their teeth. Where I was smart, they got by with mediocre grades. They were, however, popular, athletic, and a mirror image of my dad. They were taller than him, but, besides that, they were identical to the spawn of the devil himself. Small, dark-brown beady little eyes, set between a pointy nose and shielded

CHAPTER 11 ... THE AFTERMATH

under caterpillar eyebrows and foul personalities. I, on the other hand, looked nothing like him. I counted my meager blessings.

They had tried out and made the football team, which kept them out of my hair. Practicing every night gave me more time to myself to smother Marm with love without them pestering me. Every Friday night, my parents went to watch them play, and I stayed home. I had started a ritual with Marm that fall. While they were at the football games, we would spend time in the backyard under the stars. I pitched a tent, and we would "ruff" it in the backyard, falling asleep listening to the sounds of nature, wrapped in each other's arms. I knew her time on Earth was growing short, and I didn't want any regrets later. My dreams of running away with her and starting a new life, anywhere but here, had been foolish talk. I knew, as I looked into her sugar face, I would be leaving alone. And heartbroken.

Even though I semi-regretted hitting my dad, only because of the repercussions I faced, I found myself dreaming of doing it again. I had never been a violent person, but that man evoked an emotion in me that wasn't foreign anymore. I had found pleasure in knocking him out cold. It consumed my every waking minute and often woke me at night, drenched in a puddle of sweat, twisted in my sheets. I knew it was unhealthy, but common sense was out of the equation, and, the more I tried to stop my lunatic thoughts, the more overwhelmed I became, until I got to the point that it was monopolizing my entire day. The more I tried not to obsess over him, the more I did. It was quickly becoming an unhealthy obsession, and I felt trapped with no one to turn to for guidance.

I wanted to reach out to my mom and ask for direction and pointers on how to get my life back on track again, but she was treating me like public enemy number one. My grades started to suffer, and I did the only thing I could think of to escape my tortured, battered mind. I began to drown my sorrows in booze. Surprisingly, it was easy for me to purchase even though the legal drinking age was twenty-one. Since I was so tall, people equated that with age, and I was never even carded. My drinking started out harmless enough, just enough to chase away the demons. I soon found myself drinking during the day instead of attending school. And my life began to take a downward spiral into the depths of depression.

Everything that was important to me in the past, except Marm, was discarded like week-old trash. I was obsessed with the numbness that took over my mind when I was wasted. No doubts of doom or fits of anger dominated my thoughts like they had. I would drink myself into oblivion, and no one cared, assuming they even noticed. I was taking self-pity to a whole new level, and I had become a rebellious, uncontrollable teen.

Earlier in the year, I had finished taking a drivers-education class in school and had proudly gotten my driver's license and first car. All I could afford was an old Chevrolet Corvair that was a clunker—but to me it was the Lamborghini of all cars. It was my prized possession, and I spent all my spare time washing it so it shined in all its red glory. Marm would lay on the grass under the huge willow tree in our front yard, waiting for me to lift her into the front seat to go for a joy ride.

Whenever I would say, "Ready to go, girl? Time to hit the open road!" she would let out a little squeal and perk up. She loved the wind whipping through her fur, sending her ears into a swirling sea of red fur around her head, slobber covering the window, while the fuzzy red dice that hung from the rearview mirror did a dance in

CHAPTER 11 ... THE AFTERMATH

the wind. I had gotten them on the trip to Cape Cod with Theo's family and proudly displayed them, keeping Theo's memory alive. The pleasure she derived from her daily car rides were the only thing bringing me happiness and the only time I wasn't stinking drunk or drowning in self-pity, loathing my very existence.

It wasn't a good time to be me. I was letting my dad get under my skin and the pleasure he would procure from watching me self-destruct should have been enough to draw me out of my funk, but, sadly, that wasn't the case. Day after day, I was a lost cause, going through the motions of life. It was hit-or-miss if I attempted to sober myself up enough to attend classes. My grades suffered, and my teachers were no longer able to turn a blind eye. I was self-destructing right before their eyes, a shell of who I once was.

My parents were called in for a teacher/parent conference to discuss my poor performance, disruptive behavior, and absences. My dad refused to go, complaining that he wouldn't waste his time on the likes of me. It should have bothered me, but I had given up trying to please him years ago, and, surprisingly enough, I felt nothing. The night my mom drove off to school made me reflect on what should have been. I couldn't help but blame her. *I wouldn't be in this predicament if she would only talk to me and quit sweeping everything under the rug.* The proverbial rug was as steep as Mount Everest, without a chance in hell of any issue being addressed. So, I waited and hoped she came home with a solution. And more importantly, that she took the time to care.

While I waited, I sat in my room, chewing my nails to the nub, with Marm curled up by my side, I picked up a book to read. After reading the first page numerous times, I was unable to concentrate. I slammed it closed, blaming everyone but myself for my predicament.

Who was I kidding? I had only myself to blame; I could pretend like it didn't matter what my mom thought of me. It *did* matter. It had *always* mattered. I began to pace, listening to the floorboards creak under my weight. I was surprised to feel wetness on my face as tears spilled over, begging to be heard.

I wasn't proud that tears were streaming down my face. After all, I am a grown boy now, but my past indiscretions were weighing heavily on my mind. A tiny sliver of hope washed over me as I internally begged for a change. Would this be the wake-up call my mom needed to recognize I needed her love and guidance?

CHAPTER 12

THE INTERVENTION
EIGHTEEN YEARS OLD

The wake-up call I had hoped for didn't happen. As soon as I heard my mom's car pull into the garage, I ran down the stairs, taking three at a time. I made sure my dad was nowhere to be seen before I threw open the garage door, hoping my mom had the solution I so desperately needed. "Well, mom—what happened? Did you and the administration come up with a plan?" I questioned eagerly, as I tapped my foot nervously, waiting for her to answer. She looked at me with a mixture of pity and disgust at what I had become and said, "Luke, I wish I had answers, but you've done this to yourself. Grow up, and take some responsibility for once!" And, with that, she stormed past me and into the house, leaving me alone with my demons.

An intervention had been called. This is what my life had come to. Sitting in the family room, with Marm by my side, lending a paw for support, I stared at six shallow, empty faces spilling with hatred and loathing. I'm not sure why my grandparents had been called over, since they weren't really an active part of my life. I could only imagine my dad had them come to humiliate me even more. "How could you shame our family like this? After all we've done for you. This is how you repay us, by becoming the laughing stock of the neighborhood? A pitiful drunk," my dad screamed as he paced back and forth, nostrils flaring as his forehead creased into deep wrinkles.

I knew, if there hadn't been witnesses, he would have punched me. Or would he remember the last time I flattened him, out cold, looking like the village idiot? His eyes bulged out as spittle flew through the air, mixing with the dust particles that floated through the haze. Those big veins that popped out on his neck when he was pissed were back with a vengeance.

I hung my head in shame, trying to keep the tears at bay. I generally wasn't much of a crier, like I had been when I was younger, even though I took great pride in the fact that I was in touch with my sensitive side. The tears that were trying desperately to force their way out were tears of remorse, not sadness. I had let myself down. Willing myself to escape to a happier place to shield myself from his objurgation, I held my head high and pretended I was lying on a colorful beach towel as the waves splashed on the shoreline. The last thing I needed was my dad to see tears from me. One more thing to throw in my face, calling me a *sissy* or *pantywaist*.

Whereas an intervention should have been to facilitate a solution to improve my situation, it was more of a tongue-lashing to the nth degree. My mom looked like she'd been raked over a bed of hot coals, her hair unruly and frizzed out on the ends. I had come to expect bags under her bloodshot eyes, but the hair being in total

CHAPTER 12 ... THE INTERVENTION

disarray was something new. Her normal coiffed appearance had been traded for bag-lady chic.

I could only imagine the slew of derogatory remarks my dad had spewed about me to her. I almost allowed myself a moment to feel sorry for her having to listen to the nastiness my dad had bestowed on her for my misguided attempt at escaping. I shrunk within myself knowing that I had let not only myself down; I had also let her down.

Caring about my dad wasn't part of the equation at any time. We had set dynamite to that bridge long ago. Even though I knew I should respect him because he was my father, he had not earned that right. Respect goes both ways, and I had never received an ounce of love or respect from him. It was killing me to think he was deriving satisfaction from seeing me remorseful. If he'd had his way, he would have sent me away long ago or kept me locked in a cage like a poor abused dog.

I was far from dumb, and I knew alcohol wasn't the answer. I had tried it only as a last-ditch effort. It provided the reprieve I needed at the time. As my dad droned on and on, I felt like I was having an out-of-body experience. I tried my hardest to make my face look remorseful, but I found it difficult. Inside I was feeling hard edges, spikes, darkness, and hatred. Hatred for my dad and hatred for myself for allowing him to drive me to this point.

I watched and listened but never really heard what was being said. I hovered over everyone while he droned on and on, harping on the same degrading indiscretions. I get it, Dad. I was a fuck-up; now *move on* already! It was like his words passed through my consciousness like a thick, meaningless fog. Sounds of birds chirping, grass being mowed—everyday sounds but not enough to drown out the voices in my head.

I took a second to look at each person individually, seeing different emotions in each of their eyes. My grandparents sat huddled next to each other, clearly uncomfortable as they clasped their hands tightly in their laps. I took a moment to look deeply into their eyes. Life had not been kind, and they looked much older than their eighty-plus years. I wanted to see love, compassion, or even sympathy, but all that stared back at me was two little old people with gray hair and wrinkles outlining their faces as confusion and despair reflected in their lifeless eyes.

My brothers looked like they would rather be anywhere but in the same room with me. They were having a laugh at my expense as they tried to suppress their smiles and giggles. Although their mouths showed one emotion, their beady little eyes showed only disgust and hatred. I was indifferent to whatever they thought, but I did care what my mom was thinking and feeling. I looked her way, and she had her head down, wiping a tear from her eye. She made eye contact with me for a quick second, and I could have sworn I saw sympathy and concern. Was I imagining it because I wanted it to be true?

As for my dad, I refused to look him in the eye. He had made it abundantly clear how he felt about me years ago when he said he would be better off without me. Since that day, it had gone from bad to worse to despicable.

My eighteenth birthday came and went without any fanfare. What should have been a joyous occasion ended up quiet, spending it sober with Marm by myself. We had taken the day and hit the open road with the wind whipping through the windows. As far as weather was concerned, my birthday was always a bit of a crapshoot. It was technically still spring, so oftentimes, it was windy, with a bitter

CHAPTER 12 ... THE INTERVENTION

nip in the air. This particular year, it defied all odds, and the clouds cleared, opening the skies to sunshine, with beautiful wildflowers paving the landscape. I drove with abandon, trying desperately to escape my reality.

I had said long ago when I was of legal age, I would hightail it out of here, but I needed to save more money. Having to pay the assault fine had made a divot in my hidden stash. I was none too thrilled with the prospect of spending more time under my dad's roof. Now, more than ever, I felt him shoot daggers through my heart whenever I was unlucky enough to cross his path.

The intervention had done the trick—not because of what it was, but because I knew if I didn't get my shit together, I'd never be able to leave and start my new life far, far away in a land that was welcoming, forgiving, and respectful. I was hoping that this wasn't a tall order. Actually, I wasn't just *hoping*, I was *staking my life* on it.

Come June of that year, I donned my finest clothes, throwing my freshly pressed gown over the top. I adjusted my cap and strutted with pride across the stage to accept my diploma at our local gymnasium. I felt on top of the world, not only because I had jumped a huge hurdle by graduating but also because I was one step closer to putting my nightmare family in the rear-view mirror. It goes without saying that my so-called family hadn't shown up to show their support, but I was almost glad because they were more of an embarrassment to me than anything else. I celebrated by pitching the tent between some huge oak trees in a nearby campground. Marm and I shared a cake and a quart of mint chip ice cream. Boy, that girl loved her sweets! We fell asleep wishing upon the stars, cuddled next to each other. There was no place I would have rather been.

CHAPTER 13

THE GOODBYE
NINETEEN YEARS OLD

The sound of thunder and the flashes of lightning woke me out of a deep sleep. I stretched and looked to see how Marm was handling the light show, but she wasn't moving. I started to panic, jumping out of bed, flying across the room and throwing the light switch on. I reluctantly bent down to kiss her fur, scared shitless of what I might find. She didn't respond to my touch, and my heart stopped as I said a silent prayer. She was barely warm to my touch and nonresponsive to me calling her name. I pleaded with her to please wake up, as tears exploded from my eyes. An earth-shattering scream escaped my trembling body as I cradled her dead body in my arms. She was my whole life, and I didn't want to live without her by my side.

Grabbing the comforter off my bed, I gingerly wrapped her tight, as my tears soaked her fur. Stumbling downstairs, carrying her close

CHAPTER 13 ... THE GOODBYE

to me, I maneuvered each step so as not to drop her. I gently laid her in the back seat of my car and peeled out of my driveway. The storm that was passing over was brutal, with raindrops the size of saucers relentlessly pounding down, making my windshield wipers struggle to keep up. The speed limit, stop signs, and traffic lights were of little significance to me, as I screeched to a stop in front of the twenty-four hour emergency veterinary hospital.

Rigor mortis was beginning to set in as I delicately collected her from the back seat. I was soaked from head to toe from the storm that had a firm grasp on the area, but Marm was safely wrapped in my comforter, dry except for my tears that had soaked her head. We were immediately greeted by a technician as they whisked us away to an examining room. I already knew in my head what they were going to tell me, but my heart was resisting. The words, "I'm sorry, there's nothing we can do. She's gone," were like a dagger to my heart.

Leaving me in the room to say my final goodbyes crushed me beyond words. I begged her to please wake up as I sang her the song I had made up just for her. She used to love it when I sang to her, and I prayed that she could hear me one last time. After an hour of holding Marm, while I sobbed uncontrollably into her fur, Elaine, the nice technician, came to check on me, but I didn't know how to walk away and leave my heart, my everything.

Walking away was like leaving a piece of myself behind. I would never be whole again without my sweet angel Marmalade. She had been my everything, my saving grace, since I was six. I trembled and collapsed behind my steering wheel as heart-wrenching sobs racked my body, leaving me drained and inconsolable. I don't know how I made it home that morning, but somehow I managed, and woke up shivering without my comforter or Marm to keep me warm. My eyes were swollen to small slits, red rimmed, and weeping. I felt hollow and empty inside, wondering if I would find the courage to live another day.

Time has a way of marching forward when all I wanted was to reverse it to when Marm was by my side, full of life. But, instead, the hours turned into days, and, on my fourth day after losing my furry sidekick, I awoke, remembering a dream I had. Marm had come to check on me and to let me know she was running free after crossing over the rainbow bridge. She encouraged me to move on and get another dog since I had so much love and snuggles to give. She also asked me to bury her under her favorite willow tree, where we had spent many hours together. The first smile in days tugged at the corners of my mouth. I had already decided that, when her ashes were ready to be picked up, that was exactly what I would do. It was too perfect of a spot not to lay my sweet, precious girl in her temporary resting place.

The following weeks were a blur. I stumbled around in a state of despair. I had never felt heart-wrenching pain like this, and I was at a loss about how any sense of normalcy would return to my life. I wasn't ready to share my heart with another dog again, but I knew that, to honor Marm, I would get another someday in the future to fulfill her legacy.

By the third week, I hadn't heard about Marm's ashes, so I ventured on over to the clinic to inquire. I wasn't prepared for the horrid memories that would come flooding back, walking through the front door. It seemed like a lifetime ago, yet just like yesterday. I dabbed at my eyes and took some deep breaths to collect myself before making my way to the counter. I looked around in the waiting

CHAPTER 13 ... THE GOODBYE

room and saw people huddled together, wrapped in each other's arms as they said prayers of hope. Tears stained their clothes as sorrow consumed them.

Elaine, the tech, smiled broadly as she greeted me. "Mr. Travers, how good to see you. Once again, let me express to you how sorry I am over the loss of your beautiful Marmalade. She was lucky to have your undying love for so many years." I thanked her and told her how difficult it was without her by my side. I'm sure if she had a dollar for every time she heard that, she would be a billionaire. There was just something oh-so-special about the love a dog offered.

"Do you have any idea how much longer I'll have to wait to get Marm back?" I inquired. She looked puzzled and squinted, gazing at me like I'd lost my mind. "Um, she's here. She's been here for a couple of weeks. I called and left a message with your dad. I thought it was strange that you hadn't come to pick her up yet." I felt the blood drain from my face. That bastard of a so-called dad had specifically kept this information from me. I was livid. This was neither the time nor place to air my dirty laundry, so I swallowed hard and braced myself for seeing Marm again.

Pacing back and forth, starting to hyperventilate, I stepped outside to get a grip. The sun was peeking from behind a cumulus cloud, surrounding me in warmth. Sunshine had always elicited a feeling of calm in me. Losing myself in my thoughts and soaking up the rays, I was startled by a tap on my shoulder. Elaine was standing behind me with my comforter neatly folded. A polished wooden box donning a bronze name plate etched with "Marmalade" perched precariously on top. A lump formed in my throat while tears threatened to spill from my eyes. I thanked her for her compassion and collected my possessions. Running my fingertips over the box and embracing it close to my heart, I let the tears flow. My sweet baby girl was coming home.

Wanting to ream my dad for his blatant disregard for me, I knew it wouldn't solve anything, so I kept my mouth shut. This was the last straw. As soon as Marm was laid in her temporary resting spot, I should thank him for giving me the extra push and incentive to move out and be done with him once and for all.

The next morning after spending the night with Marm tucked under my arm, I knew it was time to let her be at peace. Luckily the sun was making another spectacular appearance. It would make Marm's send-off easier. There was something about rainy days and funerals that made them seem sadder. It's as if the raindrops and tears joined as one, sharing the enormous grief. The willow tree was standing tall, offering a full spectrum of shade. The same shade that helped shield Marm from the sun so many times before as she lay, sprawled out, watching me do my chores. I kissed the little wooden box as I placed it next to some dandelions while I proceeded to dig the hole.

Although laborious in nature, I didn't care that I grunted as sweat dripped down my back and temporarily blinded my eyes. I would have done anything for her. After an hour of digging the perfect-sized hole, not too shallow, not too deep, and not too wide, not too tight. Just right for my best friend. My mind told me I was doing the right thing, but my heart resisted. Knowing this was her favorite tree, it made total sense to bury her ashes here. I could visit daily, and, when I moved on, I could take her with me, so why was it so hard?

I gently placed the box, wrapped in a layer of bubble wrap and an old red paisley bandanna, in the hole, along with a bone and

CHAPTER 13 ... THE GOODBYE

stuffed pig that had been her favorite squeaky stuffie. Before filling the hole back up with loose dirt, I sat down and bowed my head in a prayer that would find her pain free, running like the wind, with an unlimited supply of apples. She loved apples and would salivate relentlessly as she begged for bites. Tears flowed nonstop. Although I had mentally tried to prepare myself for her death, I never knew how difficult it would actually be once it was upon me. I sang her favorite song and repeated endless stories of our various escapades. Neighbors came and went, and the hustle and bustle of the neighborhood began to quiet down as sunset was upon us.

Anyone would have thought I had lost my marbles if I told them that, the whole time I was sitting out there, I felt Marmalade's presence. It wasn't until she whispered it was time, that I began to pick up handfuls of dirt to cover her. Out of the corner of my eye, I saw the front porch light flick on, lighting up an image of my mom as she wiped a tear from her eye. In a funny way, I felt comforted that I wasn't the only one who would miss my best friend.

CHAPTER 14

THE MIRACLE
TWENTY YEARS OLD

Living my own *Groundhog Day* was getting to me. Without anyone to share them with, my days seemed longer than twenty-four hours. Life at home was unbearable. Living under my parents' roof wasn't an option for me anymore. The house had bad juju, and I wasn't about to wait around for it to rub off on me. Now, more than ever, I noticed it, without Marm to bring me happiness. I no longer wanted to wallow in self-pity, and the heartache of seeing Marm in every room, behind every corner was too much. I found tufts of her soft, red-golden fur in the most unexpected places, bringing a whole new round of sadness, so I pulled the trigger and made plans to move out.

I had only bad memories in this house, and the hollowness it held for me was depressing. The night before I was to leave, I set my

CHAPTER 14 ... THE MIRACLE

alarm and went out back to unearth my bounty. I hadn't counted it in a while, but I was hoping it was enough to get me by for a couple of months while I looked for a better job than the neighborhood handyman/gardener. The moon was full that night, casting shadows on the grass. A slight breeze blew the American flag that hung proudly from the edge of the house, as I sat on the patio, feeling melancholy. The feelings caught me off guard; I wasn't expecting to feel gloomy and sad. But here I was, reminiscing about what should have been.

I had done nothing wrong unless you call wanting love a crime. Nothing to cause the horrible treatment I had received day in and day out. My mom was the only one who had shown me an ounce of decency, and that was so few and far between, I could count the times on one hand. I got up, wiped the dampness from my eyes, and made a promise to myself that, from that day forward, it was all about me, myself, and I.

After digging up my stash, something flipped a switch inside of me. Knowing this was going to be the last night I ever spent under this roof had me giddy with excitement. The melancholy mood I had experienced just a mere hour before had blown away in the breeze. I tried once again curling up under my comforter to get a good night's sleep, but I was restless, so I jumped out of bed, pulled open my desk drawer, and found a tattered notebook. Surprising myself, I sat down to pen a goodbye note to my mom. I wasn't sure why I had such a strong pull to put my thoughts down in words, because, clearly, she didn't deserve it. A variety of emotions flooded my thoughts, but after twenty minutes passed, nothing I cared to share was written down. I had a fear that she would poke fun at me for sharing my innermost thoughts, adding insult to injury, so I ended up writing only my address and wishing her well. I tucked it under the lamp on my desk; I doubted I would ever hear from her again.

The next morning, I wasn't surprised to see a gray sky with threatening rain clouds about to unleash their fury; it was the exact opposite of what I was feeling inside. I wasn't about to let a storm dampen my mood. As I dug up Marm, I had a smile spread across my face and a party taking place in my soul. I waved to the neighbors, feeling a little bad that I hadn't shared with anyone that I was leaving. My parents didn't even know. Nor would they care.

I had packed up my meager belongings, loaded them in my car, and drove off, all before my brothers had woken up. I was bad at goodbyes. It would have turned into more of a *Farewell, suckers, hope I never lay eyes on you two losers again,* than a tearful goodbye. As I drove away, I glanced back and saw my mom standing on the veranda with her hand over her heart. I never looked back again.

Life on my own was lonely, but I was loving my newfound freedom. It was liberating and rewarding to know that I was solely responsible for myself. For years, I basically had taken care of myself, but this was different. I could come and go as I pleased without judgmental eyes casting shadows of doubt over me. I had managed to save a lot more than I let myself imagine and would be financially secure for more than a couple months or so. I combed the newspaper for jobs. I quickly found out the interviewing process was the hardest since I had no resume to speak of. I soon became passionate about selling myself, putting a strong emphasis on my desire to prove myself in the real world.

I had always been remarkably good with my hands, which, I later learned, was a gift from God. It was nice knowing I excelled at something others did not. Since I enjoyed being outside, I gravitated

CHAPTER 14 ... THE MIRACLE

toward anything that would fulfill my desire to merge these two things, so when I landed a job working as a crew member for a house-building company, I jumped for joy. I was honing a craft I had dabbled in at my technical woodworking class in high school but on a much larger scale. And it was a bonus to get paid. This adulting stuff wasn't bad, after all.

My apartment was a studio, which was fine with me and perfect in every way. I immediately made it my own by painting the walls a forest green and adding a rustic feel by choosing plaid bed clothes and chunky furniture. I chose to build all the furniture myself, out of pine wood I bought at the local lumber yard. Situated facing east, the morning sun filtered through the big bay window, adding to the charm. Most importantly, it was mine, and it gave me a huge sense of accomplishment; I couldn't stop smiling. Until I could get another dog, I was fine living in close quarters. The only thing I despised about it was taking my laundry to a laundromat. Tedious jobs were not my forte.

My workweeks buzzed by. I was learning new skills and shooting the shit with a couple of guys I had connected with at work. I had friends. Friends who liked me for me and enjoyed my company. I was reluctant to share much about my past life, so, when they asked me to join them for a couple of beers at the local pub, I bowed out. I was still in a fragile state after losing Marm, but I was finally feeling like my life was headed in the right direction. I wasn't about to derail it now.

Feeling like an adult, I cleaned up my humble abode, doing chores and planning the week ahead on my weekends. Waking up early Saturday morning, I stretched and peered out the window. It was going to be a beautiful day, with the sun peeking over the hill to the east. Ever since I had moved out, I started my day with an affirmation, sending good juju into the universe. This morning was no different, except I had a strong sensation that things were looking up and about to change. I had a good laugh at myself as I showered and dressed for the day, putting on a red plaid shirt smartly tucked into a pair of jeans. As I was walking through the door, I caught sight of Marmalade's dog collar that hung from my coat rack by the door. "Oh, girl, how I miss you. Your soft, red-golden fur and soulful eyes that penetrated straight into my soul. I would give anything to have you back to share my life with." I took a couple of moments to reminisce about my best friend. Her death was still fresh in my mind and had left a huge hole in my heart. I missed everything about her, including the big willow tree where she and I used to hang out.

In fact, she and the tree were the only things I missed about home. Just as I suspected, I hadn't heard word one from any members of my family after I flew the coop. It was abundantly clear that I had long overstayed my welcome.

With the sun shining bright, I knew it was going to be a day for the books. Tucking my memories of Marm away for the time being, I focused on the day ahead. I always found it much harder to be in a foul mood when the sun was warming my soul, giving me an extra promise things would go my way. Lugging my dirty clothes into the laundromat, I silently cussed myself out for being a lazy slug. Everything I owned was dirty and grimy. This was going to eat up my cherished Saturday, and thoughts of boredom trudged through my brain, as I loaded quarters into five separate washers loaded to the brim. I was alone, which I welcomed. To me, not much was worse than being forced into unwanted conversation with a stranger, with no escape route handy.

CHAPTER 14 ... THE MIRACLE

Nodding off while reading an expired *TIME Magazine* from 1985, I was abruptly jolted awake by a woman's faint voice. "Help, someone please—help me!" I jumped up, scanning the immediate area, and, in the corner, I saw a woman bent over a washing machine with her head cocked awkwardly. Her voice grew louder as I approached her, with cries of distress audible. Rushing toward her, I immediately noticed that her long, auburn hair was somehow caught in the agitator of the washing machine. Tears had formed in the corners of her big green eyes as she unsuccessfully tugged to release her hair.

"Please don't panic. I'll help you, but I need you to calm down and move off to the side as much as possible," I instructed. I began to unravel her hair piece by piece as she tried her hardest to keep her tears from falling. Two long hours later, she was free.

"Thank you so much. I don't know what I would have done without you. My name is Claire—and you are?" she said melodically, extending her delicate hand toward me. My heart skipped a beat as I laid eyes on the most beautiful woman I had ever seen. I was awestruck. Her hair, as it cascaded down her back, was the color of chestnuts, and her eyes the color of emeralds. She was dressed in a pair of chinos and a light-blue T-shirt with white Chuck Taylors on her feet. She could have been in rags, and I would have been equally as awestruck. I must have had a look of utter amazement as I took in every detail of this magical creature standing before me.

"I, I, um, I'm Lucas," I finally managed to say while taking her hand in mine. "I'm so glad I was at the right place at the right time and able to help you out of your awkward predicament. Who would have thought something like that could ever happen?" To myself, I sounded like a bumbling idiot, but she laughed, and it was music to my ears. It sounded like an angel choir, accompanied by a quartet of harps. And right then and there, I knew she was about to steal my heart.

"Luke, it's so nice to meet you. I can call you 'Luke,' can't I? I hope it's not too forward of me, but, 'Lucas' seems too formal for a man who just rescued me!" She giggled, not giving me the time to object. I really didn't care. She could call me anything as long as she called me something. It had a whole different ring coming out of her mouth. *Smitten* doesn't come close to explaining how I was feeling. Butterflies I didn't know existed had been woken out of deep slumber and began to moonwalk in my belly. I got goosebumps on my arms, causing my hair to stand on end while I stared, mesmerized by her beauty, hoping I didn't scare her off.

Finishing our laundry, we laughed the afternoon away. "Hey, Luke. What do you get if you eat too many navy beans? You end up with a dishonorable discharge!!!" I doubled over in laughter as she wiped tears from her eyes. You would have thought I was twelve the way I still loved poop humor. I couldn't let her one-up me, so I dished out one of my own. "Did you hear about the Roman emperor who never aged after he turned 19? His name was Constant Teen!!" We both laughed till our sides hurt. Come to find out she was just as much a fan of dad jokes as I was. I found this funny all in itself, because my dad *was* a joke.

I never knew laundry could be so fun. But then again, I had a very strong suspicion that if washing and folding laundry could be fun, everything would be fun with her by my side. Looking back, I feel our love for laughter and joke-telling solidified our relationship. Laughter was contagious, after all. As we parted, I had an emptiness in my heart that I hadn't felt for any human

CHAPTER 14 ... THE MIRACLE

before. It was a foreign concept that I didn't want to get used to. I missed her already.

"Let's meet for lunch tomorrow, Luke. Please?" She didn't have to ask me twice. After I gleefully accepted her invitation, she reached up and placed a fluttery kiss on my cheek. "It's been so nice to meet you. I can't remember the last time I laughed this hard." I had a smile that extended from my mouth, to my eyes, to my soul. Her lips were soft and supple on my cheek as an electric current ran through my veins. I was exuberant and filled with hope!

Until I wasn't. Driving home, I started getting in my head. My thoughts went from ecstatic to doomsville in ten seconds flat. I had negative self-esteem. In fact, it had been torn up, set on fire, and trashed. *How could she possibly be interested in me?* I wondered. I gave myself the afternoon to wallow in self-pity, contemplating what I had to offer any relationship. My parents had done a real number on me, wrecking any self-worth I had ever felt. But in spite of that, I was more determined than ever to rise above it. Tomorrow was just the day I needed to put my past behind me once and for all.

Dreaming of Claire, I woke up bright and early, drenched in sweat. Although the dream was happy for the most part, there was an underlying sadness I couldn't put my finger on. I went for a run to clear the cobwebs and to say goodbye to the last bit of self-doubt I had allowed myself. I couldn't help thinking that today was the start of my life; my daily affirmation even confirmed it, stating…"Put the past behind you, and embrace the future." Saying goodbye to Marm and asking for good vibes as I breezed out the door, I was more than eager to get started on the next chapter of my life.

Pulling into the parking lot that sat adjacent to a block of colorful, eclectic stores and boutiques, I felt my nerves start to frazzle.

Checking myself in the rearview mirror, after taking a couple of deep breaths, I was pleasantly surprised to see a calm, handsome version of myself. My pep talk, run, and cheery daily affirmation, partnered with Marm's good juju, had done the trick. The restaurant we had decided on had a façade of rustic bricks with a bright-red awning over the door. It was inscribed with *Juan in a Million* in bright-yellow mustard colors to complete the look. As it turns out, Mexican food was her favorite, too.

"*Hola amigo*," she said, cheerfully, coming up behind me and grabbing my hand in hers. I turned, anxious to see her as she wrapped me in a bear hug. I melted on the spot. She was even more beautiful today than yesterday. Standing almost five-feet-seven-inches, she stood dwarfed by my 6'7" frame. Her auburn hair spilled over her shoulders and down her back in curls. She was wearing a navy-blue sheath dress, a green sweater, matching her eyes, that was smartly wrapped around her shoulders. "You look absolutely beautiful, Claire." I gushed, turning fifty shades of red. Flattery was not my strong suit, but honesty was, so I poured my heart into my thoughts.

Inside, we were greeted with mariachi music and sombreros made out of straw and woven with colors of the Mexican flag. *This place is about as authentic as it comes*, I thought. Our conversation flowed easily, as if we'd been friends forever. Where she was upbeat, I was cynical. Where she was an extrovert, I was an introvert, but we both had a sense of humor, with a quick wit that fed off each other perfectly, laughing so hard tears ran down our faces. I was reluctant to share my horrid childhood or my brush with alcohol, so, when she ordered a pitcher of margaritas, I eagerly partook. I was a different person now, or so I hoped.

CHAPTER 14 ... THE MIRACLE

A little too tipsy to get behind the wheel of a car, and not wanting to say goodbye just yet, we opted for a stroll around downtown and into a nearby park. Wanting to hold her hand but not wanting to seem too forward, I walked with my arms loosely hanging by my sides. I was on cloud ten when she grabbed my hand in hers. Just being in her company made everything come alive. The birds chirping in the trees sounded as if they were singing love songs, while colorful flowers lined all in a row on the park strips seemed more vibrant, enveloping me in the sweetest fragrance, awakening my senses. I couldn't remember ever having been this happy before. It made me sad that I didn't have a soul to share my joy with, making me miss my sorry excuse of a mom.

Settling down on a park bench under an overhang of lavender wisteria vines, she shared that she was an only child of loving parents who doted on her. Her father was a successful attorney, and her mother an artist; she herself was interested in writing. Having aspirations of becoming a published author sounded fascinating to me, but I doubted I had the patience to ever pull it off.

"Luke, what about your family? I want to know all about the wonderful people who raised such a multi-faceted handsome guy." If she noticed my look of horror, she didn't mention it. I wanted to scream, "My parents are the epitome of evil," but I managed to skirt the issue. I wasn't ready to go down that path yet. I didn't want her to feel sorry for me. I had done more than enough of that to last a lifetime. So I explained how I earned a living. I was almost embarrassed to admit what I did, but when I told her, her eyes lit up, and she wanted every last detail.

The sun was beginning to set, casting shadows within the surrounding greenery, and fireflies began to twitter about. She surprised me when she jumped up, giggling and saying she had a surprise for me. She pulled a pocketknife out of her purse, explaining a girl can never be too careful, and carved a heart with our initials in the middle of a nearby oak tree, grinning from ear to ear. That was the moment I knew she was feeling the same vibe as me. It's true, opposites do attract.

CHAPTER 15

THE STALKER
JANE

My heart broke watching Lucas suffer over Marmalade. Oh, how he loved that dog. I wanted to wrap him in my arms and let him cry it out, but, instead, I watched from afar, a small part of me dying a slow death.

Although Lucas had never told me he was moving out, as a mother, I sensed it, dreading the day he would walk out the door forever. I wanted desperately to tell him the truth and beg for his forgiveness, but I couldn't risk Peter finding out I had broken the contract. So, I suffered in silence, focusing on the family I did have, not the one I longingly wanted.

What Peter or Lucas don't know is that I followed Lucas the day he left. I wasn't proud of my clandestine adventure, but I couldn't stop myself. The thought of losing him forever was unbearable, so I watched crouched down, hidden behind a bright-red Corvette that was parked on the side of the road, as he unloaded his meager belongings into a little apartment on the outskirts of town. He looked happy as he whistled, closing the door behind him and to my heart. I sighed once again, chastising myself for ever agreeing to Peter's unjust contract. Why was hindsight such a bitch?

The house felt empty. Even though I hadn't been allowed to show him love, there was something about him being under the same roof as me that gave me peace. His absence was unfathomable as I dug deep to keep the rest of my family intact, none the wiser. Don't get me wrong: I loved my other two sons, but it was different. They had my love from the minute they were born and knew I cherished them, unlike Lucas, who still doesn't know—and, worse, never can or will know.

I would escape to my room while Peter was at work and cry for what I had done. I prayed that Lucas would finally find peace and someone to spend his life with who could give him the kind of love he deserved but was denied. Most days, I struggled internally but put on a smile, so I wouldn't have to make up lies for my gloomy moods. I had slowly morphed into a questionable existence, not even recognizing myself most days, not understanding how Peter and the twins acted happy he was gone. I didn't share their joy.

As the days turned into weeks, I found myself missing him more and more. I wondered if he had overcome the wretched childhood I had so unwillingly bestowed upon his trusting soul. I would drive by numerous times during the week in hopes of just getting a glimpse of him to know he was all right. I couldn't believe it had come to this… I was stalking my own son. I tried to justify it as I parked blocks away, slinking behind bushes and praying I could get a window into his life.

CHAPTER 15 ... THE STALKER

One Saturday morning, telling Peter I was going grocery shopping, I snuck over to Lucas' and hit the mother lode. He was coming out of his apartment with knapsacks full of what I could only imagine was laundry. A blue t-shirt poked through the top as he lugged them to his car, which was parked at the curb. He looked healthy and, most importantly, happy.

It took everything I had to keep quiet. My stalking became an obsession—an unhealthy obsession, consumed with his whereabouts and well-being. I tried to chalk it up to concern for my son, but even I knew the difference. I had stooped to a new low and knew that, if I didn't stop, I would get discovered—and then I'd *really* be behind the eight ball. Every free moment I wasn't spying on my own son, I spent reading self-help books. They advised me to journal, but all of the thoughts I managed to write down made me look more pathetic than ever. My life was a fiasco, one blundering, idiotic mishap after another.

Paranoia reared its ugly head. Or was I being paranoid? I didn't trust Peter. I hadn't trusted his actions ever since he had discovered the truth about Lucas and made me sign his ludicrous contract. With Lucas gone, you would have thought he would ease up on the lurking and overall mistrust, but, if anything, I felt his eyes on me even more. I imagined him following me and spying on me every second of every day. I even went so far as to rip the bedroom apart, looking for listening devices. It came up clean and left me feeling like I was on the brink of losing my mind.

Sleeping had turned into a nightmare, I had dreams that left me confused and grasping for reality. I was on my own last nerve, when, one morning over coffee, I sat reading an article in the newspaper about a poor woman who had lost her child in a backyard-pool drowning accident. Obviously, she was distraught and, as a last resort, had joined a grief support group for the loss of a child, hoping it was the lifeline she desperately needed.

Hmmmm.

Interesting thought, I pondered.

Maybe this is *what I* needed as well: nonjudgmental strangers lending a shoulder to cry on while listening with open arms. A small technicality: Lucas wasn't actually dead, even though he was dead to me. I grieved for him as if he were six feet under. Wouldn't that count? I mulled it over in my mind and decided *What the hell?* As luck would have it, there was a meeting that afternoon scheduled to take place at the local library conference room. Not giving myself a chance to weasel out, I scribbled down the contact info and ran up the stairs, with a newfound spring in my step, to get ready.

I allowed myself a moment of optimism as I combed through my closet in search of the perfect outfit. It shouldn't be colorful, but black wasn't a color I wore well next to my face, so I settled on a pastel-yellow silk blouse tucked smartly into a black pencil skirt. Throwing on a pair of black kitten heels, I admired myself in the mirror. I looked a bit like a bumblebee—without the buzz but with plenty of sting. I had lost weight since Lucas had moved out, mourning him daily, so I was feeling good about myself for the first time in years.

Luckily, everyone was out of the house, so I wouldn't have to make up another lie. I was getting way too proficient at being devious these days. Oddly, I was looking forward to the meeting, even though I was sure there would be a lot of crying. Realizing it could prove risky if anyone I knew saw me, I would play ignorant. Another thing I have become proficient at, since ignorance is bliss.

CHAPTER 15 ... THE STALKER

Looking at the town through a different lens, I found I was enjoying the sights and sounds around me. Children, without a care in the world, chasing each other in the town square, giggling with abandon. Parents looking on with pride at what they had created. Images of my life twenty-one years ago started running through my mind. Young, great career, and in love. With my boss. *And* pregnant—the detail that changed the trajectory of my life. How had I been so foolish to think I could have a life with Mr. Stanford? I knew my immature, love-stricken mind hadn't made up the fact that he was as crazy about me as I was him, but to actually leave his wife for me and be the talk of the town never would have happened. I felt something wet hit my hand before I realized they were my own tears streaming down my face. My mood had gone from optimistic to remorseful in a heartbeat.

Wiping away the tears, I tucked my memories away, hopefully to never be revisited again, even though I knew it was foolish to wish such a thing. Memories of my past came as unwanted visitors almost daily. I struggled to plaster a smile across my face as I searched the parking lot for an empty spot. "I've got this," I told myself, knowing full well I was grasping at straws. Anything to help me cope with my double life was worth a shot, so I walked into the meeting with my head held high, more determined than ever to live a lie.

Flying under the radar was my plan as I chose a chair tucked in the corner as far away from everyone as possible. I wasn't sure how good my acting skills were, and not knowing what to expect had me a little jittery. As I quietly sat, I clasped my hands tightly in my lap, hoping no one would notice I was about to wet myself from fear. I had no right being here, where others had come to share their true losses—something that no parent should ever have to endure. I took a quick glance around the room, which was starting to fill up. Everyone had a hollow, faraway look of desperation etched on their faces. Some were openly crying, while others hung their heads, not wanting to make eye contact—or afraid of breaking down, unable to regain control.

My attention was drawn to the front of the room as a grandmotherly type of woman, with gray hair, cut in a pixie, and wearing round, tortoise-shell-rimmed glasses perched on her dainty nose, stood and cleared her throat. "Excuse me. May I please have your attention, everyone?" she warmly said. She oozed compassion and empathy when she spoke. "For those of you whom I haven't had the pleasure of meeting yet, I'm Dr. Hoffman, a licensed psychologist who will serve as the mediator for this group. As always, no negativity will be tolerated at any given time. We are here to offer support toward one another and to try to ease some of the burdens that are controlling your life and crushing your heart."

I let out the breath I'd been holding and felt my anxiety ease slightly as she continued. "First of all, I would like to differentiate between grief and mourning. Grief is what we think on the inside when someone we love dies. For example, this could include fear, loneliness, panic, pain, yearning, anxiety, and emptiness, to name just a few. It is the internal meaning given to the experience of loss. Know that it's OK to feel them all at once or only one at a time. There is no right or wrong way to grieve. Mourning, on the other hand, is the outward expression of our grief. Does that make sense to all of you?"

The room was silent, everyone slowly nodding their heads in unison. I immediately felt a sense of relief when I realized the loneliness, anxiety, and emptiness I had been experiencing since Lucas

CHAPTER 15 ... THE STALKER

moved out was normal. After all, the doctor had said so, and I was positive she was not here to lead anyone astray. In a strange way, it gave me validation that I wasn't losing my mind.

Feeling a wee bit guilty that I was eavesdropping on somebody else's extreme misfortune, I tried to appear invisible by donning my sunglasses and slinking down in my chair, keeping my head bent and praying we wouldn't have to introduce ourselves and share our story.

Dr. Hoffman continued on about how she was here to help build resilience and coping strategies to deal with the intense sadness one might feel throughout the grieving process and help find ways to move on in a meaningful way. *Hah! Good luck with that, Dr. Hoffman*, I said under my breath. My son was still alive and flourishing; I just couldn't see him, and that could never change. Or could it?

I got lost in a daydream about showing up unannounced on Lucas' doorstep, spilling the truth, and offering my undying love, that I hadn't noticed others around me talking. That's until the woman sitting a couple chairs over spoke before breaking down into a puddle of tears. I was jarred into the present, and, as I timidly looked up, all eyes were staring my way. I'm not proud of my next move, but I stood up like I had been cattle prodded and hastily ran for the exit, never looking back. Shame on me for being a fraud. Not just a fraud, but an imposter, hypocrite, deceiver, a phony. No matter what name you put on it, I was a devious, rotten, good-for-nothing person.

CHAPTER 16

THE ACCLIMATION
TWENTY-ONE YEARS OLD

Ever since I'd met Claire, my life had been a whirlwind and taken a complete one-eighty. The love, respect, and adoration I had been missing my whole life was showered on me, and I lapped it up faster than she could dish it out. Her fresh take on life was infectious, and I often found myself smiling from ear to ear for no reason other than I was the happiest I had ever been.

She surprised me with something new every day. I often woke up with her intertwined between my legs with a handwritten note sitting on my bedside table. Her handwriting was exquisite, as I peered at my name scrolled on the front of an envelope. Inside, there was an embossed pappus on the front of the note. It was so real looking that I had to suppress an urge to blow it while making a wish.

"Luke, you are the reason I want to get up every day. You are the reason I put my best food forward. You are my everything. Yours

CHAPTER 16 ... THE ACCLIMATION

forever, Claire." I sighed and thanked my lucky stars that our paths had crossed in the most obscure way, as I leaned over and planted a kiss on her cheek. She stirred and let out the cutest yawn as she raised her arms over her head and stretched from head to toe. Watching her gave me more pleasure than I could even fathom was possible.

I often found little post-it notes randomly placed with a play on words. In the shower I found one that said, "Let's heat things up!" One on the bathroom mirror read, "You're the best reflection of me!" And my personal favorite was in my car, near the ignition that read, "You turn me on!" They were always signed with a red heart that melted my own. I, of course, kept every single one and tucked them safely into the same box I had used to save my money in—the one I had spent hours on in shop class, intending to gift to my mom. Even though every note, and there were plenty, was corny, they spoke to who Claire was... quirky, clever, and playful. And, most of all, *thoughtful*. I oftentimes thought they would make a great little pick-me-up book for people who needed inspiration.

Our relationship progressed better than I could have ever dreamed of, spending all our time together when I wasn't working or her at the university, studying creative writing. Our personalities were so different— and yet so much alike. We fell deeply in love. We both loved to take road trips and would oftentimes hit the road singing at the top of our lungs with a bag full of snacks and drive without a plan, reveling in just being together and absorbing the beauty that surrounded us. I had never met anyone like her—with optimism oozing out of every pore.

She found joy in the most mundane things and fought for the underdog. "Do you know what my favorite flower is, Luke?" she asked me one afternoon as we sat on a green plaid blanket, under the shade of a huge oak tree, enjoying a picnic lunch. She had meticulously packed a lunch fit for a king. Setting up a charcuterie board with chocolate-covered strawberries, meats, and various cheeses, she arranged it in the middle of the park and did it with the utmost flair. She amazed me.

Not knowing what was in store for me, she made me cover my eyes and count to fifty, promising me a surprise. While I counted, she whistled a snappy little tune; when I opened them, she had a bouquet of freshly picked dandelions, confessing they were her favorite flower because they were misunderstood. She then quoted the sweetest thing. "The dandelion does not stop growing because it is told it is a weed. The dandelion does not care what others see. It says, 'One day, they'll be making wishes upon me.'"

Where had she been my whole life, and how had I ever gotten so lucky as to have her as my soul mate?

She surprised me every day with some hidden talent that she pulled out of nowhere. Let me tell you—that girl could *cook*. We spent hours in the kitchen concocting our own creations or scouring recipe books. I obviously had never had a chance to spend much time in the kitchen growing up, so I was the perfect student, eager to learn, eager to apply my newfound skills, and equally eager to partake in the finished product. She liked to make little kitchen games as well.

"Hey, Luke. I have twenty different items here that you are going to do a taste test with. All I'm going to tell you is that they can all be used for cooking and might be a condiment or a spice. Or not," she giggled as she placed a blindfold over my eyes. "Oh, yeah: I forgot to tell you: you're being timed, and with the ones you get right, you have to make me a meal." Before I could answer, she

CHAPTER 16 ... THE ACCLIMATION

started the timer and started shoving things into my mouth. We laughed so hard I couldn't tell if the tears running down my face were from the jalapeño pepper or our constant laughter. Every day was a new adventure with her.

"Hey, sweetie. Look what I bought," Claire excitedly said as she walked in through the front door after a day of classes. I looked up from where I was sitting at the kitchen table, actively building a birdhouse from scratch that I was planning on gifting to her parents. She was flushed from carrying her book bag and a handled shopping bag with colorful blue tissue poking out of the top. As she set it on the table, it made a loud thud. Throwing her book bag on the chair, she moved to the bag as I sat, eagerly waiting to see what had her so excited.

She was proud of herself, whatever it was. She proceeded to do a drumroll as she slowly began pulling it out of the bag, stopping to ask, "What do you think it is?" I seriously had no idea and told her so, but that wasn't good enough for her. She then proceeded to have me play twenty questions. She was such a kid at heart, and I adored the playful side of her. Who was I kidding? I adored *every* side of her.

Ten minutes later, I still hadn't figured it out. I begged her to throw me a reprieve, so she caved and pulled out a Kitchenaid stand mixer, two white billowy chefs hats and matching aprons, with our names embroidered in cursive while she sang "*... when the moon hits your eye like a big pizza pie, that's amore*" and finished with a curtsy and a smile that spread from ear to ear. She was beyond adorable.

Ever since she had started teaching me how to cook, I had coveted one, but I didn't want to spend the money. Whereas Claire thought I was frugal and relentlessly kidded me about it, I was secretly stashing away every penny to buy Claire an engagement ring. I couldn't contain my excitement as I jumped up from the table and wrapped her in a bear hug, kissing her passionately.

We had been talking a lot lately about moving in together, but she was hesitant about how her parents would accept it. She had described them as *old-school*, meaning they had stringent morals, and *"living in sin,"* as she put it, would go against everything they believed in. So, we decided to wait, out of respect for them. Having respect for parents was something I found foreign, but, then again, we were raised in totally different environments.

Meeting her parents for the first time had my stomach in knots. The first meeting was quite a production, at least from my point of view. I desperately wanted to make a good impression. I knew how important they were to her and she to them, that I let the old me make an appearance. Although Claire had taken my self-esteem to new heights, now, it had reared its ugly head again in anticipation of meeting the two most important people in her world. I had some scary questions: *What if they hated me? Was I good enough for their only child? Would they think she was "settling"? Could I make her happy?* You name it, I thought it.

The day of reckoning came in the early fall about two months after we started dating. I was like a schoolgirl going to prom, picking out the perfect outfit of chinos and a blue plaid button-up, long-sleeved shirt and getting a fresh haircut. I took extra care in the hygiene department, putting on multiple layers of deodorant and powder to soak up the sweat that had already begun to accumulate.

"Luke, will you please stop puttering about. They are going to see how much I love you and love you, too!" she stated matter of

CHAPTER 16 ... THE ACCLIMATION

factly. I looked up from tying my white Converse All-Stars, and she was beaming from ear to ear. "Did you just say you loved me?" I sheepishly asked. Knowing it and hearing it were two totally different things, and I jumped up, twirled her around, as I ran for the door. I opened it with her still in my arms and shouted, "Claire loves me, everyone, and I love her, too!" I wanted to share my joy with the world. I might have it plastered on a billboard on the side of the interstate, I was so excited to have found her.

Pulling up in front of her parents' house had me in a bundle of nerves. Right then, "The Sign," by Ace of Base, started playing in the car...

I, I got a new life.
You would hardly recognize me.
I'm so glad.

...when Claire jumped out of the car with as much exuberance as a kid on Christmas morning. "Come on, you!! I'm so excited to share with my parents what makes me all smiles and giggles!" Her smile was contagious and eased my fears immediately.

They lived on the opposite side of town from my parents, in a sprawling ranch-style home set on two acres. The front of the house was landscaped perfectly with an assortment of seasonal flowers adding a sprinkling of yellow, orange, red, and pink colors. On the porch, a couple of weathered rocking chairs moved slightly in the breeze. I noticed the doormat that said *Wipe Your Paws* at the same time the door opened, and a yellow labrador retriever came bounding out, jumping up on Claire while planting a big slobbery kiss right across her lips. Right behind the dog appeared two people who didn't need an introduction. I knew immediately they were Claire's parents, because she looked just like them.

Her father was tall, with an athletic build, a well-trimmed graying goatee and the same sparkling emerald eyes as Claire that crinkled in the corners as he smiled. He cheerfully extended his hand and introduced himself as Alex. His handshake was firm, and I instantly felt at ease. "I assume you're the man of the hour we've heard so many wonderful things about. I'm Alex. Let me introduce you to my wife, Sloan. And it looks like you've already met Rowdy," as he reached down and scratched behind the dog's ears, who was now obediently sitting at his owner's side. As I went to shake Sloan's hand, she grabbed mine and reached up, planting a kiss on each cheek. "So pleased to meet you, Luke," she breathlessly whispered. I caught Claire out of the corner of my eye, her hypnotic smile on full display, while she offered me a thumbs-up.

There was no denying where Claire got her good looks, because her parents made a striking couple. Both appeared to be in their middle forties, with the same chestnut-color hair that Claire had. Her mom also had an athletically fit body, and dimples as deep as the Grand Canyon were on full display in her cheeks as she smiled, showing a perfect set of sparkling white teeth. As her mom firmly grasped my hand, leading me into the house, Claire appeared by my other side, sliding my hand into hers. The house was tastefully decorated with crown molding and coffered ceilings. Dark-wood tables and rich chocolate-brown leather couches with yellow and orange throw pillows gave it a sophisticated, homey feel.

As we made our way out to their back deck, I immediately noticed, on the other side of the massive swimming pool, a horse pasture overlooking a field full of sunflowers. I almost tripped over an orange-tabby cat named Eric, sprawled contently in a sunbeam. He yawned and stretched without a care in the world. Anybody

CHAPTER 16 ... THE ACCLIMATION

who liked animals already had a leg up, in my book. The deck had a golden-reddish hue, with five steps down into a massive yard for Rowdy to chase balls in. Resting on a table in the middle of the deck sat baskets of chips with homemade guacamole and pitchers of margaritas. As I looked at Claire, she winked, solidifying what I already knew. She had given her parents a heads-up. I was hoping she had also directed them to stay clear of the topic of *my* parents. I had yet to go into depth with her, and I definitely didn't want to be grilled by Alex or Sloan.

"Claire tells us you're great with your hands," Alex said, easing into some conversation. I really hated being the center of attention, but Claire placed her hand gently on my thigh, giving me a reassuring pat, so I proceeded to explain what my job entailed and about my future plans. "Although I love working for McKinley and Sons and have learned a ton, which I'm eternally grateful for, I have bigger aspirations. I plan on opening my own business, and I'd be pleased if I could hire you to handle the legalities of it, sir." Alex laughed and said he was flattered but that his area of expertise was in criminal law, although he'd be happy to steer me in the right direction.

The afternoon couldn't have gone any better, as we enjoyed the afternoon sunshine, bottomless margaritas, easy, effortless conversation, and a play session with Rowdy. Romping around the yard with Rowdy made me realize how much I missed a furry friend. Next up on my agenda was finding a house with a big yard, so that I could get another dog of my own. Dinner was served, including some tomahawks from the grill, followed by peanut-butter cheesecake Claire had whipped up from scratch. The whole night was exceptional in every way.

Hours later, I said my goodbyes, promising to be back soon. "You've been the most gracious of hosts today, and I'm so extremely glad to meet the parents of the woman of my dreams," I gushed as Claire blushed. Alex and Sloan both gave me hugs goodbye as Claire walked me to my car. "Luke, I can't begin to tell you how proud I am of you today. I can tell my parents like you and are just as impressed with you as I am," Claire said, as she reached up and planted a kiss on my cheek. I felt invincible.

I gave myself a much-deserved pat on the back as I pulled away, promising to meet up with Claire the next morning for breakfast. I was somehow able to pull it off even though I had basically no social skills to speak of. I found this very foreign to me, but one thing I can thank my parents for was teaching me to always respect my elders. It served me well today.

CHAPTER 17

THE TALK
TWENTY-ONE YEARS OLD

Scouring the newspapers for listings of a new apartment or house to buy became my new hobby—*obsession* was more like it. I was determined more than ever to get another dog, and the sooner, the better. I had also taken up visiting the local animal shelter on my lunch break, either taking the dogs for walks or reading to them outside their kennels. On the weekends, Claire and I would go together and spend time trying to give the poor lost souls a little happiness.

All was right in my little corner of the world on the Claire front. We loved spending all our free time together, cooking, watching movies, playing games—it really didn't matter, because it was being together that was paramount. One blustery day, an unexpected cold front had blown our way, so we were wrapped up on the couch, spooning under some blankets, watching *The Princess Bride* for the millionth time, when a loud knock sounded at the front door.

"You get it," I said to Claire as I poked her in the ribs. She giggled and said, "No way, José. *You* get it!" As we playfully argued over who was going to answer the door, a much more urgent knock sounded through the apartment. Unwrapping myself, I stepped into my Uggs to see who had so rudely interrupted our together time. Throwing the door open, a cold gust blew in, causing papers on the end table to swirl in the air. Standing there shivering under an olive-green beanie pulled down to his eyes was a guy in his late teens.

"Hello. May I help you?" I inquisitively asked. A friendly smile broke out, revealing a full set of wires attached to his braces, glistening as the light caught them.

"Are you Lucas Travers?" he questioned while reaching into his black backpack. After I positively affirmed that it was indeed me, in the flesh, he handed me an envelope and wished me a good day as he departed, hugging himself tight against the wind.

"Who was that at the door, Luke, and what did he want?" asked Claire as she met me at the door with a perplexed look. Her hair was a disheveled mess as she pushed strands behind her ears. I was just as confused as she about what the stranger had just handed me. I grabbed a letter opener out of the junk drawer and proceeded to run it under the flap as I took a seat at the kitchen table. It was a business-looking envelope, with my name typewritten neatly on the front and a return address of Stanford, Bridges and Howe law firm. It didn't surprise me that I'd never heard of the law firm before, but what did surprise me was what the contents held.

I had a shiver run down my spine as Claire peered over my shoulder in anticipation on what the envelope held. I wasn't keen

CHAPTER 17 ... THE TALK

on surprises of any type. We both read in unison a letter informing me my maternal grandparents had passed and left me a large chunk of money as an inheritance. My mom was all but estranged from her parents, so I had never been close to them, making me more skeptical than ever about the contents of the envelope. In fact, I couldn't recall when I had seen them last, so, needless to say, I was surprised. And a little more than curious. The letter continued on to explain I was to appear in person at the reading of the will two weeks from Monday. I froze as anxiety gripped me, causing me to start hyperventilating. Claire looked at me, her eyes appearing the size of saucers. "Luke, oh, my word—are you all right?" she asked as she ran to grab me a glass of water and a cold compress.

It wasn't how I'd pictured telling Claire about my abusive childhood, but it was about time I addressed the elephant in the room. Panic started coursing through my veins at the sheer thought of outlining my not-so-normal upbringing. It had become increasingly more difficult to avoid the conversation since she had inquired about my parents numerous times. "Um, babe, I'm not sure where to start, but I owe you an explanation. Bear with me, because this is not easy for me to talk about, and I've never shared this with anyone before," I managed to say after my heart rate had slowed. She grabbed my left hand in hers and raised it to her lips, gently kissing me, trying to chase away my fears. As I gazed into her eyes, I saw so much love and compassion I knew it was time.

My thoughts were a tsunami of jumbled-up, painful emotions. Finding a place to start was a problem, so I decided to start as early as I could remember, outlining each year in all its painstaking detail.

"My early years were filled with everything good, including playdates, road trips, and an abundance of love," I told her, smiling, as I remembered bits and pieces of my life until my brothers came into the picture. "I was four when my brothers arrived, and, at that time, my life took an abrupt shift, spiraling me into the depths of hell." I stopped talking and tried to compose myself. The thoughts, images, and feelings were crashing into each other, causing me to feel nauseous, as sweat ran down my back, drenching my shirt despite the chilly night. Deep in thought and lost in my own world of dark despair, I dug up horrific memories I had tried desperately to bury.

Out of nowhere, the air in the apartment was stifling, stale, and acrid, threatening to cut off my oxygen supply. I felt like I was suffocating.

Underwater.

Drowning.

Unable to breathe.

I abruptly grabbed my jacket, knocking over the coat rack and Marm's collar, as I frantically made my way to the door, into the cool air, trying to collect myself. Snow had started to fall with abandon, sending saucer-size flakes floating from the gray sky and collecting on the shrubs outside my window. I stuck my tongue out and grabbed one out of the air, tasting the pureness of it. I hugged myself tight and took some deep breaths, when I heard the door open behind me. Claire was by my side, looking like she was at a loss for words and had just experienced the apocalypse from her front-row seat.

"Luke, I'm worried about you. If it's too much for you, we can continue later," Claire whispered while rubbing my back. I contemplated it for a second but knew the floodgates of anguish and hopelessness had already been thrown open, so I continued, swallowing back tears from constant rejection.

CHAPTER 17 ... THE TALK

We talked well into the night. Or I should say, I talked, and she listened, giving encouragement when I needed it to continue and sympathy when tears began to flow. It should have felt cathartic, but, instead, I had opened up old wounds I wasn't sure I would be able to close.

So many grim memories sprinkled with perseverance and the ability to turn a blind eye until I was old enough to free myself of the confines that had kept me captive and miserable my whole childhood. I was afraid I would be embarrassed when I spilled all my dirty laundry to her, but it was the exact opposite. Her compassion and genuine concern endeared me to her even more. If anything, it made us stronger and more in love, with no secrets between us.

I openly cried when I detailed the day my mom told me she didn't love me, and the night my dad said I was the black sheep of the family. But worst of all was when I was twelve, feeling all alone in the world and miserable, contemplating suicide. My thoughts then had been complicated and complex; I wondered how and if I could continue to live life unwanted and unloved. Being so happy with my life with Claire now, it was hard to believe my life had been so dark and dismal. The good, the bad, and the ugliest memories flooded back, trying to drown me once and for all, but Claire was there to guide me to a safe place. No matter what she said, I had a suspicion that no matter how hard I tried to bury this time away in a vault, it would resurface, and, next time, I might not be so lucky to have her by my side.

As I sorted through my years, I remembered the times my mom had given me glimmers of hope that things could be different, only to shun me the next time she saw me. It still baffled me what went through her mind and why she chose to bestow gifts upon me, although few and far between, and then act like I was the devil reincarnated. Hoping Claire could give me insight, I told her about my track days. "One day, out of nowhere, while I was busy packing my books in my backpack, she asked me if I had a moment. I remember wanting to yell at the top of my lungs, *I had all the time in the world for her!* but played it cool not knowing what to expect. She placed a hundred-dollar bill in my hand for new running shoes and said she was proud of me before placing a kiss on my cheek; it was the highlight of my year. But why do you think she did it?" I questioned, eagerly looking at Claire for insight.

"Luke, honestly, I have no idea. Not having met her yet, I don't have anything to go by." She could tell I was disappointed she couldn't shed any light on my mom's weird behavior, wrapping her arms tightly around my neck and kissing my cheek.

The next morning, I was drained. My tossing and turning had kept me awake the majority of the night. The times I had managed a couple of winks, Claire said I was thrashing and screaming in my sleep. Finally giving up on the idea of getting any decent shuteye, I made a pot of coffee and watched the sunrise. Standing on the patio, listening to the soft coos of the birds as they woke and the distant sounds of crickets mixed with bullfrogs, I was greeted with a playful swat on the butt.

"Good morning, my love," she lovingly whispered. "I've been thinking about our talk last night, and I really think you would benefit profusely from some therapy. I also think it would be a good idea to stop by your parents' house, prior to the reading of the will." I tensed at the thought and let out a deep breath. I knew she was right, but I wasn't sure I could willingly set foot in their house again. Luckily, Claire was the voice of reason, and, after much deliberation,

CHAPTER 17 ... THE TALK

I begrudgingly agreed. I decided I'd give it a shot, but only if she agreed to be my buffer.

Dropping to my knees, I pleaded "Please, oh, please, oh, please come with me. My parents won't be half as mean with you by my side. It's your idea, so it's kind of an unwritten rule that you go. I promise I'll make it up to you!" She laughed and said if it would make me feel better, she would be happy to accompany me. Hugging her, I felt like the luckiest guy in the universe.

Two weeks zipped by. We were sitting, eating blueberry pancakes smothered in delicious syrup that was locally made and purchased at the farm stand on the outskirts of town. It was already Sunday, one day prior to the will reading. "I'm going to hop in the shower so I can make a good impression on your parents. You did call them, didn't you?" Claire asked as I was chewing my last bite. I almost choked on it, as it got stuck in my throat. I tried to avoid her gaze, as she waited for my answer. "Luke, stop avoiding the question. Did you call them or not?"

I sheepishly looked up and confessed that I had chickened out but that I was still going to hold up my end of the bargain and go over there. I was secretly hoping they'd be out, running errands.

Hoping for a warmer day, I peered out the window up at the sky, mesmerized as the clouds nibbled away at the sun before devouring it in one big gulp. The day that had started out with a promise of sun had quickly turned into a full-blown storm. The rain was pouring down in sheets, and the wind was blowing debris into the street as I slowly maneuvered my way to my parents' house. The weather outside was the same way I was feeling inside. My insides were in knots, and I was on the verge of losing my pancakes. The angst I was feeling was indescribable, and, even with Claire by my side, looking beautiful with a smile plastered on her face, I couldn't shake the feeling I was putting us both on a collision course with a shitstorm.

Rounding the corner onto the street that had been my source of income for years, I was crestfallen to see my dad's car in the driveway. I had been hoping he would be gone, preferably in hell, where he belonged. I felt my heart beat loud and fast in my ears as I looked at Claire, who had no idea what she was in store for. "Are you sure you want to do this? We can ditch the whole thing and go to the movies instead." I begged with my eyes, hoping she would see my despondent look and give me a reprieve, but she reassured me it was the right time to face my demons. Kissing her sweetly on the lips for good luck, we made a mad dash for the front door, trying to avoid the rain puddles that had already begun to accumulate. One knock, two knocks, three knocks, and nothing. "Okay, let's go. They're obviously not home," I blurted out, already turning to leave, when the door burst open, and there stood Christopher and Brian. *Did they ever do anything apart?* I wondered silently. They had grown in the time I had been away and become handsome, coming into their own. As I stood staring at them, they were like strangers to me. I wished I could say I was happy to see them, but I didn't believe in telling lies.

I wasn't in the mood for small talk. I was here only to pacify Claire, so I introduced her to my brothers as they opened the door for us to come in, out of the storm. Surprisingly they extended their hands and shook hers while smiling pleasantly. "Are mom and dad home?" I asked before I heard my mom yell from the kitchen, inquiring who was at the door. Before they could answer, she appeared, wiping her hands on her yellow apron covered with embroidered

CHAPTER 17 ... THE TALK

sunflowers. She stopped in her tracks as she saw us, a hint of a smile playing on her lips before she started nervously looking around.

"Hello, Lucas. Who is your friend?" I must have blushed, as my face instantly felt hot. Secretly not wanting to share Claire and keep her all to myself, I graciously introduced her. "Mom, this is my girlfriend Claire. I wanted you to meet her." She reached out for Claire's hand and planted a kiss on top, telling her what a pleasure it was. She sounded so formal and had aged at least ten years with noticeable frown lines and gray hair taking over her roots. Turning to the twins, she asked, "Does your dad know we have company?" before sending them upstairs to retrieve him.

Leading the way into the family room, I looked around like I had never set foot in here before. I saw the mahogany leather couch that had been off limits and the green shag carpet that still smelled to high heaven. It seemed like a lifetime ago that I had barely existed within these walls. I was brought into the present with a squeeze of my hand and an "ahem" from Claire. My mom had taken Claire's hand in hers again and was gushing how wonderful it was to meet her. And then she turned to me, reaching up and planting a kiss on my cheek as she whispered *"I've missed you."* I almost fell over in a dead faint, but then I remembered that she was the best actress when the occasion called for it. She was surely in the running for an Oscar today.

After my mom left us momentarily as she went to get us coffee, Claire turned to me and said, "Your mom seems delightful. Is this the same woman who has made your life a living nightmare?" I was hoping her words were just heavy with sarcasm, but she looked genuine, giving credence to my mom giving an academy-award performance. Words like "delightful" and "my mom" don't belong in the same sentence. I would have never have used these words to describe my mother. Just as I was about to form a rebuttal, my dad appeared out of thin air, looking pissed that he had been rudely interrupted. He, too, had aged, which didn't bode well for him. The hair he had left was standing on end, and he was wearing a rat-tatty robe with noticeable stains down the front and used tissues spilling out of the torn pocket. He looked like death warmed over, and I secretly wondered if he was sick, hoping it was terminal.

My brothers were right on his heels, looking excited that they had a front-row seat for the action that was about to unfold. Before speaking, he took three wobbly steps toward us, grabbing his eyeglasses off the coffee table in an effort to believe his eyes. Taking the high road, for Claire's sake, I nervously said, "Hi, Dad. I've come to introduce you to my girlfriend." The ball was in his court now, and I held my breath, wondering how he would respond.

A confused look ran across his face, questioning if his eyes were deceiving him. The last time we had so much as said one word to each other was the time I'd cold-cocked him into oblivion. Not my finest moment, but I stood by the decision that it had been warranted. He opened his mouth to speak, looking like a fish out of water, gulping in air, making me silently question, again, if he was sick or drunk, or both. Or possibly just being an asshole at a loss for words. Just in the nick of time, my mom breezed in, all smiles until she caught sight of him. Her demeanor changed on the spot. And so did the air in the room.

I froze and grabbed Claire's hand to brace for the onslaught of obscenities I was sure was about to tumble out of his mouth, but he surprised me and mumbled something under his breath while turning and walking out of the room without so much as

CHAPTER 17 ... THE TALK

an audible word. He obviously didn't care about the awards show later because his acting skills were not on point, although quite dramatic. I couldn't have been more surprised if he'd handed me a million bucks. I felt like I'd dodged a bullet. A bullet that was aimed straight at my heart.

My mom looked shocked but recovered quickly, explaining he'd been resting, trying to fight off a bug. I could tell she was embarrassed by his behavior and making up excuses, but I didn't care. I was breathing a huge sigh of relief. The next ten minutes were filled with painful, awkward silence. The small smile we'd gotten from my mom when she first saw us had been filed away with all the heinous times she treated me like dogshit.

Standing to leave, Claire immediately joined me, feeling my tension. We both thanked my mom, bid her farewell, and practically knocked each other over in a desperate attempt to get to the car first. The willow tree that Marm and I had loved so much looked sad. In fact, the whole house looked like it had seen better days. Claire had the good sense not to address what had just happened. We rode in silence while I seethed under the surface. Thank God she felt my tension and knew better than to bring it up the rest of the night.

Monday rolled around faster than I would have liked. I was going to be running on fumes, having spent my night unable to relax. Rolling over in bed, I saw a cup of coffee on the night side table with a note. I started to panic, thinking Claire had left me after the fiasco yesterday. I wouldn't blame her. Reluctantly, I opened the note and breathed a sigh of relief upon reading "I'm proud of you. Love you to the moon and back." Yours forever and ever, Claire.

As I looked up, she was standing in the doorway with one of my shirts on, casually unbuttoning every button while seductively biting her lower lip, until the shirt fell to the floor, revealing her flawless naked body. And, just like that, all my anxiety disappeared.

Screeching to a stop in front of Stanford, Bridges and Howe, I glanced at my watch, noticing we had five minutes to spare before our meeting was set to begin. My much-needed distraction this morning had done the trick, and I was feeling reasonably relaxed. More than I thought was possible under the circumstances of being face to face with my family again. Although yesterday hadn't been ideal, it had served its purpose to ease the strain of today. Claire had been right again.

Walking in, we were greeted pleasantly by a young, stylish woman sitting behind a massive, ornately carved, rich dark-wood desk. "Welcome to Stanford, Bridges and Howe. Do you have an appointment with one of our attorneys today?" Handing her my letter, I watched as she punched information with her perfectly red manicured nails into the computer on her desk.

The reception area was impressive, to say the least, with twenty-five-foot ceilings surrounded by windows; some of them were stained glass, sending prisms of colorful light across the highly polished, pristine white herringbone-tiled floor. The whole persona reeked of success and wealth, making my decision to wear my best suit and tie the right one. Claire was conservatively dressed in a black blazer over a silk pale-blue blouse and pencil skirt hitting right above her knees. She had meticulously corralled her hair into a low ponytail tied with a pristine white silk ribbon. She was the epitome of stylish elegance.

Handing my letter back, I was instructed to head up to the sixth floor and turn left out of the elevators. My meeting was set to take place in the office of Gregory Stanford, one of the firm's partners.

CHAPTER 17 ... THE TALK

I felt out of my element but quite at home both at the same time, which was odd. I couldn't shake the niggling feeling that I'd been here before, even though that was impossible. There was something about the feeling of power and justice that appealed to me.

"Penny for your thoughts?" Claire asked as the elevator doors opened onto the sixth floor.

"I'm both scared shitless and equally in awe of my surroundings. I could get used to hanging out here every day," I said as I openly gawked. Not only was there rich, dark wood everywhere I looked, adding the air of elegance, but it also smelled like money.

Stumbling about for a bit, we found our way to another reception desk. Another impeccably dressed young woman ushered us to an office that sat in the corner of the building, taking up enough room for four offices combined. Windows lined the walls overlooking the downtown area and a breathtaking lake that skirted the edge of the town square. I could see for miles from this vantage point and felt on top of the world, figuratively and literally.

I was drawn out of my trance when an unknown voice greeted me from behind while gently tapping me on the shoulder. "Excuse me. May I be of assistance? I'm Gregory Stanford, and this, young man, is my office. Who might you be?" I turned and came face to face with a man who looked slightly annoyed, looking me straight in the eye. That, in itself, never happened because few people I met ever shared my stature. He looked strangely familiar, too, which I found unusual, as I was certain we'd never crossed paths before.

Slightly thrown off for a second and feeling intimidated by Mr. Stanford, I regained my presence of mind and answered. "Sir, please let me introduce myself. I'm Lucas Travers, and I'm here for a meeting with you regarding a reading of my grandparents' will." I watched as his left eye faintly twitched and he did a double take.

"Did you say 'Travers'? Did I hear you correctly?"

"Yes, sir. That's exactly what I said. Should I know you from somewhere?" I was puzzled at this point because I could see the wheels turning in record time through his head.

Ignoring my question, he regained his composure and ushered us into the conference room, where my mom was sitting and my brothers anxiously pacing. I looked around, expecting to see my dad lurking in the corner, but, thankfully, he was nowhere to be seen. My attention was immediately drawn to my mom as a gasp escaped her mouth and she turned white as a ghost, gulping for air.

The gray hair from yesterday had been touched up. She was dressed to the nines, and her makeup had been skillfully applied. She didn't remotely resemble the mom from yesterday, and I suspected that she had dressed to make a good impression. Mr. Stanford stopped inches from her, reaching down to embrace her in an awkward hug. The air got sucked out of the room as sparks flew around the two. We were all forgotten as the two of them stood transfixed on each other, acting like two lovesick teenagers.

It was more than obvious they knew each other, becoming animated and all smiles. I couldn't remember any other time that I'd seen my mom so happy—at least none that was locked in my memory vault. After what seemed like forever, they separated and got down to business. No explanation was given on what had just transpired, and I chose not to ask.

CHAPTER 17 ... THE TALK

Mr. Stanford flipped an invisible switch and became all business as he explained the will in great detail all while stealing quick glances toward my mom. I watched her out of the corner of my eye as she sat with a whimsical smile plastered on her face, looking like the cat that ate the canary. There was something I was missing, but, honestly, I didn't give two shits anymore. My life was with Claire now, and I was more than ready to start the next chapter.

CHAPTER 18

THE NEW BEGINNING
TWENTY-TWO TO TWENTY-FIVE YEARS OLD

The next months were a much-welcome whirlwind. I had made steps in the right direction to start my own business, which I planned on naming Golden Ray Construction Company. It was a nod to Marm, since she had been a golden retriever. And, of course, a ray of sunshine. After looking endlessly, I found the perfect little house to buy, situated off the beaten path on the west side of town. It was on the opposite side from my parents, which made it extra appealing, and not far from Alex and Sloan, which was an added bonus. Things were looking up for sure.

It was one of those *You know it when you see it* kinda things. It was a three-bedroom olive craftsman style with a wide porch that wrapped around the whole front of the house, set under deep eaves. I visualized us sitting out on the front porch, watching our children play under the willow tree that was identical to the one in

CHAPTER 18 ... THE NEW BEGINNING

my parents' front yard. I already had plans to bury Marm in what I hoped would be her final resting place. The house itself was flawless in every way, especially the corner brick fireplace that sat nestled in the family room, and the chef's kitchen that looked out over the fenced backyard, perfect for our kids and dogs to play in.

I had to suppress a laugh as I visualized Claire and me in our aprons, mine with the "L" for Luke, shaped like a ladle, and hers with the "C" for Claire shaped like a colander, with flour smeared on her face, trying to fine-tune our homemade pasta.

Claire and I spent nights and weekends planning for the future and making the home our own. Honestly, that woman turned everything she touched into perfection; I watched in awe as our house became a home filled with love, happiness, and hope—that we would soon fill it with children of our own.

One night, I lay in bed, tossing and turning, my thoughts consumed with pulling off the perfect engagement. I had already asked and gotten my blessing from Alex. After picking out an exquisite engagement ring, all I had left to do was not botch one of the most important days of my life. Claire wasn't the type to want anything remotely flashy, so I settled on a one-carat, princess-cut diamond that matched the sparkle in her eyes. Hopefully, if all went as planned, we would soon be picking out our wedding rings together. I was bursting at the seams just thinking about becoming hitched to my saving grace.

Claire's studies were going splendidly, pulling in straight A's and loving every minute of it. I was in complete admiration of how she tackled everyday life with enthusiasm, diving right in with the most positive of attitudes. If there was a less-than-savory side to her, I was yet to see an inkling of it.

The harsh winter gave way to spring. It was my favorite time of the year because the sun was back in all its glory, shining brightly, lighting up the days and casting shadows on the beautiful wildflowers that plentifully bloomed in abundance, dotting the landscape near and far with every color known to mankind. All was right with the world, and things were going my way after years of struggles. So much so that I couldn't believe my good fortune. Only one thing was left to make my life complete.

Picking a bouquet of dandelions mixed with some sunflowers and baby's breath, I wrapped them in some muted yellow tissue paper, finishing it off with a brown raffia bow. Even though I was learning to be a good cook, I wanted this day to be perfect, so I had relied on the professionals to whip up an assortment of picnic foods. Placing them in the wicker picnic basket, I grabbed a bottle of Dom Perignon and two crystal champagne flutes. I carefully wrapped them in a tartan-red plaid blanket and headed to the car. I nervously checked my pocket for the upteenth time today, feeling for the unmistaken feel of the ring box. Today was the day I had dreamt about, and I was equal parts giddy and scared shitless.

We had agreed last night to meet by our favorite oak tree, situated next to a quaint little lake on the outskirts of town. The lake often glistened in the sun and was so still it resembled a mirror, reflecting the near-cloudless sky. Ever since we randomly stumbled upon it one day as we were out exploring, we had claimed it as our own, even getting brave enough to take a polar plunge last winter. I double checked the back seat to make sure the boom box was there with my cassette mix tape in place. I had spent hours taping love songs appropriate for an engagement. Feeling confident I hadn't forgotten anything, I sped away, leaving my past behind me and driving toward my future.

CHAPTER 18 ... THE NEW BEGINNING

Being a bit of a perfectionist was my downfall at times. I knew the proposal would be perfect without the champagne, flowers, picnic goodies, and music, but I couldn't help myself—only the best for Claire. So when she pulled up, I nervously greeted her with the flowers tucked innocently behind my back, as her smile lit up my soul.

She was a vision of glorious beauty dressed casually in boyfriend jeans and a butterscotch-yellow pullover sweater. Her hair was curled on the ends and pulled up on the sides with yellow barrettes shaped like daisies. Wrapping her arms around my neck, she kissed me passionately—like it had been weeks instead of hours that she had last seen me.

Taking a step back, she took a long, hard look at me while playfully biting her lip. "Whatcha got behind your back there, Luke? Are you hiding something from me?" She grabbed my arm, and I dropped to one knee, handing her the flowers and pouring my heart out. "I never knew what happiness was until I met you, Claire. You're everything good and pure that I want in my life forever." I had planned a whole speech but was suddenly overcome with emotion, feeling as if my heart would explode with all the love I had for this amazing woman. Taking a second to compose myself, I continued, "I love you more than words can explain. Would you do me the honor of becoming my wife?"

"What? Really? You want to spend the rest of your life with *moi*?" She laughed, knowing full well how I couldn't live without her. She then proceeded to jump up and down, screaming, "Yes, I will be your wife, you wonderful, handsome hunk of a man!" I couldn't wipe the smile off my face, nor did I want to.

I'd always read that we should live in the moment but never totally understood until now. The proposal is a blur of happy tears, promises to be together forever, I love you's, and the all-important "Yes," while "Unchained Melody" played softly in the background. We both cried as I hugged her tight, promising her my undying love. I didn't have a lot of happy memories to compare it to, but I couldn't imagine ever being happier.

Who knew planning a wedding could be all-consuming? We only wanted something simple, so, after hours of looking at brides magazines and weighing the costs, Claire had a great idea.

"Luke, what do you think about having a small affair at the courthouse? All that really matters is that we become husband and wife, so why all the hoopla? We'll invite our families to share in our special day, and you can get Don, your best friend at work to stand up for you; I'll get Helen, my bestie from childhood to stand by me. What do you think?" She said with a mischievous smile, posing like the famous sculpture, *The Thinker*.

I laughed and agreed on the spot, except for our families being invited. Mine were still leaving a bad taste in my mouth. When I raised my concerns, she was adamant, mumbling something about olive branches. So, I reluctantly accepted the stipulations, mainly because I was yet to find fault with any decision she made, and, most importantly, neither one of us wanted to wait. We started making plans for a beautiful summer wedding on August 14 of that year.

I opted for an invitation through the mail for my family. I still wasn't sold on the idea of them attending and acting like a wet blanket on my special day, but I kept my mouth shut and hoped for the best. Alex and Sloan were over the moon to our faces, but I had a feeling in the pit of my stomach that they didn't think I was good enough for their precious little girl. I was more determined than ever to prove them wrong. I had high hopes that Golden Ray Construction

CHAPTER 18 ... THE NEW BEGINNING

Company was going to be next-level success. One thing I'd learned about myself through the years is that I am a survivor and that, once I put my mind to something, I could and would succeed. Or die trying.

Long days and sweltering heat drifted by at record speed, and, before I knew it, the big day was upon us. I had received a response from my mom saying they would be in attendance, so I braced myself for the onslaught of nastiness that my dad would spew. I was certain he would find it impossible to keep his mouth shut when he knew he had a golden opportunity to ruin my day.

"Luke, I know this is silly," Claire said one day prior, looking like a schoolgirl with her hair in braids tied with bright fluorescent pink ribbons on the ends, "but I want to be traditional. No spending the night together tonight and definitely no seeing me beforehand in my wedding dress."

Pulling her into a big bear hug, I kissed the top of her head, inhaling the intoxicating scent of lavender, and laughed. "I don't think you're being silly at all, you beautiful, hot woman of my dreams."

Every time I think I've reached the epitome of happiness, something else comes along and makes me giddy beyond my wildest dreams. My wedding day was everything I dreamed about and so much more. I got to the courthouse early, wanting to surprise Claire and decorate with flowers. The joke was on me, because, as soon as I rounded the corner, my nose led the way down the long hallway adorned with framed pictures of past and present city officials, into the interior room, where the ceremony was to take place.

She had already worked her magic, as I stood in awe of how the room had transposed itself into a wonderland with whimsical fairy lights intertwined amongst the furnishings. There were hundreds of white candles in various shapes and sizes enclosed in clear-glass containers, sparkling and filling the room with wonderment. A picture we had taken of each other the day of our proposal had been blown up, sitting on an easel, filling the room with our joyous smiling faces. And if that wasn't enough, a massive bouquet of red, white, and pink roses shaped like a heart stood at the makeshift altar, filling the room with a sweet aroma. As I looked closer, I saw that some dandelions had been sporadically placed, adding Claire's personal touch. It was as if I had walked into my own personal fairytale.

I had gone to great lengths to make my appearance something she would be proud of. I had a fresh haircut and a charcoal-gray suit that cost more than my first car. She loved me in pink and always joked that only real men wore pink, so I had chosen a pastel-pink oxford shirt with a paisley tie matching the suit and shirt. A pink pocket square poked smartly out of the pocket, finishing the look to perfection. If I had to say so myself, I cleaned up well.

We had decided to write our own vows, and, as I sat rereading mine, waiting patiently with fifteen minutes to spare, the air changed in the room immediately as I felt an evil presence lurking. I knew without turning my dad would be there, but I was determined to not let anything ruin this day for Claire and me, so I turned with the biggest smile I could muster up. There stood my family, looking more like they were attending a funeral other than a happy occasion.

"Thank you for coming to share my special day," I eagerly said, reaching out to shake my dad's hand and give my mom a peck on the cheek. I was the one competing for the Oscar today, and I had a strong suspicion my acting skills would be on point. Miracles do happen, because my dad shook my hand and wished me well. My mom looked on, nervous as a whore in church, noticeably swallowing, followed by a slight grin with a twinkle in her eye. I still had

CHAPTER 18 ... THE NEW BEGINNING

my suspicions something was up, but I was hoping they were just happy I was going to be someone's else's problem now.

Keeping it quaint and small, my pal Don showed up, giving me a hearty pat on the back, followed by Helen, Claire's bestie. Pleasantries were made as the judge that was overseeing the ceremony popped his head in, introduced himself, and found his place next to the heart-shaped flowers. His handshake was firm, and he offered me a little wink as I looked him in the eye. The peaceful aura surrounding him put me at ease, reassuring me I was in good hands.

I was nervous. Not nerves indicating I was doing the wrong thing—quite the contrary. Jittery nerves because this was a big step and one that I had wanted my whole life. *Happy* nerves—if that was even a thing. I smiled at myself, wondering if it was just me, or was Claire feeling nervous anticipation, too? I took a couple of deep breaths as we made my way to our spots.

It was "go time," as music started playing from a boombox that had been hidden in the corner. Claire had thought of everything as "I Can't Help Falling in Love" serenaded us.

Like a river flows
Surely to the sea
Darling, so it goes
Some things, you know, are meant to be

Through the years I had shed many sad tears into Marm's fur, but this was different. These were ecstatic tears of joy, and nobody could have prepared me for the emotion I felt as tears freely flew upon seeing Claire in her wedding dress. Her beaming parents on either side, accompanying her down the small aisle, was the most majestic sight I had ever seen. She glowed like an angel, and I wouldn't have been a bit surprised if she had sprouted wings. I heard audible gasps taking in her beauty. I took a quick glance at my Mom and saw her brush a lone tear from her cheek as she looked on with admiration. Not only was Claire a vision to behold, but her heart was pure, making her beauty run deep.

Claire had chosen a simple Chantilly lace white gown that had a sweetheart neckline showing off a string of pearls I had given her as a wedding gift. Her dress flowed in layers as she gracefully floated toward me. Her hair was gathered in a French bun at the nape of her neck, while wispy curls cascaded down the sides of her face. She was not one to wear a great deal of makeup, and today was no exception. She had a light dusting of blush and a couple of strokes of mascara accentuating her gorgeous eyes. She finished off her look with rose-colored lip gloss catching the flicker of the candles just so. Her best accessory by far was her smile, and I had to remind myself to close my mouth as I bit my lower lip in anticipation.

If this is what heaven felt like, I didn't want to wake up. Reciting our vows, forgetting about the others in the room, we gazed lovingly into each other's eyes, promising to love and cherish each other till death do us part. She was the puzzle piece I needed to become whole. Everything about the ceremony was perfect as we kissed and took a little bow as we were introduced as Mr. and Mrs. Lucas Travers.

Our life was just beginning, and I couldn't wait to fill our home with children of our own. It would be a little like a do-over, giving my children the love, respect, and attention I had never received. I felt like a charlatan, undeserving of the love we shared, but Claire was always there to reassure me that what we had was real and much deserved.

CHAPTER 19

THE HEARTBREAK

Every day was better than the last. We found ourselves in a very enjoyable routine. By day, I worked in sun and sleet, making a name for myself in the construction business. Claire attended classes and spent precious bits of time here and there working on a manuscript she planned to publish in the near future. All was more than perfect in our little corner of the world, as we cherished each other to the fullest.

Because of Claire's insistence, I started seeing a therapist to try to come to terms with my childhood. It had taken an extreme emotional toll on me, and, even when I wasn't aware, the smallest of things affected how I saw life and tried to get the big picture. They were things I wasn't even cognizant of, but they were ingrained in my soul and heart.

One day we were out spending the day, enjoying each other's company, without a care in the world, when we came upon a petting zoo, part of a traveling carnival set up on the outskirts of town. A childlike squeal escaped Claire's lips as she bounded out of the car in a full sprint toward the animals. Her exuberance for life was uplifting as I chased after her, giggling all the way, until I saw her kneeling down with her arms wrapped around a black sheep. I stopped dead in my tracks and started to shake, not seeing the animal for who it was but for what it represented to me. Memories flooded my mind, and I was a child again, sitting on the stairs, listening to my parents talk shit about me. How I was a loser. They would be better off without me. They called me a black sheep.

A *black sheep*. The outcast, freakish one. And why was it so vivid of a memory? The mind is a funny thing and tends to remember bits and pieces that have affected us in both positive and negative ways. I fell to the ground, wrapping my arms around myself, rocking in a soothing motion and blinking away the impending tears. I was on the verge of losing my way when Claire was suddenly by my side, whispering in my ear.

"Honey, what has made you so upset?" she questioned as I tried to shake the feeling that I wasn't a child anymore but instead a grown-ass married man with a beautiful wife I loved unconditionally and a very successful business. She grabbed my hand and led me to a nearby picnic table positioned under a giant maple tree that was offering shade, while the leaves blew in the breeze that had taken hold throughout the day. She looked me dead straight in my eyes, and I saw a myriad of emotions play across her face. She looked scared and concerned most of all, but behind her beautiful eyes shone enough love to chase away any bad memory. I bowed my head, breaking eye contact out of embarrassment for the weak moment she had just witnessed. I mumbled that I was sorry if I acted

CHAPTER 19 ... THE HEARTBREAK

childish and un-man-like, but all she could say was "Love means never having to say you're sorry," while getting up and reenacting our first date by carving a heart with our initials inside on the side of the maple tree. And just like that, my memory was tucked away, hopefully to never resurface again.

Unfortunately, as days passed and circumstances arose, images of childhood memories began to surface again, one after the other. They were sometimes fragmented memories I was able to push aside but other times were full-on meltdown moments. I had taken to talking in my sleep, and, on numerous occasions, I woke up abruptly, gasping for air, shaking uncontrollably, only to be calmed by Claire's reassurances and loving embrace. I saw the troubled look on her face as I struggled. Not only was she concerned for my mental well-being, as I had increasingly become more agitated, but seeing the pain I was in and my concern that I was becoming unhinged had her grappling for answers. Although the memories were crippling, not once did I ever lose sight of what was most important, which was Claire, my one and only.

After months of pleading and convincing from Claire, I bit the bullet and made an appointment.

My therapist assured me occurrences like these were normal and part of the healing process, since we had begun a deep dive into my past. Sitting in the waiting room for my 4 p.m. appointment to begin, I cautiously looked around. I still had not gotten accustomed to being here and felt a certain shame that I hadn't been able to shake the past on my own. The office was tastefully decorated in calming blue hues, with leather-bound chairs in an assortment of coordinating colors scattered about. They were by far the most comfortable chairs I had ever sat in, lending themselves to a quick catnap. As I sat snuggled in, I couldn't help thinking it was almost like receiving a hug from an inanimate object.

In the corner of the room, a refreshment center had been set up with different sweets and an assortment of herbal teas ready to be made. My favorite part was the eclectic collection of mugs that had been collected throughout the years. All had uplifting affirmations or motivational sayings and quotes. It was a glimpse into the "personality" of the office. I opted for a snickerdoodle cookie and steeped some peppermint tea in a bright red mug, on which was printed *YOU MAKE THE WORLD A BETTER PLACE JUST BY BEING IN IT.* I was already starting to feel better!

There was only one other person waiting. It was a woman in her fifties, with a stylish grayish bob, busily working her fingers meticulously around some needles, knitting from a large ball of multi-colored yarn that sat in her lap. I was nervous today, fidgeting and uneasy. A took a sip of my scalding hot tea in an attempt to wash away the bile in the back of my throat. My insides were stripped raw—I knew that my session would once again open up more painful memories.

I nibbled on my cookie and thumbed through a *TIME* magazine, looking at the pictures but not reading anything. The receptionist sat quietly behind an antique cherrywood desk in the other corner of the room, next to the entrance. She was a grandmotherly type, wearing a perpetual smile plastered across her face. She had a look that radiated comfort, and I envisioned her baking homemade cookies in her off time when she wasn't tending to her garden.

To calm my uneasiness, I decided to take a stab at a game Claire and I played often. We both loved to people-watch, and, oftentimes when we were out, we would try to guess someone's occupation by the

CHAPTER 19 ... THE HEARTBREAK

way they dressed and handled themselves. If we were lucky enough to gather bits of conversation to help with our consensus, that was a plus. The competitive side of Claire came out in full force, often resulting in her blatantly striking up a conversation to try to prove her guess. She was relentless and left me with sore cheeks and a stitch in my side from uncontrollable fits of laughter. We even went so far as to keep score with a tally sheet, stuck on the front of the refrigerator with a golden-retriever magnet, resembling Marm, proudly displayed. After all these years, I had finally managed to have something of importance to me shared in such a prominent spot, displayed for all to appreciate.

As I took a quick clandestine gander at the woman in her fifties sitting on the other side of the room, I made a quick guesstimate that she was not only a new grandmother knitting a baby blanket but a successful real-estate agent by day and avid reader by night. Come to think of it, she did resemble an advertisement I had seen on a bus-stop bench recently, causing me to chuckle under my breath.

I was brought out of my thoughts when "Luke, I'm ready to see you now," was whispered in my ear as I felt a soft embrace on my shoulder. I looked up into the eyes of my therapist, Dr Brandi Hawthorne. She was not a lot older than myself; I judged her to be about thirty-five. She had come highly recommended—"the best in the biz"—helping her patients to regain sanity, one session at a time.

The therapy was already beginning to make a difference, and I wondered to myself why I hadn't taken the plunge earlier instead of waiting and internally suffering, dying a little more every day. I had been seeing Dr. Hawthorne for about a couple of months and instantly liked her. She's what the guys in high school would have referred to as a smoke show, with eyes the color of the sky on a bright sunny day and a little button nose that struggled to hold up her studious cat's-eye glasses. She was one of those types that didn't know she was hot and focused all her attention on her craft, which I found refreshing.

Her office immediately eased my mind as I gazed at a variety of ocean scenes, creating a Zen effect. Soothing music was barely audible in the background, with a fluffy sand-colored couch sitting in the middle of the room on a blue shag rug the color of the sea. Sand and surf had always had such a calming effect on me. So much so that I researched and wrote a paper in school, interested to learn why it held such healing powers. Not surprising when brain imaging had been done, it linked water with your brain, releasing feel-good hormones, including dopamine and oxytocin. Not only that, but the sound of the waves had been proven to relax the mind, activating a part of the nervous system that slows down the brain and helps promote relaxation. The whole effect eased my nerves immediately, and a false sense of calm took over.

"Good afternoon, Luke. I'm so pleased to see you this afternoon. I feel like we've been making some promising progress these last couple of months," Dr. Hawthorne said while patting the couch for me to take a seat. Our sessions were an hour long; basically, I would share what was troubling me on each individual visit, while she asked ever-more-probing questions, trying to get me to open up. I'm not going to lie: I had trouble with that. To me, "sharing" meant reliving my nightmare of a childhood. It often left me drained and emotional after a session. She was always insightful and reassuring, which I found not only helpful but encouraging; still, I was a mess. I was quickly getting fed up with my past coming back to haunt me. The last thing I wanted was to bring Claire into my warped

CHAPTER 19 ... THE HEARTBREAK

childhood or give my horrendous parents any of my precious time and headspace, but I knew that therapy was a necessary part of my life now—like it or not.

By any stretch of the imagination, Claire and I were far from old, but time seemed to be flying by at warp speed, causing us to get into a bit of a rut. Although it was a good rut, it was still a rut. Work, school, therapy, weekly dinners with Claire's parents, and sleep—day after day on repeat. One Saturday we both woke up early and simultaneously said, "Let's go get a dog today!" Great minds do think alike. We threw on some sweats, grabbed our coats, and were out the door before our coffee—we were so excited at the prospect. I missed Marm more than I could put into words, and Claire missed the constant companionship of Rowdy, who still lived with her parents, unwilling to part with him.

We were both passionate about animal rescue, so I set out toward the local animal shelter. Our problem wasn't going to be finding a dog we instantly felt connected to but, instead, narrowing it down to one. "Luke, I'm so excited we're finally going to do this! I'm over the moon that we're getting our own dog! I hope we don't have trouble making up our minds! We need to stop at the pet store on the way home!" I instantly knew how thrilled she was, because a constant stream of comments were exploding from her mouth, not waiting for a response. She did this only when something really had her on top of the world. Like everything else she did, I found it endearing, as I watched her face become more animated by the second. I let her ramble, laughing out loud at her as we pulled up front.

"Well, Mrs. Travers, are you ready to find our fur child?" But she was already out of the car, running to the entrance with more exuberance than someone who had just won the state lottery. The shelter was a no-kill shelter, but it still wrecked me. There were aisles upon aisles of perfect animals beaten down and thrown out like trash. As long as I live, I will never understand people who mistreat an animal. I took a second to say a silent prayer that they all would find a home soon.

We were familiar with the layout from volunteering, but we took our sweet time talking to each dog, giving them encouragement. The ones that cried actual tears ripped me to shreds, and, more times than not, we both shed a couple of tears right alongside them. Once again, I was thankful that Claire loved my sensitive side as much as I loved hers.

Before we knew it, hours had passed, and we were alerted that the place was closing down for the day. The moment we were dreading was upon us. We both wanted to take them all, but we settled on a golden retriever that looked like Marmalade and a yellow labrador retriever that resembled Rowdy. Both were a bit on the timid side, unsure of their fate at this point, and we could hardly wait to shower them with the love—and happy life—they deserved.

Claire sat in the back with the pups on the way home, smothering them with nonstop kisses. "Hey, babe, what do you think we should name our kids?" she said, burrowing her head into their fur. The golden was a female, so I threw out a couple of names. I always thought people's names for dogs were cute, and, with the holiday season quickly approaching, my mind wandered there. "How about 'Holly,' 'Belle,' or 'Faith'? And for the lab, 'Jingle,' 'Nicholas,' or 'Joseph'?" I saw the twinkle in her eye as she realized why my mind had gone where it had. Christmas was both of our favorite holidays. "I love it! Christmas names for our two Christmas miracles!" she enthusiastically replied, while wiping off a face full of dog slobber.

CHAPTER 19 ... THE HEARTBREAK

And just like that, it was settled. We had become a family of four, naming the pups Holly and Joseph, Joey for short. If it were only that simple to get a human baby. We had been hoping and trying, but, unfortunately, every month we were left with a heartache and disappointment. Claire was especially starting to get discouraged, which was out of character for her. As time marched on, I tried to take her mind off of it and focus on Holly and Joey. They were flourishing and had made remarkable progress. It only reaffirmed what I already knew—that if you gave a dog love and attention, they would return it tenfold.

Claire graduated, and I was the proud husband watching with admiration as she walked across the stage to collect her diploma. It goes without saying my parents didn't come to show their support, even though Claire had called them personally, extending an invitation and leaving tickets for them at will call. Knowing how sensitive she was, and, after extending an olive branch, I knew it hurt her feelings, but she was all smiles and full of dreams for our future. She was hell-bent on having a baby, even though, secretly, I loved our little family just the way it was.

"Luke, I know I'm probably overreacting, but I've made both of us appointments to see fertility specialists. I never thought I would have a problem, but something feels off to me," Claire casually said while popping a brussel sprout into her mouth while eating dinner I had whipped up from scratch. I saw the pain in her eyes, and, even though I thought it was premature, I agreed.

Is there anything worse than not being able to conceive? I know this sounds melodramatic because, of course, there is, but my heart felt as if it might break when I watched Claire break down in a pile of sorrow and tears month after month. I always did my best to lift her up by surprising her with little trinkets and doting on her. But I could feel her slowly start to develop some depression, when the unthinkable happened.

The day was gray with a relentless drizzle and a stiff breeze that bit through my layers of clothing as I congratulated myself for securing a huge contract to build a new housing subdivision. This was a major coup that required a proper celebration, so, after stopping to grab a bottle of Dom Perignon, I rushed home, barely able to contain my excitement. From the driveway the house looked mostly dark with only a faint light shining through the shutters that covered our bedroom windows. Throwing open the door, I was greeted with silence, which was strange since Holly and Joey usually greeted me with boundless energy and shrieks of joy at the end of each day.

"Claire? Hey, babe—where are you? Come on out. I have something wonderful to tell you!"

Silence. Nothing. I kicked off my shoes and hung up my parka, suspecting she was in the tub with headphones on, the pups lying joyfully by the tub. They very rarely let us go anywhere without them trailing, tails wagging. I heard the wind whistling through the trees as I bent down to throw kindling into the fireplace to start a fire. Claire loved fires. We often spent many a stormy night wrapped up in each other's arms, cuddling with the warmth of the fire enveloping us as we shared our dreams and aspirations.

"Claire, Joey, Holly—where are you guys?" At the mention of their names, I heard a couple of woofs from the bedroom but still no greeting, so I grabbed a couple of champagne flutes, the Dom, and eagerly went to find my family. Approaching the door, I swore I heard a whimper and some scratching, which seemed weird and out of character. A cold draft blew from under the door, and I got

CHAPTER 19 ... THE HEARTBREAK

an eerie feeling that something was askew. I always had a bit of a sixth sense—not what I would consider full-on ESP but close to it—and, as I reached the door, I was in a full-on panic.

A dull ringing filled my ears and the *thump, thump, thump, thump* of my pulse echoed through me, mimicking the bass drum of a symphony orchestra.

Throwing the door open, I immediately saw Claire, still and lying on the floor, fully clothed, at the foot of the bed. A grimace had formed on her lips, and her beautiful eyes had a look of terror. She must have been carrying a cup of tea, because a dandelion embossed cup lay broken into shards of glass, among a pool of amber liquid. Holly was licking her face, while Joey was whimpering and pawing at the ground, raising his eyes to me as a tear dropped on Claire's hand.

Not to frighten the dogs, I whispered, *Everything is going to be all right*, as I gingerly bent down to carefully scoop Claire up and place her gently on the bed. She was cold to the touch, and the first signs of rigor mortis were beginning to set in, making it almost impossible to release what she was clutching in her left hand. As I pried it out, I audibly gasped as I looked straight at a vivid blue line on her pregnancy test. Claire was pregnant with my child—a child that I would never meet. My heart shattered into a million pieces as I caressed her hair, begging her to wake up. I knew right there and then that my life would be changed forever.

CHAPTER 20

THE MELTDOWN

"Distraught" doesn't come close to describing my mental state. My life might as well have been over, because my reason to live died the day a brain aneurysm claimed Claire's life. My throat felt so thick and heavy that I could hardly breathe. It felt like a nightmare, where you want to scream but can't summon your voice. I couldn't sleep. I couldn't eat. I couldn't catch my breath half the time, and I spent my days and nights wondering what I could have done to prevent it, knowing full well there was nothing. I needed answers, but there were none. I was numb and grief-stricken.

Joey and Holly were confused, wandering from room to room, looking for her and lying on her favorite blanket. I knew firsthand that dogs showed human emotions and felt pain as humans do, but I couldn't explain to them that their beloved mom hadn't left them by choice—or me, for that matter. Wanting to escape my reality, I went for daily runs with the pups, but it did little to soothe our souls.

CHAPTER 20 ... THE MELTDOWN

I contemplated ending it all, like I had when I was twelve and miserable. This was a whole new misery and nothing like I'd ever felt in the past. The only thing that kept me on this side of the ground was Claire. I knew how upset she would have been if I gave up. She would want me to carry on and find another love when the time was right. The thought of spending my life with anyone other than her was downright crazy talk and something I wouldn't even entertain. When I wasn't out for my daily jog, I spent my days curled up in a fetal position, hugging her pillow, which still had her lavender-vanilla scent. I was inconsolable and heading for a collision course that would change the trajectory of my life.

My business, which I had taken so much pride in having built it into the reputable company it was now, started faltering. I refused to show up to work, causing deadlines to be missed. It began to suffer, and I didn't care. Uncharacteristically, my mom tried to reach out, but her phone calls fell on deaf ears. Alex and Sloan offered what little support they could through their unfathomable sorrow. Although it was appreciated, I could see the doubt in their eyes—that I had never been good enough for their precious angel, and now I had let the unthinkable happen. We were all crushed beyond words.

And that's when it happened. Innocently enough, I started drinking again to drown my sorrows and camouflage my pain. When I drank, it was the only time my heart didn't hurt and my mind didn't stray to *what could have been*. What *should have been*. And the unavoidable *what never would be*. My pain had taken on a whole new meaning; I knew that, every time I raised a beer bottle to my mouth, I was flirting with danger, but I couldn't stop. Worse than not being able to stop was not *wanting* to stop. So, it continued day after day. Night after night stinking drunk, only to wake in a pool of my own vomit, not remembering what had transpired.

I had lost touch with reality and was unable to take care of not only myself but also of Joey and Holly. Alex and Sloan took them home with them one night after they saw them roaming by themselves down the street. It only added insult to injury, but I knew it was the best thing for them. They would have constant companionship and pets galore. I knew in my brain that it was for the best, but my heart spoke differently. I mourned for them as I drank myself into the deepest, darkest depths of hell.

Somehow word of my present state got back to my parents, and, when I returned home one night, I was greeted by my family, along with Alex and Sloan. The looks of disgust on their faces should have been enough to sober me up, but I had given up caring what they thought years before. Another intervention was staged, in hopes I would see the light, turn over a new leaf, and get my life back on track again—one Claire would be proud of. But not even her name could bring me out of my self-inflicted funk.

My parents walked out, shirking any responsibility for me—but not before my dad got in one last dig. "I always knew you were a loser. You should have been the one to die, not Claire." So much hate packed into such a small package.

Alex and Sloan did the same, turning on their heels, wishing me a good life, but not really meaning it. Empty words falling on deaf ears. As they departed, they slammed the door, causing the hanging framed picture of Claire and me on our wedding day to tumble to the ground. Just like my life, the frame lay shattered into a million shards of glass. I sat hovering over it as tears streamed down my face.

CHAPTER 20 ... THE MELTDOWN

"Why did you leave me, Claire?" I screamed till my throat was raw.

My jaw clenched so tight it hurt, my teeth grinding together. Black spots clouded my vision. I didn't owe them an explanation. Nor was I under any obligation to care what they thought. Then the unthinkable happened.

Hearing Claire's voice made me turn around. Startled, I began to search for her, knowing I was imagining it. But it was so real. And I wanted and needed to believe she'd come back to me. She whispered how much she loved me and how sorry she was that she'd left me and taken our precious child with her. She was a beautiful vision as she pulled me into a hug and planted the sweetest, most tender kiss upon my lips. And then she had the best idea as she floated off to heaven.

CHAPTER 21
THE BRIGHT IDEA

Having Claire visit that night of the intervention was the best thing to happen to me since she'd passed. She reminded me of the time the Army recruiters had come to my high school and given a talk. They piqued my interest, with their promises of exciting travel, the GI bill, and an opportunity to learn discipline. They would provide me with a roof over my head, three square meals a day, *and* a paycheck; it sounded too good to be true. I'd always heard that, if it sounded too good to be true, it probably was.

Clearly, I needed help, because my path to self-destruction was getting me nowhere fast. Nowhere *productive*, anyway. I was better than that, but it was so tempting when I hurt so bad. Claire's visit wouldn't leave my thoughts, and it was weighing heavily on my mind—so heavy that, one morning, after coffee, I showered and set out with an open mind to the local recruiter's office. After I had been so impressed back in high school, I had done a tad bit of

CHAPTER 21 ... THE BRIGHT IDEA

research of my own. One thing I read was to be prepared: I wrote out a variety of jobs that would be of interest to me as well as a list of basic questions for the recruiter. I knew exactly where the list was, so I grabbed it, and out the door I went, with, hopefully, more promise than I felt. It certainly wouldn't hurt to see what they had to say.

I looked like hell. My most recent bender had left me dehydrated but puffy at the same time. My eyes had dark circles and wrinkled bags under them. I couldn't attribute that all to the alcohol, though. My tears and sleepless nights hadn't done much for the state I was in. I could feel Claire's presence, sitting right beside me in the car, and it gave me the encouragement I needed not to turn the car around and head home. Sitting at home was doing nothing good for my mental well-being. I saw her in every room, with her contagious smile that lit up the darkest of days.

After rolling down the windows to let the cool morning air in, I reached over to adjust the sound on the radio. I sharply inhaled as the speaker cracked a little and our wedding song, "Can't Help Falling in Love," filled the car. If I hadn't felt Claire's presence before, I certainly did now. I reached over and put my hand on her seat, willing her to come back to me. I would have staked my life on what I felt next. My hand instantly felt warm as a thumb stroked the back of my hand. My one true love was here in spirit to give me the encouragement I needed to make a potentially life-changing decision.

Surprised at how good it felt to be part of the living instead of wallowing in self-pity and drinking myself under the table, I allowed myself a smile and a much-deserved pat on the back. I had a very strong premonition that today would change my life forever—a change that would define me through the rest of my life.

BLACK SHEEP

The Army recruiting office sat squarely in the middle of the town square, which was bustling with activity, filled with shoppers eagerly searching for the next big deal. School was just around the corner, bringing summer to a close, which meant moms and dads had their kids out for back-to-school shopping. I stopped and smiled, watching as the kids chased each other around, squealing with excitement. I eased my weary bones down onto the bench that sat opposite the ice-cream store, *Dippity-Do-Da*, with the colorful pink and brown awning. I wondered if the colors they chose had subliminal meaning, since those were the same colors Baskin-Robbins used. Well, it had worked on us, because it had been a favorite of mine and Claire's. I knew it wasn't by coincidence that I had chosen this bench, with a view of our store. The whole morning had been filled with serendipitous moments and subtle hints that Claire hadn't truly left me. Her physical presence was gone, but her spirit would remain in my heart forever.

The meeting with the recruiter went as expected. He was the very picture of a quintessential military guy. He sported a crew cut and a neatly trimmed mustache that came to the edge of his lips; he had a spiel that would make you eager to join. Fit as a fiddle, he was a model of discipline and health. A bell sounded as I entered the sparse room, alerting the recruiter that he had a potential enlister in his presence. As he shook my hand and introduced himself as Sergeant Hagins, I felt uneasy. I took pride in being a good judge of character, and, even though he had a friendly smile, I felt as if he had a quota to meet and he didn't care about me any more than the next schmuck who walked through the door. In all fairness, I guess I didn't blame him, but I wanted and needed to feel like I was important.

CHAPTER 21 ... THE BRIGHT IDEA

I knew he would try his damndest to get me to sign on the dotted line immediately, but I had reservations and some still-unanswered questions that only I could answer. But, truthfully, I didn't trust my judgment. So I promised the recruiter I would get back with him soon. I jumped in my car and headed over to Alex and Sloan's house. I desperately needed a play session with the pups. I was hoping Claire's parents would be receptive to my visit, since the last time I saw them, they had not been my biggest fans.

Nerves started to get the best of me as I rounded the corner. Last time I was here, Claire was alive and by my side. The street felt sad, as if the weeping willows were indeed shedding a tear at the loss of the best person to ever grace this street. Despite the cooler temperatures, sweat began to pour down my back, leaving a stream of moisture soaking through my pale-green Oxford shirt. I had spent countless visits here, but today felt different. I had a strong suspicion that I was being judged and needed to prove myself. Honestly, it was not a task I was certain I could pull off, but I conjured up all the determination and strength that I could and plastered a timid smile on my face.

An apology on my part was in order, since I had gone off the proverbial deep end after Claire died. I felt that it was all justified—except for the drinking, which had clearly gotten out of control. I didn't necessarily have an addictive personality, except when it came to alcohol. I wasn't proud of my behavior, which, admittedly, bordered on addiction. I knew I needed to come to terms with my problem before I ended up in worse shape than before. Dr. Hawthorne had gone out of her way, taking my calls at all hours of the day and humoring me with my stories about a love gone too soon. But she wasn't at all accommodating when it came to my alcohol consumption, though. It seemed like everyone was on the same page there.

I was contemplating my next move when the door creaked open, revealing a brooding Alex. He looked pissed.

"What are you doing here, Luke? Didn't we say everything that needed to be said the other night?"

I was taken aback and must have shown it, because his expression softened slightly, revealing a hint of a reprieve as he loudly exhaled. Luckily, before he could utter another word, the three dogs came barreling full-steam ahead, jumping up on me and covering me in slobbery kisses. Dogs really were the best medicine one could ask for—*and* a much-needed distraction from the grilling I was about to receive from Alex.

Bending down to partake in the lovefest, a strong sense of betrayal weighed heavily on my heart. Even though I had met Joey and Holly's physical needs, I had failed to support them emotionally. Finding it hard to admit I needed help, I had let my responsibilities suffer. I felt ashamed. Discouraged. And defeated. Something needed to change ASAP, and it needed to be different from anything I had ever experienced before. Something to get my head back in the game of life and out of the depths of death. I needed discipline. A purpose. Camaraderie. A change of scenery—all things I knew the military would offer.

It was like I had a come-to-Jesus moment and miraculously knew what I needed to do, without any guidance from Alex and Sloan. Because of all I have been through, I've come to accept and appreciate the seasons of change and know that, when something ends, something unique and beautiful grows in its place. It doesn't mean it hurts any less, because, believe me, it's devastating. I guess it's just one of the few benefits of grief. It reminds us to love fiercely,

CHAPTER 21 ... THE BRIGHT IDEA

despite knowing all that it costs, and to live in the moment, because, sadly, we cannot go back. If that were possible, I would be there in the blink of an eye.

Lost in thought, I looked up to four confused eyes staring at me like I had lost my marbles. It was Sloan who spoke first.

"Luke, you look like you've just seen a ghost. Are you OK? Can I get you a glass of water? Please come take a seat in the family room."

I felt foolish that I had even gone over there. But I followed her into the family room and plopped down on the big, comfy leather sofa.

I cleared my throat and dove in. "First of all, I owe you an apology for my behavior as of late. I'm better than that, and I know in my heart that Claire would be appalled, and that deeply saddens me. Frankly, I came to ask both of you for advice. As you're both aware, I've been in an incredibly dark place, unable to find my way out of my mind-crushing grief. I know this might sound odd, but Claire has never left my side. Physically, yes, but she's with me all the time, and she gave me a great idea the other day."

Taking a breath, I took a second to look at them. Watching them nudge each other and give each other a look of "Oh, geez," I knew they didn't understand. Not that I'd expected them to—or cared for that matter. I knew what I was feeling was real, and that's all that mattered to me. "I can see that you think I'm a third of a bubble off, but I wanted you to know I'm joining the Army, and I'll be gone for a while at boot camp. Unfortunately, I won't be by to see the pups. When I said I had come to ask for your advice today, that's what I wanted to ask you... if you thought enlisting was a good idea. But somewhere between leaving the recruiter and now, I've had an epiphany. I hope you can understand."

BLACK SHEEP

With that, I stood, wrapped my arms around the pups, shook Alex's hand, and planted a peck on Sloan's cheek. I had a date with a recruiter and a checklist a mile long in my brain that needed writing down ASAP. My life was about to take a one-eighty, and my head was already beginning to swim with the changes and possibilities in store for me.

CHAPTER 22

THE WILD RIDE

A plethora of emotions ran at full throttle through my mind. I was crushed by the sale of the house that Claire had made into a home. Memories flooded over me as I signed away my ownership, leaving behind my one shot at the happiness I had craved my whole life. Having it for four glorious years as husband and wife wasn't nearly long enough when I thought we would have a lifetime and a family. Life was cruel. Life was unpredictable. Life was a whirlwind of ups and downs. Life was about to change and take me on the wildest of rides I had yet to partake in.

After leaving Alex and Sloan's, I made quick work of beelining my way back to the recruiter's before I changed my mind. Sgt. Hagins acted as if he knew I'd return and already had my ASVAB (Armed Services Vocational Aptitude Battery) placement exam set out, with a couple of freshly sharpened #2 pencils ready. I had already decided that my job of choice would be a Carpentry and

Mason Specialist, so that once I got a passing score, my new career would be underway.

The night prior to being shipped off to basic training, aka boot camp, I sat alone in my car, staring at the big willow tree in my parents' front yard. Many thoughts and memories, both bad and good, flooded over me. I could see an outline of myself as a broken and battered teen, holding Marmalade's ashes in my arms as tears filled the hole I placed her in. The more I tried to remember the positives from my childhood, I was left searching for answers I knew I'd never find. I had been and always would be the *black sheep* of my dysfunctional family. And oddly enough, after countless hours of therapy, I wore that badge proudly.

Deciding I would be the bigger person, I wrote my mom a note explaining my latest adventure. And just like the last time I wrote to her, when I moved out, I was at a loss for words. I wrestled with wanting to tell her how she had wrecked my childhood and how all I ever wanted was her love, but I decided to let it go. I knew it wouldn't change anything.

Although my years under her care had been more than awful, I couldn't help feeling that a tiny sliver of her *actually* cared about me. A glimmer of love here and there shone through at the oddest times, always to disappear as fast as they came. Or maybe it was wishful thinking on my part. I opted to hold on to that for the time being. Either way, I was doing it for Claire. She, always the optimist, had wanted desperately for me to reconcile with my parents, even after I told her it would never happen. She was my gleaming, bright, shining, perfect angel.

I wiped yet another wayward tear from my cheek as I climbed the steps to the veranda. I got a strange feeling standing there, like

CHAPTER 22 ... THE WILD RIDE

I was trespassing and never truly belonged. I placed the note under the welcome mat that had sunflowers etched around the edges, being extra careful to leave a corner peeking out. And then I turned, saluted the door, and walked away, maybe forever. Disturbingly, I felt fine with it.

My thoughts were far from suicidal anymore—again, thanks to therapy—but I had an eerie feeling that, once I left, I might never return. Definitely not in the same capacity as now. I had a strong suspicion the military would change me. Needing this change in the worst way, I turned and said good riddance to the only childhood I had ever known—one filled with disrespect, hate, and avoidance, but mine nonetheless.

After a fitful night of sleep, I pondered over my decision, knowing it was too late to turn back now but not being able to stop myself from contemplating it. I was still at odds with my decision, but I put on a brave face and checked out of my motel, looked around, and bade farewell to Piedmont, hopefully once and for all. The taxi was punctual as I glanced at my watch. It was eight a.m. sharp, and I was on my way to the airport to catch a flight to Fort Jackson, South Carolina, which would be home for the next ten weeks for my basic training.

My emotions were all over the place. I was excited to start the next chapter of my life but apprehensive about what it might entail. I knew it wasn't going to be a walk in the park—quite possibly, it could be the toughest, most challenging ten weeks of my life. Most of all, I was sad. I hated leaving the pups and Claire. In a strange way, I felt like I was deserting them. The funny thing about thoughts and feelings is that they have a mind of their own. Joey and Holly loved the new life with their grandparents, and Claire would always be with me, tucked neatly into a special part of my heart that was reserved for her only. Taking a couple of deep breaths, I moved forward, trying my best to push the troubling thoughts aside.

Air travel was something I had never experienced, so even that was making me a bundle of nerves. I was a mess. So many firsts were coming at me fast and furiously, not giving me time to adjust. Or dwell. Dwelling unnecessarily and overthinking issues had always been a downfall of mine, but there was no time or place for either. Knowing that was a good thing, because more times than not, overthinking left me confused, but a strange part of me missed it. I had always found it difficult to give up old habits.

The plane sat on the tarmac as I sat in the airport, impatiently running my hands through my thick head of hair. I knew I would be saying goodbye to that soon enough, as crew cuts were part of the indoctrination into basic training. Another first. As I nervously peered around, I decided to play mine and Claire's old game of trying to guess a stranger's occupation. I needed the distraction—*and* it made it seem like she was sitting next to me.

I was absentmindedly twirling my wedding ring around and around my finger, wishing with everything I had that things could be different, when suddenly, I felt an eerie presence around me. I cautiously looked around, half expecting nobody to be there, blaming it on a case of nerves gnawing at me. But, to my surprise, sitting on the seats adjacent to me was a woman dressed in a tattered, stained, drab, khaki-colored coat. Her head was bent, and her hands were covered in dirty gloves, nervously twisting within each other. Atop her head was an odd choice of hats, but there, in all its Sherlock Holmes glory, sat a brown plaid deerstalker. It looked out of place, but, then again, so did she. I felt like I was eavesdropping on her

CHAPTER 22 ... THE WILD RIDE

innermost thoughts, but I couldn't shake the feeling that I had come in contact with her in my past. Her mannerisms were familiar, in a strange, indescribable way.

"Excuse me, ma'am, but do I know you from somewhere?" I felt a profound pull toward her. She didn't appear to hear me, as she nervously tapped her Keds-clad foot, keeping her head down and avoiding eye contact. Cautiously taking a step closer to where she was sitting, I was mesmerized by the intrigue she was projecting. Just then, I was jarred out of my trance when I heard the PA system announcing my flight was boarding at gate 3B. The spell was broken as I picked up my bags and headed toward my destination, still wondering if my mind was playing tricks on me.

She stayed on my mind as I boarded the plane, storing my duffel bag in the overhead compartment and squeezing myself into the narrow seat by the window. I was a goliath of a man, and this seat was anything but comfortable for me. But I knew complaining would get me nowhere quick, so I pulled out my Walkman and settled in for the two-and-a-half-hour flight, all while saying a silent prayer I would get there in one piece.

CHAPTER 23

THE NEAR MISS
JANE

Oh, my Lord! I almost got caught! What was I thinking when I followed Lucas to the airport? Would it be worth it to finally have my secret out in the open? I wanted to believe Peter had mellowed or had turned over a new leaf once Lucas had moved out of the house, but I knew better. If anything, the more time that passed, the more belligerent he became, picking at the smallest of things and making my life hell on earth. But the fact remains that I'm scared shitless of him, so I stay and live the life of a dutiful wife and mother, while my heart pines for Mr. Stanford.

After all these years, one would think I wouldn't let him invade my innermost thoughts, but I welcome it. It's an escape for me that I don't have in real life. I know in my head that it's not healthy, but I like to play the "What if?" game. Although I have a ton of "what ifs," the one that tugs at my heart strings is the "What if I could tell

CHAPTER 23 ... THE NEAR MISS

Lucas the truth?" Beg for his forgiveness and welcome him into my arms and heart. What a glorious day that would be.

This morning started out innocently enough. Today, like any other day, at the crack of dawn, my favorite time of the day because I have solitude and can let my mind wander, I opened the door to retrieve the newspaper. It was always like an Easter egg hunt, never knowing where I would find it tossed with abandon. I often wondered if the neighborhood carrier was quite possibly reckless and a bad aim, or maybe he was choosing to play a little game with me to add a touch of fun to my otherwise mundane, vanilla life. I made myself laugh at that one. Mundane, vanilla life? If outsiders only knew what my past indiscretions had caused. I guess there's truth to the saying, *You never know what goes on behind closed doors.*

But this morning, it wasn't the paper that had my attention, but instead a note addressed to me in Lucas' hand, peeking out from underneath the doormat. A small squeak escaped my lips, giving me hope that he had forgiven me and wasn't sure how to tell me face to face. Quickly looking around to make sure I was alone, I wrapped my tattered yellow robe tighter around myself, and tore the envelope open like it contained a check for a million bucks.

Inside, it read...

Mom,

Not that I think you'll care one way or another, but I want you to know that I have decided to join the Army. There's nothing left for me here in Piedmont, and I need to focus on getting my life back on track. I leave for basic training tomorrow morning by airplane to Fort Jackson in Columbia, South Carolina. Not that you will, but don't spend a second worrying about me. I'll be fine.

Luke

I hadn't realized my hands were shaking until I reached up to brush a tear off my cheek. I was crushed that he thought I wouldn't care, but, then, why would he think otherwise? Peter had made sure I stayed true to the contract. That damn contract. I wish I could strike a match to that wretched piece of paper and watch it burn to ashes.

Regaining my composure, I tiptoed into the house, silently shutting the front door, not wanting to wake Peter or the boys, and made my way up to the attic one stair at a time, avoiding the loose ones Peter had promised to fix years ago.

Making sure I was painstakingly quiet, I began searching through the stacked boxes that sat collecting years of dust under the exposed beams. Peter had been a bit of a thespian in college, performing in numerous plays, not wanting to throw anything away, so I was certain there was a forgotten box containing odds and ends. I needed to find an outfit that I could go incognito in and make it snappy if I wanted to get to the airport before Lucas departed. The thought of never seeing him again tore through my heart and gave me the incentive to dig through box after box, until I stumbled upon the perfect outfit to stay hidden, so I could stalk him from afar.

Throwing on a pair of jeans and a tee, I tied my Keds and quietly walked out the front door, with my disguise tucked securely under my arm. As luck would have it, the airport was close to our house and small enough that I wouldn't have a hard time locating his departure terminal. My heart was racing a million beats per minute as I drove furiously, knowing I would never forgive myself if I missed seeing him, which could potentially be for the last time. Not if I had anything to do with it.

A half hour later, I screeched to a stop, grabbed a parking space, and set out in a full sprint, donning my disguise as I made my way

CHAPTER 23 ... THE NEAR MISS

closer. The airport was bustling with unwanted activity as I dodged crowds of people giving me perplexed stares. I had to admit I looked a bit odd in Peter's old, dingy khaki trench coat, a filthy pair of gloves, and the first hat I could find. If I remember correctly, it was called a "deerstalker" hat, and it was from a Sherlock Holmes play Peter had performed in. It completed the odd disguise to perfection, jauntily perched on my head, with my hair neatly tucked underneath it.

Feeling like a bag lady who had just scrounged through the dumpster behind a Goodwill store, I kept my head down, not wanting to draw more attention than I was already getting. I located Columbia, South Carolina, on the departure board and made my way toward the waiting area closest to the tarmac, trying to locate the plane. If the information was correct, I didn't have much time; the plane should be boarding within fifteen minutes or so. It was risky, but I raised my eyes, scanning the area, looking for my handsome son. The place was swarming with people joyous in anticipation for their next adventure.

Starting to get a tad panicked, I tried to settle my nerves as sweat dripped down my back. I thought I had missed my golden opportunity to see him one last time when I spotted him sitting alone, with his head bent down, absentmindedly twirling his wedding ring around and around on his finger. A small gasp escaped my lips, once again drawing unsolicited attention. I quickly covered it with a cough and made my way adjacent to where my Lucas was sitting. He looked deep in thought and lost in his own world, but the sight of him brought a much-needed smile across my lips. Oh, how I wanted to rush up to him and give him a hug, tell him I was sorry and, most importantly, that I loved him with all my whole heart, but instead I sat admiring him and how he had grown into his own. He was a spitting image of his real father, which dredged up memories of a lifetime ago.

I had a fleeting, ludicrous thought that I'd called his name—he looked up like he had heard something. Either that or he felt my presence. I don't think I said his name out loud, but I couldn't be sure of anything anymore. I had lost touch with reality a long time ago. I abruptly looked down, busying myself by twisting my hands nervously in my lap. I felt eyes burrowing down on me, and then he spoke. "Excuse me, ma'am, but do I know you from somewhere?" he inquired with that same rasp in his voice that Mr. Stanford had. I froze and continued to fidget, pretending like I hadn't heard him, when they called his gate to begin boarding.

And, just like that, he collected his things, turned with one last glimpse my way, and ambled off toward the gate and out of my life. As I watched his tall silhouette getting smaller as he walked farther away, I whispered, "Be well, my son. Be safe, my son. Be happy, my son. I love you!" They were words he would never hear but ones I needed to say.

CHAPTER 24

THE TEST

My first flight was anything but enjoyable. I had a charley horse in my left calf and a cramp that felt like a bucketful of biting crabs in my ass cheek, not to mention the jitters that couldn't be contained. I didn't dare have an alcoholic drink, as I knew I would need my wits about me, so I relied on my Walkman with Claire's and my playlist to soothe my restless soul. This attempt failed miserably and, in fact, had worked the exact opposite. It had left me sad and melancholy, missing her touch. Just as I had one foot firmly planted in the rabbit hole, getting ready to tumble in, an overhead announcement sounded over the PA system. We were starting our descent and would be touching down shortly, leaving me no time to contemplate my pitiful life.

Luckily, the landing was smooth and uneventful, giving me hope that the day had taken a turn for the better. Collecting my things, I hobbled off the plane and hailed a cab to begin my new life.

The landscape looked different from what I was used to, and there was a heaviness to the air that caused me to break out in a sweat instantly. I had read that the south was humid, but not having ever experienced it on my own, I was unaware of how uncomfortable it would be, as the mugginess made it difficult to breathe.

The taxi came to a screeching halt, sending a spray of water— from the last afternoon thunderstorm that plagued the region that had accumulated in the gutter—into my face. It was not how I wanted to show up on the base, but I pulled a handkerchief from my pocket and wiped my face dry, determined to keep a positive attitude. The driver was of middle-eastern descent with a black pencil-thin mustache, full long beard, and large brown eyes hidden under a pair of black bushy eyebrows that matched his beard. He was wearing a blue turban that coordinated with his Los Angeles Dodgers T-shirt and wore a smile that exuded warmth and friendliness.

When he spoke, his accent was strong but pleasant. "Welcome to South Carolina, sir. What brings you here?" I was in no mood to talk, partially because I was a nervous wreck but also because small talk was not something I was proficient at. I answered politely, put my headphones on, and gazed out the side window, watching the greenery pass, hoping he'd get the hint. He didn't. He wouldn't shut the hell up, so I anxiously nodded in agreement to whatever he said, fighting off the urge to vomit all over the back seat. Between sweating bullets, being nervous about my next adventure, and not being able to get the taxi driver to put a lid on it, I was starting to lose my shit and have a panic attack. I hadn't had one in ages, but I knew the feeling all too well.

The twenty miles it took to get from the airport in Columbia to Fort Jackson seemed like an eternity. But, as he pulled up to the

CHAPTER 24 ... THE TEST

entrance gate, I had miraculously managed to calm myself enough that I no longer felt like I was having a heart attack or about to hurl. I bade him farewell, wishing him a good day, and took a second to get my bearings and formulate my next step.

The first thing I noticed welcoming me on base was the biggest American flag I had ever seen, blowing slightly in the stagnant breeze. I felt a wave of patriotism run through my veins, causing a warm sensation. Or was that the humidity? Either way, I felt proud—proud to be an American, as I stood up a little taller, wearing the badge of honor in my heart. Everywhere the eye could see was a sea of camouflage—BDUs (battle dress uniforms)—and that's when it finally hit me that I was part of this life now. No looking back—only marching forward into the unknown.

Checking in felt surreal. There was a sign that proudly claimed Fort Jackson to be the U.S. Army's main production center for Basic Combat Training, training roughly 50 percent of all soldiers. I took comfort in knowing I would be in good company. The recruiter, Sgt. Hagins, had told me that basic training would be a ten-week program of blood, sweat, and tears—and most definitely not for the faint of heart. I felt up to the challenge and hoped that I wouldn't embarrass myself. I needed this in the worst way for my self-esteem as well as my mental health. It was time to focus on making myself into the best soldier I could be.

Looking around, my mind got lost taking in my surroundings until I heard an "Ahem, may I help you?" uttered by a man behind a rich, dark walnut barrier separating me from the spacious room, filled with numerous desks with papers stacked neatly in piles. A credenza of the same color set nestled up against the wall, displaying a number of trophies in various sizes and shapes. A man about my age, wearing some Army fatigues with his name, Sgt. Whittaker, stitched onto a name tag, stood, impatiently tapping his fingers waiting for my response. He was clean shaven, tall, and lanky. He looked the picture of health, without an ounce of fat anywhere in sight. He smiled at me, easing my nerves.

"I'm so sorry I kept you waiting. I'm in awe of my surroundings and got caught up in the moment," I managed to say, trying to give him my undivided attention. "I'm Lucas Travers, reporting for basic training." I looked on while he thumbed through some paperwork, my heart rate escalating by the second. At first glance, it looked like I was going to be a part of a huge "class." I took solace in that and hoped that I would make some much-needed friends. Even though I'd had friends in the past, I was what anyone would consider a "loner" right now, but not by choice. Claire had been my best friend, and, when we were together, I didn't feel the need to hang out with the guys. But I was finding it increasingly lonely and needed the camaraderie a couple of buddies would offer.

"Here we are. I see you here. Welcome to Fort Jackson, where your life is about to change. For the better, of course," he added with a chuckle that was reflected in his eyes. He reached out to shake my hand. "This is what is known as week zero, also known as reception or basic-training reception battalion. All this really means is paperwork, immunizations, a physical exam, haircut, getting your uniform, and having your first physical training test, all while getting you acclimated to your surroundings. It generally takes three to seven days but can take up to ten, depending on when the next basic-training schedule begins. Enjoy this busy time, because, once your training actually starts, you'll be too exhausted to see straight. I'm sure your recruiter informed you about the

CHAPTER 24 ... THE TEST

ten-week program, right?" he questioned while gathering stacks of informational pamphlets.

Was it too late to run? I thought, questioning my sanity for thinking this was the answer.

"Yes, sir. I've been forewarned that my life is going to be anything but a walk in the park, but if I'm being brutally honest, I'm a little nervous," I admitted, reluctantly, while picking at a hangnail on my left thumb. He let out a guffaw and smiled from ear to ear. "First of all, you don't have to call me 'sir,' and secondly, if I had a dollar for everytime someone admitted that, I'd be a millionaire. Trust me when I tell you, you're going to be just fine. I will, however, offer you a bit of unsolicited advice, for what it's worth. Soak it all in, and show up with enthusiasm and a willingness to be the best you can be. Before you know it, you'll be sitting at graduation, a full-fledged soldier." I thanked him profusely, letting him know I would return shortly to get further instruction, but, for the time being, I took a deep breath as I made my way to check out the mess hall. I was famished.

There was an indescribable electricity to the air that I couldn't put my finger on. The place was abuzz with activity as I eagerly took it all in, suddenly eager to get this show on the road. To say I was anxious would have been an understatement of major proportions, but I figured that was mostly due to the unknown. As I made my way past barracks lined up like soldiers, one after the other, I noticed a flurry of activity off to my right. Groups of would-be soldiers marching in unison in tightly formed lines, toting heavy packs on their backs. Other recruits, sweating from head to toe, were running through obstacle courses and rappelling what looked to be at least a forty-foot tower. I was unsure how to respond, so I proudly saluted everyone I made eye contact with, feeling pride swell within me.

The next week was a blur. Between orientation and all the other tedious tasks, I found myself feeling a tad homesick. Homesick for *what*, I wasn't sure, since I had no one left in Piedmont that cared a damn about me, or I them. Except for the pups, of course. I missed their boundless energy and undying, non-judgmental love. I dug deep, trying to put my finger on this foreign feeling. I felt a hollowness, leaving me confused. I shirked it off as not understanding what should have been. No amount of therapy would ever be enough to change the fact of what was and had been leading to the confusion and emptiness I still felt.

I was assigned a bunk in a barracks, which I shared with forty other recruits. The camaraderie didn't come as easy as I thought it would. Chitchat was frowned upon, and lights were out at nine p.m. every night, leaving me little time to get to know anyone. I hadn't gone to bed that early since I was a little kid, but I welcomed it every night, because I was exhausted from the day's activities. One thing I found out very quickly was that the Army was big on schedules, most importantly sticking to them, down to the minute.

Each recruiter's basic training was an intense ten-week course that focused on transforming a civilian into a well-trained, disciplined, physically fit, and motivated soldier, with emphasis on the importance of teamwork. The ultimate goal was that, after graduation, each trainee would be well versed in the seven Army values of loyalty, duty, respect, selfless service, honor, integrity, and personal courage.

My drill sergeant was not a warm-and-fuzzy kinda guy, but, then again, that didn't surprise me. His job was to whip a bunch of average joes into fit soldiers. That was a tall order, and it left him no time

CHAPTER 24 ... THE TEST

to mince words. Nor should he. Honestly, the first time I met Staff Sergeant Aitchison, he scared me a little. OK, more than a little. I had to grab my hands to keep them from shaking. He intimidated me with his steely gaze, crew cut, and no-nonsense attitude. It was abundantly clear he wasn't here to make friends.

In a subconscious attempt to sooth my frazzled nerves, I reached up to run my fingers through my hair but came back empty-handed. My new buzz cut felt strange to me. Within a second's time, I was quickly reprimanded, reinforcing the rule that hats must remain on at all times when outdoors. I was already missing the freedom to do as I wanted, when I wanted. Claire used to poke fun at me for lounging around in my boxers, but I was all about comfort.

I silently cussed my parents for teaching me the social skills of a gnat. I felt out of place and awkward. My legs were numb with trepidation. My stomach was weak and queasy. I didn't want to draw attention to myself, so I concentrated on my breathing, willing myself to focus on the present. This is my life now, not back in Piedmont, living my dream with Claire by my side. Damn it! I really missed her—and my unborn child I would never meet.

Everything seemed so close to the surface. I swallowed my pain and somehow managed not to let my mind go there—the deep, soul-crushing place of pain associated with losing a child. I thank my psyche for protecting me, because, no matter how hard I tried, I was sure this would be the catalyst that would send me back to drinking. I wasn't sure I would ever find my way out again.

Prior to enlisting, I did my due diligence and read multiple articles that hinted at the same thing: the military was an acquired taste. Not everyone was equipped mentally and/or physically to handle the rules, restrictions, and regulations. It required a great deal of discipline to toe the line, but if I were being brutally honest, I liked that about it. In a convoluted way, it offered me what I had been lacking my whole life and made me feel as if someone cared about me and what I was up to. The Army was cheering me on so that I would succeed in the real world. It was kind of a match made in heaven.

My days were long and short at the same time, if that makes sense. Long because we were woken up so early. It almost seemed illegal. But short, because they flew by in a flash. A typical day, except for Sunday, started promptly at 4:30 a.m. Not a second before or a second after. We had thirty minutes to prepare ourselves and report to formation at 5 a.m. Physical training (PT) was from 5 until 6:30 a.m. After that, it was breakfast time, before meeting up with our drill sergeant to train until lunch at noon. You guessed it: After lunch, there was more training.

Having been an avid runner for years bode well for me, for two reasons, actually. I had kept my requisite body fat down to less than 20 percent, and I aced the fitness standard of running a 1.5 mile in 18:30 minutes or less. If you failed at either of these things, you were placed in a fitness-training company for additional training. You then had two chances per week to pass. I never asked, but I had a strong suspicion that, if you continued to fail, you'd be thrown out on your ass. They weren't playing games.

I quickly learned that everything was done with precision and a purpose, clear down to the shower we took. We were allowed two minutes from start to finish, which hardly seemed like enough time, but I learned to adapt quickly. Complaining would be frowned upon, and the last thing I wanted was to put a target on my back and draw negative attention to myself.

CHAPTER 24 ... THE TEST

We had Sundays off to do whatever we wanted. While the majority of the guys spent the day writing letters to their families or calling them, I tried to busy myself with activities that kept my mind occupied. Most of the time, this involved running, exploring my new surroundings, and reading. I loved to learn—always had—and, more times than not, found myself perusing the shelves at the library, lined with knowledge and escapism from reality. Downtime and I were archenemies. The more downtime I had, the worse I felt, and more times than not jumped down a massive rabbit hole, wondering what I could have done to change the miserable outcome of my present-day life.

The ten grueling weeks of BT were divided into categories—the red, white, and blue phases. No explanation was given or needed as to why those colors were chosen. Phase one, the red phase, encompassed weeks one through three and was also called the adaptation phase. The fundamentals, traditions, and ethics were taught for what it meant to be a soldier. We were taught the Warrior Ethos and the Soldier's Creed, and we were expected to be able to recite them on a moment's notice. Briefings were held on basic first aid, as well as sexual harassment, and sexual-assault-awareness and -prevention programs. It was a good thing I loved to learn, because the amount of information they threw at us on a normal day was pretty intense. As much as I enjoyed that part and excelled at it, I loved the physical training even more, testing my strength and stamina to its limits. At the end of the three weeks, we were awarded an Army Unit Patch that was worn on the left shoulder of our uniform. I swelled with pride.

Weeks four and five were phase two, known as the white phase. Assuming all the basics were in place, it was now time to dig deeper and focus on self-discipline, teamwork combat skills, night training, hand-to-hand combat and weapons training, basic rifle marksmanship, and more physical training. By now I could officially say I was getting the hang of things and starting to meet a couple of guys I could shoot the shit with during our downtime. I still didn't feel comfortable sharing my backstory and wasn't sure I ever would, but it was nice to have others to talk to who shared my passion for sports and exercise.

One thing I wasn't getting the hang of was the weather. The humidity was brutal, causing me to instantly sweat a monsoon the moment I walked outside. It was uncomfortable and drenched me from head to toe, sweating in places I didn't know one could sweat. You could pretty much count on a thunderstorm rolling through every afternoon, which I learned to welcome, because after the brief seconds the grey clouds pissed bucketsful of rain, it cooled slightly before it turned hotter than the devil himself. It also nourished nature, turning everything a vibrant green.

My best buddy and barracks mate was Aiden Fitzgerald. Of Irish descent, he had a shock of red hair and enough freckles you could play connect the dots on his lily-white face. He was pencil thin, tall, with eyes the color of a four-leaf clover, but what you noticed first was his infectious smile that went from ear to ear, divulging a gap between his two front teeth. When he spoke, it wasn't a surprise that a whistle came out mixed with his words. We often spent our Sundays hanging out, trying our damndest to stay out of trouble. I jokingly referred to him as "my lucky charm," because, wherever he went, good things were sure to follow, lending credence to the old adage *"the luck of the Irish."*

He was born and bred in the south, calling Alabama his home, where he was the oldest of seven kids and son to loving high-school

CHAPTER 24 ... THE TEST

sweethearts. On paper, we had nothing in common, but it worked between us. We soon became inseparable, finishing each other's sentences and laughing at each other's quick wit. It felt good to let loose after our intense training sessions.

Before I could turn around, I was entering the third and final six through nine weeks, known as the blue phase or Warrior Phase. These weeks were meant to serve as a final transformation from a civilian into a soldier. The skills I had been taught thus far were honed and tested, along with some new tasks, including advanced weapons such as machine guns and how to throw a live grenade. This was the nitty-gritty real-life war stuff, and I couldn't get enough. The first one to show up to training every day and the last one to leave, I lapped it up. I had to rein in my thoughts time and again, because I found myself daydreaming what it would be like to throw a live grenade into my dad's room, blowing him to smithereens. I wasn't proud of my thoughts. I hated the fact that he had made my life so miserable that I envisioned bestowing harm upon him. That wasn't who I was. It was not one of my finest moments, and, unfortunately, it happened more often than I would have liked.

To close out this phase, we were put to a test on a multiple-day navigation course, meant to prove our survival, fitness, and soldier skills. The tasks were grueling, all 212 of them, but, once you passed, you were rewarded with an Army Black Beret and deemed a full-fledged 100 percent qualified soldier. I was beyond proud of myself to say the least, and beaming with pride.

The final phase, week ten, was graduation week, also known as recovery week. Quite frankly, it had been the fastest nine weeks of my life. Not only had it been intense physically, but it had been taxing on my mind and taken its toll on my mental state. Bittersweet, I was conflicted about how to feel. My mind sped from ecstatic that all my blood, sweat, and tears had paid off, to sad. It was unequivocally apparent to me now that I had nowhere to go. Nothing to look forward to. No place to call home.

With my head bent, resting in my hands, perched on my knees, I sat on my bunk, pondering my next step, I felt a presence near me—someone watching but not speaking. I wasn't in the mood to talk to anyone, because I wasn't sure how to put into words the despair I was feeling without spilling my guts about my past. I hadn't shared any of it, not even with Aiden, and I had no plans to modify that. I was hoping that, if I ignored them, they would go away. But, after a couple of minutes, I heard my cot squeak as someone sat down beside me.

Draping his arm around my shoulders and giving me a hearty pat on the back, Aiden let out a deep sigh and spoke. "Luke, I've known for a while that you've been keeping secrets about your family and your past, and I want you to know I'm here if you need me, but, brother, I love you all the same if you don't. Nothing can change the amount of love and respect I feel for you." I didn't know how to respond. The last person who had accepted me for me was Claire. Bar none, no questions asked. It made me a little misty. I cleared my throat as I looked him square in the eye, thanking him with unspoken words.

Wrapping up loose ends and getting paperwork sorted gobbled up my time leading up to graduation. It was scheduled to take place outside at nine in the morning; the weather forecast threatened thunderstorms. No surprise there. Talk about raining on my parade. I chuckled at the irony of it. Pacing back and forth, worried that someone would notice the lack of family—or *any* support—in

CHAPTER 24 ... THE TEST

attendance, for that matter. We were allowed to invite whomever we chose, no tickets necessary. I had wrestled with the idea of inviting Alex and Sloan, but, in the long run, I opted against it for no good reason, except I didn't want to explain how I knew them. Claire needed to stay in my other life, buried in my heart and memories that ran in a perpetual reel over and over.

The ceremony itself was semi-quick and to the point, lasting only about forty-five minutes. Streamers in red, white, and blue were strung from light poles and a live band was set up in the corner of the stadium, playing patriotic tunes. As we all filed in, dressed in freshly starched, perfectly pleated uniforms, I took a look around at my fellow recruits, taking our seats on the uncomfortable steel chairs. I saw my friends trying their damndest to look stoic and reserved but failing miserably. The look of pride swelled within us all, and we were beaming from ear to ear. We had done it—we'd accomplished ten weeks of brutal physical tests and learned to be soldiers, ready for war at a moment's notice.

Feeling a tad nervous, I let my mind wander, settling on the bleachers, where the spectators sat sweltering, waving makeshift fans and hats crafted from the programs. It was a packed house. Out of the corner of my eye, I saw a woman standing at the top of the stairs, alone, wearing a monstrous sun hat covered in sunflowers. Her eyes were covered in what appeared to be designer shades, so it was difficult to assess where she was gazing. Her hand was resting upon her heart. I continued to pan the crowd, but an indescribable force willed me back to her. As I locked eyes with her, she turned and ran down the stairs, tripping as she reached the bottom. I heard a squeal, and then she vanished. Right before my eyes, she was there and then gone. I felt an eerie shiver, despite the temperature in the nineties. She reminded me of my mom. Was it the sunflowers? They were her favorite, after all.

Shaking the incident out of my mind, I heard my name being called. As I walked across the platform, stopping to shake Staff Sergeant Aitchison's hand, I secretly wished I had someone to share this momentous occasion with. Could that have been my mom? Before I could give it any more thought, a flyover of fighter jets pierced the sky, and whoops of congratulations filtered through the air. As a collective group, we all shared one big group hug before proudly gazing in awe at our Army Service Ribbon (ASR) we had proudly earned.

CHAPTER 25

THE PLAN
JANE

Nervously sitting in the back of my taxi, I gently massaged my ankle, wincing in pain. I silently prayed I hadn't broken it, leaving me the impossible task of having to explain my latest blunder to Peter. He was no dummy, with a deceitful side a mile longer than my own. I was an amateur in comparison. Avoiding eye contact with the driver, I shrunk within myself, reliving my last twenty-four hours.

Taking pride in myself for becoming a mediocre sleuth, it was blatantly clear I had a lot left to learn. My recent fiasco had divulged a couple of rookie mistakes. Now I was backpedaling, trying to cover my ass. Twirling my thin gold charm bracelet around my wrist, I cursed myself for being careless. And clumsy. Had Lucas noticed me in the crowd? I specifically wore that crazy oversized sun hat to shield my identity. Maybe it was the sunflowers? Did he even know they were my favorite?

Whatever the reason, it was inconsequential now. The damage had been done, or so I thought. Reliving the moment step by step in my mind's eye, I might be over-exaggerating. Or am I? So many questions left unanswered. The one and only thing I was certain of right now was how unbelievably proud I was of Lucas. He did it, despite a lifetime of obstacles that were thrown at him day in and day out. Mr. Stanford would be proud, too.

Often, I wondered what Mr. Stanford would have done differently if I had only grown a pair and confessed my pregnancy to him. Certainly, my life would be different, but would I have opened a can of worms that could have never been closed? Catching myself in my daydream, I noticed we were stopped in front of the airport, the driver staring at me over the crusty backseat.

"Hey, lady—are you all right? Should I get help?" *Oh, trust me—I need help all right*, I wanted to say but instead politely declined. Collecting my one small bag, I left him a generous tip and thanked him profusely. The last thing I needed was unwanted attention.

After my near miss at the airport when Lucas was leaving for boot camp, I vowed to be more careful. Peter catching wind of my clandestine "meet-ups" with Lucas would spell disaster—for us both. I was not concerned about myself, because, truthfully, more times than not, I would choose death over living with the tyrant Peter had become. Or had he always been like that and I had turned a blind eye? Either way, I needed to stay alive and keep my mouth shut to protect Lucas. He had finally broken free and had his whole life waiting with open arms.

CHAPTER 25 ... THE PLAN

Ten weeks have passed since my ill-fated encounter at the airport, where I said my heart-crushing, silent goodbye to Lucas. I left that day defeated and despondent thinking that could potentially be my last goodbye. I remember driving home in a haze, angry with myself on how I had let things get this far. Why should I have to worry about ever seeing my own flesh and blood again? If it weren't for Peter, my Lucas' life would be so different. But you know what they say about *hindsight and all that BS*.

As I rounded the corner, the hustle and bustle of the day had just begun. Feeling the sadness of watching my firstborn walk away, I barely noticed my neighbors with their briefcases firmly grasped in hand, trudging to their cars to begin another day. There were moms yelling at the top of their lungs for the kids to hurry up or they would be late for school. The same old grind, day in and day out. But not for me.

Nope.

Not anymore.

I had a plan.

Oh, how I would love to snuff Peter right out in his sleep. Put a pillow over his ugly little face and feel him take his last pathetic breath, but I wasn't a murderer. Even though I despised his very existence, I would continue being the mother and wife for appearances only. In a small way, it was getting easier. Peter was gone a lot. Was he having an affair? That was doubtful, with his foul personality and impish physique. I never asked—quite frankly because I didn't care. Not two shits. I loved that he was gone a lot. The twins, too. Their school activities kept them occupied, which gave me plenty of time to put my plan into motion.

My plan was simple. It wasn't even much of a plan, really. Feeling my heart rip from my chest, making me think that I may never see Lucas again lit a fire under my ass to rectify that situation. Spending every spare moment at the library scouring and researching Army life and reading up on Fort Jackson made me feel like I was part of Lucas' life. I called the base with the pretense of checking things out for my high-school son. I got to know his schedule inside and out, clear down to the date that was set for graduation. I was back to my old stalking ways but on paper this time.

Time passed slowly leading up to graduation. I had been sneaking money from the weekly grocery shopping trips, so I had plenty for an airline ticket and expenses once I arrived in Columbia. The thought of seeing my son graduate was all I could think about. I was obsessed. Happy tears sprang up in my eyes, and I wore a goofy smile whenever I let my mind wander to the actual day.

But there was one little problem. What would I tell Peter? My parents had long passed, and I was an only child, so I couldn't use visiting relatives as an excuse to be gone overnight. Friends were nonexistent in my life. Peter had made sure of that. I weighed many scenarios over in my mind, and I finally settled on one that I hoped and prayed was fail-safe.

It wasn't much of a stretch, but I had decided I would pick a fight. Not just any fight but one that would send Peter into a tailspin. Get him so pissed he would lash out, but I would be prepared this time. He was, after all, a creature of habit, like we all are to a certain degree. I knew that, when he was spitting fire and seeing red, he would take off, speeding away, sending debris flying in his wake. Although I was almost 100 percent certain he would be gone for a couple of days, since that was his *modus operandi*, but I needed

CHAPTER 25 ... THE PLAN

to be one million percent certain he didn't come home and find me gone. I needed to take one for the team. Let him hit me. It was a bit extreme, but it's not like it was completely out of the norm. When he had hit me in the past, I retreated to my room and gave him a wide berth. He would expect nothing out of the ordinary if he were to venture home unexpectedly.

I was almost giddy with excitement as I planned for my "escape." I went shopping—and not at the usual department stores, but to the high-end shops that carry all the designer labels. I had a total *Pretty Woman* afternoon. I loved that movie, and, honestly, nothing was too good for my Lucas. I spent a day of pampering at the local salon, getting the works. It was a slice of heaven that I was going to incorporate into my everyday life after this was all said and done. That is, if I didn't get caught. If the unthinkable were to come true, I might not be let out of the house to see the light of day ever again. I could kiss goodbye ever seeing Lucas again—that's for sure, because I would be a prisoner in my own home.

Tickets bought, check.

Hotel room booked, check.

Suitcase packed, check.

Directions printed, check.

Nerves under control, nope.

Feeling on top of the world, double-check.

D-day was upon me, and I was starting to panic. Could I actually pull this off? I wasn't keen on fighting, and I most certainly wasn't keen on having pain inflicted upon my body. I hope I wasn't delusional, but if I knew the punch was coming, I felt certain I could semi-deflect it, and it would cause only moderate damage.

The graduation was set to begin at 9:00 a.m. tomorrow, so I booked the last flight out of Piedmont, scheduled to land in Columbia just before midnight. A good night's sleep and I could arrive at the graduation in plenty of time, hopefully rested and sans a black eye. I had taken that into consideration, though, and purchased not only the ultra-sized sun hat but also a designer pair of shades to cover imperfections. It felt good to splurge a little.

Dousing myself in Peter's favorite perfume, I seductively waited in my finest black lacy negligee for him to return from work. Notes of patchouli and musk permeated the air, causing me to feel nauseous. It had been a while since we had been intimate, so I knew he would take the bait. Men were predictable that way. The mere thought of sleeping with Peter was enough to gag me, but, for my plan to work, I would have to pull off an Oscar-winning performance.

The twins were at baseball practice and wouldn't be home for hours, giving me ample time to work my magic. Even though slightly rusty, I was confident I still had it. Enough to get Peter right where I wanted him, begging for more. I heard his car pull into the driveway. It was go time.

Draping my bare leg over the arm of the chair, dangling my freshly painted red toenails over the side, I swallowed my pride. Gulping down the bile that was rising in my throat, I seductively winked at him as he walked through the door.

"Hey, handsome—do you want to have a roll in the hay before dinner? The boys won't be home for hours, and I've been missing our together time."

He stopped in his tracks, raising an eyebrow as a wicked, lecherous grin emerged. I wanted to jump for joy. It was working! Throwing his briefcase down, he hit the entryway table, sending the vase of sunflowers crashing to the ground.

CHAPTER 25 ... THE PLAN

Jumping up from my chair, I approached him, carefully avoiding the broken glass littering the floor. He was falling into my trap easier than I could have imagined, as he started loosening his tie while grabbing ahold of my waist. Wasting no time, he pulled me up the stairs, throwing clothes over the railing as we made our way to our bedroom.

"Hey, tiger—slow down and enjoy the moment, won't you?" I barely squeaked out as he clumsily threw me on the bed. I was caught off guard and gasped when he was on me faster than a fly on dog poop. One hedonistic grunt, and then it was over. Very anticlimactic if I had cared, but, as it was, I was relieved.

"What the hell was that? Do you not have enough stamina to last longer than a teenage virgin?" I was egging him on, on purpose. I knew his ego was bigger than the universe and that he would get pissed. The more pissed off, the better the plan would work. "Maybe you need to see a doctor about your ED problem, huh? What do you think? I didn't realize you had such a problem, but, then again, I should have guessed, since you have Little-Man Syndrome." I kept hurling the insults at him left and right. He was walking toward the bathroom door, away from me, when he stopped dead in his tracks. I watched as his neck muscles tightened and he gripped his hands into fists.

"Shut the fuck up, Jane. If you were the least bit attractive, instead of looking like a hag all the time, I could last all night. I just wanted to get it over with!"

Jumping off the bed, I pushed him from behind as I hysterically laughed. "Yeah, right—you sorry excuse for a man. And I use the term 'man' loosely."

Everything happened in slow motion. It was as if time stood still as he whipped around, his face contorted, with spittle flying out of his mouth. Before I knew it, he had his fist in the air ready to connect with my nose. I deflected his fist enough to lessen the blow, but only slightly. Blood spurted out of my nose, and I yelled in pain. He bent over me and spit in my eye before grabbing a fresh set of clothes. I looked up to see him storming through the door before he slammed it, causing the windows to rattle in their panes. I sat for a second, dumbfounded but happy.

Slowly getting up to assess the damage to my face, I first went down to the end of the hall to peer out the window that looked over the front yard. I got there just in time to see him peeling out of the driveway. He was so calculable.

Running downstairs, I grabbed ice out of the freezer and immediately put it against my nose, applying pressure to stop the bleeding. I was laughing like a lunatic but, I couldn't help it. I was so damn proud of myself. Surveying the damage in the downstairs mirror, I wasn't distraught. I had seen worse. I might have a black eye, but I was reasonably sure it wasn't broken, and the pain was already dissipating. No matter how much pain I would feel later, after the adrenaline wore off, it would be worth it.

Allowing myself fifteen minutes to gain my composure, I couldn't have asked for a better outcome. Peter was gone, and I was a free woman—free to do as I wanted. Jumping in the shower, washing off the putrid perfume, I kicked into gear so I could be ready for the taxi when it arrived at seven. I scribbled a note to the boys that their dinner was in the fridge and not to worry—I would be back in the morning. I took off with a newfound freedom that had my head in the clouds.

The rest of the night went off without a hitch, and I knew Lady Luck was shining down on me as my plane taxied into the gate at

CHAPTER 25 ... THE PLAN

Columbia, South Carolina, right on time. After a short ride to my hotel, I checked in and allowed myself my first breath of relief, as I threw myself on the pristine white down comforter that covered my king-size bed. All had gone as planned for this mother on a mission. I would never be able to explain my reasons for being a horrible mother to Lucas, but that wasn't going to stop me from loving him from afar and supporting him whenever I could.

Why are alarm clocks so annoying? I was in a deep sleep, dreaming of Mr. Stanford, when a shrill, relentless sound invaded my space. Rolling over, I rubbed my eyes only to be rudely reminded of the punch that had connected with my nose last night. Was that just yesterday? It seemed like a lifetime ago. I was giddy with excitement as I poured myself a cup of coffee and switched on the morning news, not believing my good fortune of actually being here. As I looked around, I hugged myself tight, reveling in my surroundings and not believing I had pulled it off. It was going to be a great day.

Dancing into the bathroom, I jumped in the shower singing "U Can't Touch This," while luxuriously soaping my body and steaming up the mirrors. Giving myself a pat on the back for having the foresight to splurge on the expensive foundation that promised to cover the worst of blemishes, I meticulously applied my makeup. Happy with the outcome, my bruised face was hardly noticeable.

In one of the many articles I had read, Sunday church attire was the preferred dress code for the graduation. I had picked out a black silk sheath dress with a smart yellow gauzy wrap that matched the sunflowers on my hat. Throwing on a pair of black kitten heels and shoving my belongings into my new black Coach shoulder bag, I blew myself a kiss in the mirror, pleased with my reflection.

Sweat began to pour down my back the second I emerged from my air-conditioned taxi. I dabbed moisture off my upper lip, reminding myself this day wasn't about me. The Army base was huge. Looking around in awe, I loved the fact that I was getting to see where my baby had spent his last ten weeks.

Cautiously walking up the semi-steep stairs of the bleachers, I took my place in the top row. I was dead set on getting a bird's-eye view from this location, in hopes of making it easier to pick out Lucas from the group of recruits. Even though I had gotten here a half hour early, the stands were filling up quickly. Everyone was in good spirits, giving high fives and congratulations to each other while sharing stories of their loved ones. I felt out of place. And nervous, reminding myself I was just another face in a sea of others.

Tapping my leg up and down, I put my hand on my knee to calm my frazzled nerves. That was easier said than done, so I gave up my seat, electing to stand in the corner instead. Grabbing the sun hat as a last-minute purchase had been genius. Not only was it shielding me from the elements, but I was also incognito, although the sun hat made me stand out at the same time. Weird how that worked.

Looking around, I tried to retain a calm demeanor, so as not to draw attention to myself. A much-welcome chuckle escaped my lips at the thought of it. I was a good thousand miles away from home, despite the fact that nobody even knew I was here. My identity would remain under wraps—of that, I was certain—unless I would somehow come face to face with Lucas, which I wouldn't let happen.

At precisely 9:00 a.m. a band that was set up next to the stage started playing "God Bless America," as a group of soldiers marched in precision, taking place in some uncomfortable looking chairs on the field. I scanned the group for Lucas. It had always been easy

CHAPTER 25 ... THE PLAN

to spot him in a crowd because of his height, and today was no different. My heart was in jeopardy of exploding out of my chest as I was overcome with emotion. I dabbed at my eyes and placed my hand over my heart, swelling with pride.

Just then he looked up, panning the crowd. He looked so handsome in his uniform. I wanted to wave and yell at him, but I kept stoic. He looked away, and I breathed a sigh of relief that he hadn't seen me. But just as soon as he turned away, he turned his head around at whiplash speed, staring at me with a perplexed look on his face. There was no way he could know it was me. Or could he?

I panicked and ran down the stairs, tripping at the bottom and falling to the ground, twisting my ankle! I hadn't been thinking clearly and made more of a spectacle of myself than if I had stayed put. Totally embarrassed, I expected to see everyone laughing and pointing at me. Peter had really done a number on my self-esteem.

Pleased to see I was not the brunt of anyone's jokes, I brushed myself off and found a semi-hidden spot to finish watching the ceremony. It was perfection, all wrapped up in the most prideful moment. My Lucas had done it. He was now a soldier in the United States Army. I wanted nothing more than to hobble onto the field, throw my arms around him, and explain everything, but, instead, I bid him a silent farewell, hoping he would be safe.

Feeling sadness sweep over me, the whole morning had been bittersweet. I limped away, swallowing my pride, and I retreated back into the hollow shell of my former self. The confidence I had exuded earlier, when I had blown myself a kiss, was gone, buried deep in one of those dusty boxes in the attic.

CHAPTER 26

THE FRIEND

Saying goodbye to my home away from the home I never really had was ambivalent to me. The Army allowed us all to spend a day or so with our loved ones before reporting to our new station as full-fledged soldiers. Having nowhere to go had never hit so hard. I fumbled with my duffle bag, full of my belongings, as I wiped sweat from my brow; I was embarrassed that it had stained my shirt under my armpits. Although it was still technically morning, it was already a scorcher, giving me a good reason to move on.

Startling me out of my reverie, I heard Aiden yelling from afar as he sprinted toward me. "Hey, chap—I want you to meet my family. We're headed to a celebratory luncheon and would be honored if you would join our crazy, rambunctious lot. Will you?" He looked like a kid in a candy store, eyes huge and searching. I started to decline. I didn't want to be a turd in the punch bowl and ruin everyone's time. But before I could answer, I was surrounded by a

CHAPTER 26 ... THE FRIEND

slew of jumping, punching, laughing kids, all with the same color hair as Aiden's. I felt like I had been plunked down in the middle of a strawberry patch, ripe for picking. I couldn't help but get caught up in the ribbing they were giving one another, and I immediately felt like part of the clan, eagerly accepting.

Aiden's parents were everything my own parents, sadly, weren't. When they welcomed me with a hug and a peck on the cheek, it wasn't hard to see where the red hair in the family had come from. Conversation flowed freely. I couldn't remember having a better time, feeling welcome and loved. Not since Claire, anyway. But this was different. This was what a family should be. I could feel the love and admiration for one another. Aiden had definitely won the sperm lottery. And, for the first time in my life, I felt a tinge of jealousy.

Parting ways and saying my goodbyes with Aiden was rough. He had been my right hand for ten weeks, and I was going to miss his no-nonsense attitude. "Aiden, you're the brother I wish I had. Promise me you'll keep in touch," I said, feeling brotherly emotions come over me unexpectedly. Knowing full well no matter how much we cared for each other, we would lose contact. We had chosen different career paths, which resulted in different base assignments.

My Advanced Individual Training, AIT, was set to start ASAP. I would then begin my Military Occupational Specialty, MOS, and train as a carpentry and masonry specialist. A plethora of reasons had spoken to me when I was deciding on whether to enlist, and one at the top of the list was to see the world. That hardly meant Missouri, but here I was, boarding a bus to Fort Leonard Wood, Missouri, where I would start a nine-week training program before learning my craft. Boot camp had sounded daunting. *This* almost sounded like a walk in the park in comparison.

Immediately, I started second-guessing my decision to take the bus. I should have given myself a swift kick in the ass for listening in the first place. My internal monologue was taking my mind off the road. It would be the last time I ever listened to myself when I had lamebrain ideas.

See the country, I said.
It'll be fun, I said.
You'll save some money, I said.
Blah, blah, blah.

It wasn't fun, and the countryside was boring. Actually, if I was honest with myself, the scenery was rather pretty. Lush, green hillsides, meandering rivers, and sunshine. It was *me* that was in a foul mood. The realization that I was alone in the world had hit extra hard lately, leaving me with doubts about my future. I dug deep and tried to find something positive about this godforsaken bus ride from hell. It was reasonably empty, leaving me with my pick of seats. Not only was I able to stretch out, but I also didn't have to make small talk. A win-win. Nothing sounded more annoying than traveling with a jabbering imbecile for 855 miles, for almost 14 hours. However you chose to look at it, it was an ungodly number.

I sat in a window seat, mesmerized as the landscape flew by, ticking off one more mile.

"Hey soldier—do you mind if I take this seat?"

I ignored the voice, hoping they were talking to someone else. I felt a presence lurking over me.

"Ahem, excuse me—mister? May I sit here please?"

Aggravated, I slowly looked up to see a teenage girl with murky-brown, lake-water-colored eyes, curly, strawberry blonde,

CHAPTER 26 ... THE FRIEND

shoulder-length hair, and a complexion that looked like it had struggled with acne and lost the battle.

She excitedly waited for my answer, tapping her red Converse sneaker, as I took a look around the bus. It was more than three quarters empty, so, why for the love of God, did she choose me to sit by? I felt trapped. I didn't want to be rude. But then again, why not? I didn't owe her anything.

"Well if it's all the same to you, I'd rather be alone."

She looked crushed as her smile, displaying a mouthful of crooked teeth, turned to a frown, and a tear formed in the corner of her eye.

Oh, damn. If there's one thing I hated, it was seeing a girl cry. Especially at my expense.

And this, my friends, is how I met Paige Sherman. Feeling awful, I changed my mind as a look of defeat washed over her pale face.

"Well, on second thought, why not?" I said, with way more enthusiasm than I was feeling. She let out a high-pitched *"Yippee!"* as she reached over, planting a timid kiss on my cheek. I could feel a blush creep into my cheeks.

Not wasting any time, she settled into the seat on the aisle, pulled open her fuchsia knapsack, and drew out a deck of cards, a steady stream of questions spilling out of her mouth. I struggled to keep up, let alone have time to answer.

Come to find out she was from Columbia, on a road trip to Missouri to visit her grandma. Feeling a tad overwhelmed, she had just needed someone to talk to, and, as she put it, I looked *verklempt*, like I had lost my best friend. She wasn't far off and more than a little perceptive. Especially for her age. Or maybe her age was *why* she was perceptive. Life had not yet had a chance to kick her in the teeth and shatter her dreams.

We talked. We laughed. We slept. And we played more "War" than I ever thought possible. Turns out, we both had a competitive side, and she was keen on keeping score. She loved a good dad joke, and her laugh had the most infectious vibrato to it. She shared her high-school crushes, asking for my advice. I kept my past hidden. Even though the bus ride was a long one, there wasn't enough time in a *year* to tackle that subject.

As Paige took a catnap with her head nestled on my shoulder, I couldn't help but feel some external factors had come into play with us meeting. I'd been intrigued but skeptical about "guardian angels" in the past, but I felt certain this was precisely what had happened. Of all the buses and all the times for her to be placed in my path, this was, indeed, divine intervention. I had always had a strong belief that people come into your life for a reason—when you needed them the most. There was no other explanation. My guardian angel had been working overtime.

My mind drifted back to when I was twelve and Ivy had been my saving grace. She helped me through some of my darkest days, and, then, *Poof!* she was gone. The same with Theo. I still missed that guy and his parents. Claire had shown me what love was all about. She had taught me more about myself than I knew was even there and helped me see in which direction my career path should go. Then there was Aiden. I needed a friend in the worst way, and, somehow, my guardian angel placed him in my path.

Paige stirred as I looked down at her fondly. I felt like I had known this bright light for a lifetime. Last, but not least, I would be remiss if I didn't mention Marmalade. Out of everyone and everything that had been miraculously placed in my life, Marmalade had saved my life on more than one occasion.

CHAPTER 26 ... THE FRIEND

Fondly remembering them all, I couldn't help wondering what was in store for me next.

"Paige, you have been just what the doctor ordered to make this bus ride fly by. I wish you were my sister!"

With that, she blushed fifty different shades of red and took my hand in hers. "Luke, I feel the same. I knew there was something about you that I would connect with. I'll give you my address and you can write to me, OK? Please?" I accepted, not making any promises, but telling her I'd try. She was the friend I didn't know I needed to pass the time.

As we pulled into the bus station, weathered, exhausted, and famished, all I could think about was a hot shower, a hot meal, and stretching out on a soft, comfy bed to get uninterrupted sleep before reporting to my newest station. Making sure Paige was welcomed by her grandma, I gave her one last squeeze, thanking her for making my ride enjoyable. Then, I hailed a taxi.

Fort Leonard Wood was located in south-central Missouri in the heart of the Ozark Mountains and adjacent to the Mark Twain National Forest. As I looked through narrowed eyes out the back seat of the cab, I saw green scenery and rolling hills. I felt a tinge of excitement take hold. The base was small compared to Fort Jackson, with roughly five thousand active-duty soldiers. I was proud to be one of those soldiers, and my heart swelled as we drove through the front gates of my new home.

In pure military fashion, I was checked in with precision and shown to my barracks, where I had my own room. Being handed a pamphlet on what would be expected of me while living here, I threw myself onto the bed, eagerly opening it, taking a mental inventory of my surroundings. It housed the basics. A twin XL bed, which, for obvious reasons, I was thankful for, even though I still hung off the end, was positioned under a large window with stark-white metal mini-blinds.

It looked out into a cemented courtyard with terra-cotta pots housing an assortment of colorful perennials around some picnic tables. A row of barbeques were lined up next to steel drums acting as trash cans. There was not a piece of trash anywhere in sight. Rounding out my furnishings was a chest of drawers, a weathered-looking wooden desk and chair sitting flush against the east wall, while a nightstand with a sorry-looking lamp giving off muted light was nestled next to my bed.

It was sparse, at best, but I knew I could easily make it my own. We were encouraged to add our personal touches, and I already had ideas to breathe some life into it. I wasn't much of a party animal, and knowing I would spend the bulk of my off time here gave me extra incentive. Grabbing my backpack, I ran down the stairs to hail a cab. There was no time like the present to start my new life.

Fort Leonard Wood was flanked by two towns that ran adjacent to it, St. Robert and Waynesville. I knew nothing about either one, so I left it up to the taxi driver to choose for me. Next thing I knew, I saw a sign on the side of the road, welcoming me to St. Robert. It looked small but was picturesque, with colorful boutiques offering an assortment of wares. A mile or so down the road, the taxi hung a left and pulled into a large parking lot at a Walmart SuperCenter. I felt like a kid on Christmas morning—or at least what I *surmised* most kids would feel.

The cute little town I just witnessed had vanished. Even before I walked into the store, I immediately noticed trash littering the area. Candy-bar wrappers, cigarette butts, empty, smashed soda

CHAPTER 26 ... THE FRIEND

cans, and that horrendous, pungent stench. It smelled like urine that had been baking in the sun all week. I was not impressed, to say the least, but I was determined not to let anything dampen my spirits. For the next two hours, I combed every aisle at least twice just to make sure I hadn't forgotten anything. It had been a while since I had been shopping. Since Claire, actually. I missed our trips to the mall buying odds and ends for our home. I missed her. Desperately.

My cart was overflowing by the time I was done. No one was going to accuse me of forgetting anything! With my training due to start on Monday, it left me the weekend to get my humble abode spruced up. I went to work setting up my new TV, stereo system, and a cushy Army-green corduroy beanbag chair. I attached a patriotic red, white, and blue-colored tie-dye flimsy cotton-scarf thingy over my blinds as a makeshift drape. It reminded me of the hippie-dippie era. Even though it had been two decades ago, I had always felt a certain pull toward their free spirit, love-thy-neighbor persona. I thumbtacked a couple of posters onto my wall to add the finishing touches. Standing back and admiring my handiwork, I was more than pleased.

As I unpacked my bag, I pulled out a framed picture of Claire and me on our wedding day. She was breathtaking, with an angelic aura encompassing her. *"I'm so proud of you, Luke. I love you with my whole heart."* My heart fluttered as I looked around, knowing I was hearing things but wanting it to be real. I felt a warmness wash over me as the bed creaked slightly. And then I felt the gentlest kiss upon my lips. I grabbed for her as she evanesced and faded away. What had just happened? As I reached up to rub my eyes, I was surprised to find they were moist. Kissing the picture, I tucked it gently inside my bedside table. I would never be in the right frame of mind to share my memories of Claire with anyone, so it was best to keep my past a secret.

Training started, and I was soaking all the info up like a sponge. A lot of it I already knew, but you're never too old to learn. There was talk around the base and on all news channels that there was unrest in the Middle East—even a possibility of war. Knowing this was a distinct possibility sent chills down my spine. Not that I was a coward, but I lived more by the motto *Make Love, Not War*.

Tensions were running high. Relaxing in my room after a long day of classes, I flipped on the nightly news. Things were heating up, and it looked like the inevitable would soon become a reality. I had an urge to write to my mom. It was a foreign feeling. One that left me confused. The more time I spent away from home, the memories of her abuse faded a tad, as I tried to dig through the rubble of my so-called childhood and concentrate on the tiny glimmers of hope and love she seldom bestowed upon me. Yes, they were few and very far between, but I grasped onto those like they were my lifeline to normalcy.

She had always been a stickler for watching and reading the news, and, I figured she'd be worried. I hoped anyway, but honestly it was a crapshoot. I visualized her in her tattered yellow robe, the one that had cheery sunflowers embroidered on it, combing over the newspaper with bloodshot, weary eyes. I wrestled with what to say and ultimately decided to wait until there was a definitive answer. Let her stew a tad longer. And, just like that, I was back to letting the bad memories consume me. She needed to suffer just like she had made me suffer.

With all the gossip on base, it sounded like it would be sooner rather than later that I would have to make the tough call and decide

CHAPTER 26 ... THE FRIEND

if she deserved my letter. Quite frankly, she deserved to rot in hell, right along with my despicable father, who had done nothing but hurtful things to me my whole life. It was growing more difficult every day to even call him my dad. I always heard *Blood is thicker than water* and that you were supposed to love your parents, but didn't it go both ways? As far as I was concerned, neither one of them had earned my love and respect.

Geography had never been my strong suit, so when I heard talk about Iraq and Kuwait, it seemed like another whole universe. I spent hours at the base library, educating myself on foreign affairs. But, unfortunately, nothing could have prepared me for the shock and utter despair I felt on August 2, 1990. A war was being waged by coalition forces from forty-two nations, led by the United States, against Iraq, in response to Iraq's invasion and annexation of Kuwait. Saddam Hussein became a household name. The president of Iraq was a martyr who ruled with fear, intimidation, and violence. The U.S. claimed that the intent behind striking Iraq was to disarm that country of weapons of mass destruction, to end Saddam Hussein's alleged support for terrorism, and, supposedly, free Iraqi people.

I remember where I was at the exact moment the Gulf War had been declared. I was sitting in the mess hall; an announcement was made over the loudspeaker to congregate in the gymnasium. As we all pushed and shoved each other out of the way, nerves were at their highest. A lump had formed in my throat, making it nearly impossible to talk. So I kept my head down and found a spot on the wooden bench sandwiched between a couple of other soldiers who looked as if their world had just collapsed. It felt that way.

What we had trained and prepared for was upon us. Something I never thought would happen in my lifetime *was* happening. There was talk of deployments. I said a silent prayer that, by the grace of God, I would be spared and be able to remain stateside. Feelings of guilt washed over me for being so selfish.

The loudspeaker crackled before the base commander spoke. "Attention, all. As you all have heard by now, a war was waged today by coalition forces from forty-two nations led by President George H. W. Bush and the United States against Iraq's invasion of Kuwait. I'm sure you have many questions and concerns, and want to know what this means to you as part of the United States Army. I wish we had all the answers, but, at this time, we are unsure of the progression this will take. We urge you to get your affairs in order, including an updated will. More information will be forthcoming as it comes to light."

I was numb, having an out-of-body experience as I listened to my superiors outlining our next steps. Get our affairs in order? A will? A cold sweat covered my body as I tried to grasp and compartmentalize what I had just heard. Audible sighs and gasps were uttered around me as reality began to sink in. I pinched myself, thinking I was having a nightmare, but no nightmare could be this devastating.

Walking back to the barracks was surreal. Soldiers were all around me, but we walked in silence, all caught up in our own thoughts. I'm not sure how I made it back. I immediately headed for my nightstand and took out my picture of Claire. Maybe there was a silver lining in all this madness. If I were to die in combat, I would be reunited with her forever.

The next months passed slowly, waiting to hear if more troops would be deployed. I felt like a walking, talking, eating zombie. I was going through the motions of existence but not feeling anything. Nightmares consumed my sleep. I lost weight and morphed into a

CHAPTER 26 ... THE FRIEND

lesser version of myself. Counselors and clergy were made available for those who were at their tipping point. I chose to shrink within myself and implement the coping mechanisms I had been taught in my many years of therapy. Having survived my childhood, I was more than confident I could survive anything thrown my way.

The only bright spot in my dismal existence was my correspondence with Paige. She sent me a constant stream of letters outlining her escapades, always bringing a much-needed smile and chuckle to my day. Oh, to be young again, with the indestructible mindset only young people possessed. I even wrote back. A promise is a promise, after all, and is sacred in my book.

The news I had been dreading came on November 29, 1990. My orders came through with news of my deployment to Saudi Arabia in December. Talk about a crap Christmas—this was going to be one of the worst. A plethora of emotions came over me. I wasn't just scared—I was petrified. Full of unanswered *what ifs*, I walked around with the weight of the world on my shoulders, knowing my fate was out of my hands.

Figuring there was no time like the present, I sat at my desk, trying to find the words to put down on paper to my mom. I wasn't sure why I felt the need to let her know, but it tugged at my heart strings, and, deep inside, something was telling me it was the right thing to do.

Dear Mom,

Knowing how you love to keep up with current affairs, I know you are aware the U.S. is at war. I was hoping I wouldn't have to tell you this, but I got orders for a deployment to Saudi Arabia. I passed basic training with flying colors, so I'm prepared. Well, as prepared as one could ever be when faced with uncertainties. The fact remains that it's war, and I most likely will be on the front lines, fighting for our country. I'm honored to represent the United States but terrified of what I might be a part of. On December 15, I will fly out. There are too many unknowns at this time, so I'm not sure when I'll be back on U.S. soil, if ever. I'll be cognizant of my surroundings and try my damndest to come back in one piece, but I can't make you any promises. Try not to worry. I hope this finds you well.

Love,
Luke

Folding it into thirds, I kissed it before placing it in the envelope, hoping that would bring me luck.

Before I could even turn around, December 15 was upon me. I gathered on the tarmac with others from my platoon, boarding a plane for Saudi Arabia. Spirits were high but guarded. The only thing I could be sure of at this point is that I was about to have the worst Christmas of my life, and that was really saying something.

CHAPTER 27

THE MAYHEM

Stretching my legs, trying to work out the cramps in my calves, I breathed a sigh of relief that the twenty-plus-hour flight had come to an end. My nerves were on edge, and I grabbed my hands to control the shaking. We made it without any incidents, despite my in-flight visions of being shot down. I felt grateful for small mercies. Hopefully, this meant that Lady Luck had packed a knapsack and decided to join us all.

Immediately, I noticed a difference in the terrain. In every direction I looked, there was sand and flat land. It was brown for miles as camels roamed freely, dotting the horizon. So much for my dreams of having a white Christmas, because it was a sunny and very windy fifty-nine degrees. The wind was relentless as it blew mercilessly, blinding me and threatening to blow my hat off. Tumbleweeds swirled in the air. I was thankful the military had strict dress-code guidelines, requiring our pants to be bloused within our combat boots. Without those guidelines, I was certain I would have had a boot full of the fine sand rubbing my toes raw. I would later learn there were two semi-annual windy seasons called *shamals* with wind velocities averaging thirty miles per hour. Unluckily for me, one was from December to January. Maybe Lady Luck had stayed stateside after all.

Our lodging made me immediately miss the barracks. We were assigned to a tent, where we had the very minimal basics. A cot to sleep on with a drab-white pair of sheets and Army-green wool itchy blanket, a makeshift closet/dresser and a locker to store our personal belongings. The water was scarce and most likely tainted with chemicals, so, instead of having free running water, our drinking water was housed in "bladder" water tanks. When we showered, we were instructed to keep our eyes and mouths closed to avoid contamination. Having an open wound added another whole level of concern. Missing the creature comforts of home had never been so evident.

Luckily, I had managed a bit of training in my career field, because it was put to good use the minute I "settled in." My official title was "combat engineer." It sounded all highfalutin', but all it really consisted of was performing a variety of military engineering to include tunnel- and mine-warfare tasks as well as construction and demolition duties in and out of combat zones.

The days were long. And dusty. The nights were longer. And lonely. Finding it nearly impossible to get anywhere near comfortable on my too-short cot, I tossed and turned, counting endless amounts of sheep to no avail. The nights were filled with air raids and the sound of bombs echoing off the sand. When I managed a couple of hours here and there, I woke up with massive dream crumbs made

CHAPTER 27 ... THE MAYHEM

of sand, lodged in my tear ducts. I prayed that Claire would come visit me in a dream, but she had enough sense to stay away from this godforsaken hellhole.

The waiting game was the worst. Bits of information filtered through our camp, all pointing to the inevitable. I was positive we would be sent to the front lines—but *when* was anybody's guess. Morale was at an all-time low. Men walked around in an apocalyptic-like state, barely making an effort at small talk. Some wanted to leave, and others were chomping at the bit to serve their country and use the skills we had been taught in basic training.

The one highlight was when we received care packages. Care packages consisted of a variety of things, but one of the most popular was cookies. The camels even got to know the mail trucks. The troops would feed them goodies and cookies, so the camels would sprint over, looking for a handout.

News from the States was limited and hard to know if it was propaganda or not. Lately the skinny from the States was that there were a lot of pissed-off people thinking the U.S. had no business in the Middle East. Thousands of anti-war demonstrators protested the United States attack on Iraq. Across the world, millions of people took part in demonstrations, strikes, sabotage, desertion, and other acts of resistance. It was a sad time for the world.

Christmas came, and, even though it wasn't the white Christmas I wanted, it was even better. The USO and Bob Hope showed up and put on a show to beat all shows. It was just the medicine everyone needed—a night filled with nonstop jokes. The base erupted with laughter when Mr. Hope asked, "You know what 'Saddam' is spelled backwards? That's 'mad-ass'!" It was a festive night complete with Santa hats; everyone was able to forget, for the time being, that there was a war going on and open a present. Back in the States, volunteers had worked diligently organizing the care packages to add some joy to our lives. It was heartfelt and appreciated more than we could express.

Someone found their creative side and built a makeshift Christmas tree out of sandbags, spray-painted green with an odd assortment of decorations, including kitchen utensils, a roll of paper tape, and a star crafted out of tin foil on top. The mess hall served turkey with all the trimmings, and, at midnight, we all gathered together, giving thanks. Before the festivities were over, a group of Marines remixed the lyrics to "Jingle Bells," singing, "Dashing through the sand, with an M16 in hand, terrorizing the land, looking for Hussein. Treads on the tracks will ring, giving troops a fright, opening up the door, we get out and fight." It was a far cry from a traditional Christmas, but it would be one I would remember all the same.

The days dragged on, and the troops became impatient, until we were told on the morning of February 14, of all days, to pack up our things and join a convoy headed to the northeastern corner of Saudi Arabia bordering Iraq. The same men I had witnessed looking forlorn had now done an about-face and were downright giddy with excitement. I didn't share in their exuberance.

The weather hadn't cooperated for even one day since we landed, continuing to blow sand with such velocity that it ended up in places I never thought possible. By the time we pulled into our new, temporary base, we were all parched and wind-blown. I gave up wishing for decent living conditions, reminding myself we were at war, after all. We were briefed, and we learned that air assaults had been taking place since the middle of January, but it had now become apparent that ground reinforcements were needed. Looking around

CHAPTER 27 ... THE MAYHEM

at my fellow comrades, I saw a variety of emotions. Some looked like they had been accosted in a dark alley, while others looked like they had just hit the winning home run to win the World Series. I was somewhere in the middle.

For me, "D-Day" took on a whole new meaning and would always be February 23 now. As my platoon stood at the ready for the orders to move out, we were dressed in full combat attire with our military-issued M16A2 Assault Rifles grasped firmly in our hands. It was go time, as we inched our way over the border into Kuwait and northern Iraq. Emotions were all over the place but mostly optimistic. I was still skeptical and unsure of what we might encounter once we arrived at our destination.

My eyes couldn't believe what I was witnessing, as I tried to catch my breath. Mayhem and total destruction reigned all around. Everywhere I looked, I saw blood—so much so that I fought off the urge to vomit. Dodging a body that had been blown up, his dog tags lying three feet from his lifeless body, I managed to roll into a trench as gunfire exploded around me. One thing basic training had taught me was that the rules we learned existed for a reason. They were to be followed to maintain order and help each other out. It was all about being a team—and, if I was anything, I was a team player.

With that in mind, I scooped up a man who had fallen at my feet. His face was half gone. An empty eye socket hauntingly stared at me. Tightly pressed lips strained across his face, masking pain, as a blood-curdling scream pierced through the air, fighting to be heard among the bombing and gunfire. Pandemonium was surrounding me, as more men fell like dominoes. Seeking out a medic, I dodged bodies, trying my hardest to avoid the empty stares of death.

Amid the chaos, I searched for a familiar face. Troops from our allies were intermingled with each other, fighting as comrades for the same cause. Upon finding my platoon, I wasn't sure how I had allowed myself to get separated. They looked worse for wear. I felt how they looked. My hands were covered in blood, and the smell of death was all consuming. I heard grenades hit their intended targets, while flashes of gunfire pierced through the night sky. We had been at it for hours, and all I could think about was *Why?* Why were men losing their lives when they had so much at home to live for?

We diligently fought off the enemy, and, after three treacherously long days and nights, we claimed Kuwait City. Our job here was done, and we were instructed we would be moving out back to our camp in Saudi. Mixed emotions flooded over me once again. I was ecstatic to leave behind this hellhole of a battlefield but distraught about leaving so many men behind. Those men had taken an oath to protect and serve but didn't deserve to die.

Weary wouldn't begin to describe how we felt as we walked around camp, trying to put the pieces back together. Grief was visible on everyone's face, but no one talked about it. It was too painful. Too raw. Too fresh. We went through the motions of living, barely getting by. My appetite was nonexistent. Food was antithetical, making me nauseous. War had changed me. The smell of burning flesh, sounds of agony, and the total ugliness of death played on repeat, holding my thoughts and dreams hostage.

I felt as if I had been bamboozled by my own government. Promises of seeing the world, learning a trade, and building camaraderie seemed like a distant memory. Now Stateside for therapy, I sat cocooned in my barracks, a shell of my former self, dealing with unimaginable trauma. And not dealing well, I might add. The sleep

CHAPTER 27 ... THE MAYHEM

I managed to get was filled with nightmares. I woke up screaming on the floor in a fetal position half the time, not sure how I got there. Any little sound made me jump out of my skin, hitting the ground, expecting to be blown to smithereens. And in a tragic way, I was one of the lucky ones.

Past therapy sessions had taught me that I was going to have to find a way to talk about it—or it would eat away at me. I would never be able to file it away, where it belonged, if I didn't face my horrible experience and sort through the rubble. But, for now, I was certain it was too early.

Combing through every news article I could find, I tried to make sense of what I had witnessed. So many different reports came from the government regarding lives lost. I'd heard one hundred fifty-four on up to more than two hundred. If it had only been one, it would have been one too many.

CHAPTER 28

THE THERAPY

My courtesy seven days off after returning from Saudi were coming to an end. I took stock of my mental state, pondering if I was capable of functioning as the soldier I had been groomed to be. I looked around, wondering what I was doing. Where I was headed with my life? The war had really done a number on me. Trying to put the pieces back together was not coming easily. I took solace in the fact that I wasn't alone. I was told that it was a normal response, but I felt less of a man. Somehow, with all my past experiences, I felt like I should have been better prepared for a life of disappointments.

Assuming all of my deployed platoon who had seen the ugliness of war were struggling, I was afraid to ask. Struggling to come to terms with the good fortune of coming out alive, and struggling to accept the shallow truth that friends had not been so lucky. I had

CHAPTER 28 ... THE THERAPY

struggled through most of my life, so I was no stranger to dealing with destruction and heartache. But this hit differently.

This was a whole other level of disconnect and sadness—one I could not begin to grasp. I felt like I was losing my mind. Frantically clawing my way out of a hole, buried alive in dirt. Or drowning, gasping for air as my soul left my body. I was starting to spiral out of control. If that happened, I was certain I would not make it out to the other side—the side that was a productive citizen. Instead, I would become a nuisance, a drain on society.

The pain I was feeling was so real I could taste it. It was sour with a bitterness that left a burning in my throat, causing a gagging reflex. I would have thought the whole thing was a nightmare, but I knew I was awake. I heard faint voices in the hall, a slamming door, a toilet flushing in my connected bathroom, a phone ringing over and over again, but I was not feeling anything. I was numb.

As I sat holed up in my room, surfacing only to nourish myself, I fought the urge to give up. I was better than that. If I could overcome my childhood, I could do this. But how? Was I strong enough to overcome this alone?

Waking up with a start, I felt warmness surround me. "Luke—come on, baby. You are stronger than you think. If you don't want to do this for yourself, do it for me. Make me proud. I love you, sweetheart." Claire's voice was music to my ears. Reaching out to feel her embrace, she vanished right before my eyes, but not before planting the sweetest kiss upon my lips. I swore I could taste her strawberry-flavored lip gloss.

Far be it from me to disappoint Claire. Jumping out of bed and into a hot shower, I felt determined to tackle my issues before they tackled me. Mapping out my day with a newfound clarity, I made my way to the library first to do a little research on PTSD. My motto before the war had always been *mind over matter*, but, then again, I had never witnessed men get their chest blown open and die while clutching their dog tags, whispering their *I love you's* to their soul mates back home. Visions of blood and guts clouded my vision.

The library was empty except for one of my platoon mates, sitting lost in thought, with headphones on, staring at a computer screen. I pulled up a chair next to him, logging on to a separate computer; he turned, shocked to see me. He looked awful. Travis Buehller was close to my age, but short and stocky with bushy eyebrows that fought with his round-rimmed glasses. He was the silent type, who kept mostly to himself, but we'd shared a meal or two in the mess hall.

"How's it going, bro?" I asked as I gave him a hearty pat on the back. He shook his head side to side as he ran his hands over his almost-bald head before answering. A smile tried to appear but missed its mark as he mumbled, "Not great. How about you?" I took a peek at his computer screen and saw he was scrolling through articles on PTSD. So, I was right: I wasn't the only one suffering in silence, searching for answers.

"Honestly, not great, either. I see what you're researching. I came here to do the exact same thing. You know what they say, great minds and all." I said with a chuckle, but all I got as a response was a blank, vacant stare. He had it bad. As bad as I had it before Claire's pep talk. Don't get me wrong: I was still hanging by a thread, but I had a newfound hope in her words that I intended on taking to heart. I owed it to her. And me.

"Let's go grab a coffee and have a chat before we do any more research, OK?" Feeling a sudden urge to take him under my wing was something that had come out of left field. Surprisingly, he agreed,

CHAPTER 28 ... THE THERAPY

and we spent the better part of the evening sharing our feelings and what our plans were for the future. We both felt disenchanted with the military and what we had seen in Saudi—although, in all fairness, the military hadn't lied to us. They had prepared us for battle, even though the battle was more than we could comprehend. It almost felt better to point the finger and blame someone. Deciding that our next plan of action was to join a support group and hold each other accountable, we shook on it, binding us to the agreement. Just having a game plan took a small burden off my heavy shoulders.

Time flew at record speed, and, soon, the weeks had turned into months. I was muddling through but not what I would call excelling at life. Travis and I had, indeed, joined a support group, and, although it helped to share our innermost thoughts, it didn't take away the nightmares that plagued me a good portion of the week. For some strange reason, I was thinking the support group would miraculously make me forget about the horrors that I had witnessed firsthand. Boy, was I wrong.

I was sadly mistaken about the benefits I would receive, and I continued to wrestle with my demons. I was beginning to think I would be doomed for the rest of my life. I was unable to shake the devastating feeling that I was letting Claire down, and it weighed heavily on my mind.

The therapy group met every Tuesday evening at the chapel on base. In any given week, there would be any number of soldiers, ranging from ten up to fifty. It was a safe place for us all to openly divulge our fears and our innermost thoughts in a non-judgmental forum. The one thing I found beneficial was that I wasn't alone. Or crazy. We were told it was natural to feel afraid during or after a traumatic situation, because fear is a part of the body's fight-or-flight response, which, in turn, helps us avoid or respond to potential danger.

Understanding PTSD and why my body was reacting in such a way was going to be paramount in my recovery. So, when I learned being easily startled and feeling tense and on guard were normal responses, I breathed a sigh of relief. My thoughts were shared by others as we grappled for a bit of normalcy in our lives.

My studies continued, and learning was therapeutic to me—as it always had been, although I noticed my attention span was miniscule at best. It was yet another symptom I seemed to be suffering from. It was something I had never dealt with in the past, and, unfortunately, at the end of the day, I was still a mess. My sleep was erratic, and my normal good nature was being put to the test on a daily basis. Even the smallest, minutest things sent me into a tailspin.

I spent all my downtime combing through article after article on PTSD and which coping mechanisms were most successful. Living in the state I was in was not an option—not one I was willing to accept. So, when I stumbled upon an article talking about Eye Movement Desensitization and Reprocessing therapy, also known as EMDR, I stopped dead in my tracks. *Was this the answer I had been looking for?* I wondered.

Devouring the article, I caught myself holding my breath as my heart pounded loud enough to wake the dead. The therapy was reasonably new, with clinical trials taking place just two years ago. The article went on to explain that it was a method involving the movement of your eyes in a specific way while you process traumatic memories. One interesting fact I was drawn to was that the therapy did not require talking in detail about a distressing issue but instead focused on changing the emotions, thoughts, or behaviors that result

CHAPTER 28 ... THE THERAPY

from a distressing, traumatic experience. This, in turn, allows your brain to resume a natural healing process.

Hmmmmm. I was encouraged, giving myself hope that I wasn't a lost cause, after all. Not having to talk openly about my trauma was indeed an extra, added bonus worth more than its weight in gold for this socially inept introvert.

Since your brain stores normal and traumatic memories differently, it needs to be addressed differently. Often the brain stores trauma memories that don't allow for healthy healing. Think of it like a physical wound that your body hasn't been allowed to heal. Because it hasn't had a chance to heal, your brain didn't get the message that the danger was over. Standing with my hand over my mouth, I felt like there should have been a lightbulb flashing over my head and someone shouting from the mountaintops, "Incoming important information!!" It seemed so simple, yet complex at the same time. Feeling a tad perplexed why my support-group leader hadn't talked about this, I chalked it up to it being new and not mainstream treatment yet.

Just like your body is sensitive to pain from an injury, your mind has a higher sensitivity to things we see, hear, smell, or feel during a trauma-related event. I hit the "Print" button with more aggression than intended, and the button protested with a loud clang. It sputtered and let out an exhausted hiss before it died.

Kaput.

Damn, I thought, weighing my options. I could write all the info out longhand in the notebook I had packed in my backpack or I could fess up to the librarian that I had gotten a little too excited and overzealous and, in turn, accidentally broke the machine. That would require talking to someone, though, which was not on my list of favorite things to do. My moral compass won out in my internal struggle, as I shamelessly hung my head and went in search of help, convincing myself that it was the honest thing to do.

Back in the barracks, I read word for word over and over, until I was well-versed on everything the therapy entailed. I was feeling more optimistic than I had felt in months, leading me to have a voluminous appetite and a spring in my step as I headed to the mess hall. I ran into Travis and shared my newfound knowledge, but the more I talked about it, the more convoluted it sounded. The optimism from just an hour earlier had turned to pessimism in record time. I'd been programmed from my childhood not to ever have anything go my way, so why would this be any different?

I didn't want to feel sorry for myself, but if I had to be brutally honest, pretty much everything I touched or came in contact with ended badly. Not just for me, but for others, too. I felt cursed. Cursed by the gods of doom.

CHAPTER 29

THE DECISION

Not all days were created equal. Or nights, for that matter. I can't tell you how many times I woke up on the floor, clutching my head, with my heart racing, trying to avoid a grenade that had landed inches from me. The nightmares were so realistic, leaving me in an indescribable funk for the entire day.

I was getting better at camouflaging my moods, though—at least on the outside, for appearance's sake only. I didn't want to talk about it anymore. I was sick of talking about it. Sick of thinking about it. Sick of reliving it, day in and day out. I stopped going to the support group and avoided Travis. He was getting better, and I didn't need the constant reminder that I was a failure, yet again.

My time here at Fort Leonard Wood was over. I had graduated from my training program, and I was now faced with the decision about what direction my life would go. Wrestling with my future, I had no one to talk to about which road I should follow. I really didn't feel like moving to another base and starting over. But what?

In my despair, I sat down and decided to write a letter to Aiden. Even though we had promised to stay in touch, life had gotten in the way, and our friendship had fallen into the cracks of life. The last I'd heard, he had settled in nicely at Fort Richardson in Anchorage, Alaska. He had been fortunate to avoid the war. Jealousy reared its ugly head every time I thought about his good fortune. Even though he was my friend, it still felt odd asking him for life advice. I was a grown man, for God's sake.

I ripped up the letter and instead went to the chapel. The last time I had prayed was when Marmalade was sick, but some unknown force propelled me there, searching for answers. Bowing my head and closing my eyes, mostly to keep the tears from spilling out, I bared my soul.

The chapel was quaint. It housed only ten rows of pews on two sides, separated by an aisle that was covered by rich red carpet. The red complemented the rich walnut, intricately carved pews that had cushions matching the richness of the carpet. Stained glass windows surrounded the space, casting colorful prisms of light. A massive stone cross sat front and center on the altar. It felt like a safe haven. Non-judgmental and forgiving. A warmth enveloped me as I made myself comfortable.

Growing up without religion as part of my life, I felt out of place—although totally welcome at the same time. An odd sensation, but who was I to judge? I was just happy with the opportunity to throw my dilemma out into the universe. There were way too many questions fighting each other in my mind. I prayed like I'd

CHAPTER 29 ... THE DECISION

never prayed before, searching for a way to end the cacodemon that haunted my days and nights.

"Excuse me, but I couldn't help but notice how distraught you are. Is there any way I can be of assistance? A shoulder to cry on? An ear to bend? Advice to be given?" I jumped at the sound of the deep, angelic voice that sounded like a chorus of alto gospel singers. Standing before me was an older gentleman who oozed gentleness and more spirituality than Jesus himself. He was mostly bald, with gray tufts of hair that floated on the top of his head like a halo. When he smiled, his whole face lit up, creasing the corners of his hazel eyes. I immediately felt at ease.

"May I?" he questioned while motioning to the space next to me on the pew. He extended his hand. It was covered in age spots and wrinkles, showcasing his life's journey. "My name is Harry Gray. I'm the part-time chaplain here. I was once a soldier like yourself but turned to the Lord after a stint in World War II. It changed me. I knew I had to do something to help myself, so I enrolled in seminary school. The rest, as they say, is history," he said while patting me on the back.

There was something about him that allowed me to promptly drop my guard. I reached out and shook his hand, which was soft and warm but a hearty shake nonetheless. "I'm Lucas Travers, but please call me 'Luke.'" I felt like I'd known him my whole life and couldn't help wishing he'd been my father instead of the piece of crap I had.

Opening up hadn't always come easy to me, so I was shocked when three hours had passed and a *Reader's Digest* version of my whole life had been laid out on the table. We talked—well, mostly, *I* talked, and Harry attentively listened, interjecting only when necessary. Talking about my childhood was something I'd shared only with Claire and Dr. Hawthorne, my therapist in Piedmont. Opening up to Harry seemed like the right thing to do. Oddly enough, I wasn't ashamed when tears flowed like lava from a freshly erupted volcano. The genuine concern in his eyes was heartwarming. Needing it more than I ever imagined, I couldn't help thinking I was witnessing one of those moments where the right person had been placed in my path at the right time. Whatever it was—my guardian angel intervening, Claire pulling some strings from up above, or serendipity—I was here for it.

Harry was warm, insightful, and a great listener, but, most importantly, he was an older version of myself. He had lived my life, just years earlier. Our childhoods were similar in the respect that he was a bit of an outcast as well. Searching for a way out and needing to find his own identity, he had joined the military, where he promptly was sent to war. He'd fought for his life, on the front lines, watching men fall to their gruesome death at his feet. PTSD wasn't a foreign concept to him. He knew it intimately and dealt with the aftermath years later. It's like he knew me from the inside out; so, when he offered advice, I was all ears.

"Son, if you want my honest-to-goodness opinion, I'll offer it to you, for what's it worth," he winked, while offering a lopsided smirk and a chuckle. What I really wanted was for him to adopt me on the spot, no questions asked, and I told him so, which got a belly laugh that sent his gray tufts of hair swirling like they were working a hula hoop. "In all honesty Luke, sometimes the hardest part of the journey is believing you're worth the trip. I think you need to find yourself. There comes a time in one's life that you have to stop trying to please others. Let them doubt you, but don't ever

CHAPTER 29 ... THE DECISION

doubt yourself. At the end of the day, it's you against the world. Be gentle. Be kind. And respect what your body is telling you it needs. A medical discharge can be arranged due to your PTSD."

I hadn't even thought about a medical discharge. When I enlisted with the recruiter, I had signed up for a two-year service commitment. I remember thinking that I would honor that commitment—no matter what.

"I'm afraid I'll feel like a failure if I quit. What will everyone think of me?" I questioned him with quizzical eyes, searching for more of the knowledge that he seemed to dish out in spades. "Who cares what anyone thinks? The road to success is paved with doubters and haters. Prove them wrong," were his words of wisdom. And, you know what? That's exactly what I intended to do. Or die trying.

After bidding farewell to Harry and thanking him profusely for his time and advice, I ventured back to the library, in search of answers on medical discharges. Between the library and Harry, I had found my two best friends. Obviously, they were different from each other, but so similar in many ways. They both were full of knowledge, wisdom, answers, and escapism—all things that were crucial to my next steps. Prior to my trip to the chapel, I felt as if I was floating in a sea of despair, but he had thrown me a much-needed life preserver, allowing me to stay afloat another day.

CHAPTER 30

THE SEPARATION

Taking the proper steps to separate from the military was laborious. Even so, after extensive research, upon Harry's suggestion, I was certain this was the right direction for me. It wasn't a quick process, to say the least—in fact, it was dragging on while I was hanging out in limbo, growing more impatient as I ticked off days on my calendar. My next base assignment had been put on hold while the Medical Evaluation Board made their determination on whether I was fit for duty. And even then, they didn't have the final say. The final step would be for an occupational health team to make the final separation, determining that I, indeed, *did* suffer trauma while serving my country.

Sitting in front of boards was not my thing. I got nervous and broke out in a sweat that beaded on my brow, rolling down my face while I was being grilled with questions on my mental state. Well—I wasn't *actually being grilled:* it was more like being

CHAPTER 30 ... THE SEPARATION

questioned. I hated being the center of attention, though. If I wasn't already having problems, this would have created a multitude of them. I was pissed at myself for not being able to overcome my issues on my own, playing the blame game. I couldn't help but think it had something to do with my childhood. I liked to think I was a badass and showed determination and resilience, but, ultimately, I was a beaten and broken shell. The EMDR treatment hadn't been successful for me, leaving me more distraught than ever. Not only were the nightmares horrifying, but I had started to notice a number of physical ailments plaguing me on a daily basis.

I was a mess but more determined than ever to get back to my old self. As I sat in my barracks room, a knock sounded on my door. *Ugh.* I wasn't in the mood to talk. Everyone meant well, but I hated letting people see the less-than-jovial side of me.

"Lucas Travers? Are you in there? I have a special delivery letter for you."

Needless to say, I was intrigued. Jumping up, I threw the door open, to see a pimply faced young girl standing there, holding an envelope-sized package, grinning from ear to ear. Thanking her, I clutched the envelope, pondering its belongings.

Expecting it to be news about my discharge, I was shocked when I tore open the outer envelope only to see an inner envelope covered in sunflowers and my name written delicately in my mom's hand. Instantly my heart rate rose, and time stopped. I had to chastise myself for feeling scared to read its contents. Secretly hoping something bad had happened to my dad, I ripped the sealed flap with trembling hands. A waft of my mom's floral perfume filtered through the air, and I was instantly transported back to my childhood—not a good place to be. Swallowing hard, I removed the yellow-tinted stationery and read…

Dearest Lucas,

    I've thought of you often since you told me you were off to war. I've become obsessed with the news, searching for any information I could learn on your whereabouts and well-being. I finally had to hire a private investigator to determine your status. Pleased to know you returned safely. I hope this finds you well. I beg of you, please don't tell anyone, especially your father or brothers, that I've reached out.

    Love,
    Mom

That's odd, I thought, while I sat rubbing my forehead, trying to piece together *why* she had reached out and furthermore, *Why it was such a big secret?* I had mixed emotions. Again. Part of me was happy she cared enough to find me, but a big part of me was pissed that she never showed me love when I lived under her roof. Thinking this was a cruel game she was playing, I chose to put it out of my mind—I ripped it into shreds and flushed it down the toilet. I had enough going on already—I was too busy to play her wretched mind games.

    Seven months and seven days after I had returned home from Saudi Arabia, I got my medical-separation discharge papers. I contemplated the timeframe and decided it was an omen, since lucky number seven had to have come from somewhere. I began the tedious job of packing up my stuff while I listened to "What a Fool Believes" by the Doobie Brothers. Was there some foreshadowing there? The title was painstakingly accurate on all the facets of my life. It seemed like I was always in search of the elusive dream that

CHAPTER 30 ... THE SEPARATION

would lead me to my Happy-Ever-After. But the sad reality was that I'd never achieved it. When I *did* achieve it, with Claire, it was promptly taken from me. I had a strong feeling my luck was about to change. Especially when I looked over at my nightstand and the clock read 7:07.

Saying goodbye to Fort Leonard Wood wasn't bittersweet in the least. I had never fit in here, always feeling like the odd man out. I would, however, miss Harry. Since our initial interaction, we had met up numerous times. He always had the right thing to say and the most soothing aura, oozing positivity. So, it came as no surprise when I went to say my goodbyes that he had made a "goodness basket," as he called it. He must have the world's best memory, because it was filled with all of my favorite things that I had mentioned in passing. I chuckled as I visualized him rifling through a compartmentalized mental rolodex that lived in his head, cataloguing all my favorites. I felt like a heel because I had nothing for him except my undying gratitude. He accepted that with open arms and a big bear hug.

"I'm going to miss you, son," he gushed, with tears dotting the corners of his eyes. "Our talks have been the spotlight of my otherwise mundane, sedentary life. I'm beyond pleased that we've become friends and that I've been instrumental in your decision-making as of late." I couldn't keep my eyes off the basket, finding it hard not to devour the homemade peanut-butter cookies on the spot, but I managed to stop salivating long enough to ditto his feelings. He had indeed been a godsend placed in my path at the most desperate time. Another serendipitous moment and a friend to add to the people I've met on my way to finding myself.

Leaving the nightstand last to pack up, I emptied its contents into a brown packing box, taking my and Claire's wedding picture in my hands. "I love you, my special angel," I whispered to the picture, wiping a tear from my cheek. "I hope you're proud of me and the decision I've made." As the last sentence left my lips, a gentleness washed over me, and I felt a presence sitting in my lap. My Claire had never left my side.

One of the hardest decisions I had to make was *Where was I going to go?* I was a man without a home. I always wanted to live on the west coast; I hadn't given up on my childhood dream, but I also had a strong premonition that the time wasn't right just yet. With no other immediate options, or at least none that made sense, I opted to head back to Piedmont. I had—at least—Joey and Holly to welcome me back. Contemplating whether I would reach out to my mom left me in a state of turmoil, confused yet again on the mixed signals she gave me. I finally decided that, at the end of the day, I was better off without her mind games. The town wasn't big by any standards, so the chance of running into her *was* a possibility. One I decided I'd face if and when the time came.

Saluting the flag that was waving proudly in the sky, I climbed behind the wheel of the small U-Haul I had rented. I was sad it had come to this. I really thought this had been the answer when I signed on the dotted line a mere seventeen months earlier. Just goes to show you how unpredictable life can be. With that thought, I started my trek across the country, not knowing what I would find once I arrived.

CHAPTER 31
THE LIST

There's something to be said about the open road and road trips, with their endless supply of snacks. Giving me time, all thirteen hundred miles or so, to think wasn't ideal for someone in my mental state, but, on the flip side, I had more than enough time to try to sort out a plan for my future. It's like I was starting from scratch, not having the military to fall back on anymore. That ship had sailed and capsized.

Driving was something I had always enjoyed, especially with Marm's ears flopping in the wind as she joyfully hung her head out the window. I missed her every single day, and reminiscing about her made it even more painful. Or was it my tortured state of mind that had me painfully aware of all the feelings? I needed to rein it in, because I was starting to irritate myself.

Driving was a "Either you love it or hate it" kinda thing. The infrequent family trips I had taken as a child were always overshadowed by my dad being the epitome of Mr. Cranky Pants. Bitching and cursing the whole entire time he sat behind the wheel, finding fault in everyone except himself. Looking back on it now, that was just who he was as a person: Mean-spirited, vindictive, and foul-tempered, to name a few of his not-so-stellar traits. It's a wonder I came out of my childhood as unscathed as I did. A smile played on the corners of my mouth as I thought about the time I knocked him out. It wasn't one of my finer moments but one in which I took extreme pleasure.

Although any fond memories of my childhood were few and far between, one thing I do remember positively about the road trips were the games we played while sitting crowded like sardines in the back seat, dripping sweat. My dad didn't believe in using the air conditioner, giving some lame excuse about it using more gas. So, my brothers and I took turns sitting by the windows to try to catch a breeze blowing through while playing *Name the Alphabet*. Starting at the beginning, with "A," we had to find something outside that started with that letter. Once you spotted one, you yelled it out, and you got a point. Whoever ended up with the most points by the time we finished "Z" was declared the winner and awarded a window seat for the duration of the trip home. I had quite an eagle eye and won more times than not, which angered my brothers to no end. I didn't care. Fair was fair. It was one of the only times in my childhood that I recall being part of the family.

Giving myself a high five for deciding to drive, I marveled at the landscape that flew by me as I barreled down the interstate. America was gorgeous. Even with all its problems, there was no denying its beauty. Rolling, vibrant green hills, with wildflowers sprouting out sporadically with no rhyme or reason for miles, and, then just

CHAPTER 31 ... THE LIST

around a corner, it could turn to scrub brush. The ever-changing scenery kept me guessing and daydreaming.

When I originally planned my itinerary, I figured I would drive all day and pull over to rest at night, putting me in Vermont within three days, but, after my first day, I reevaluated. What was the big rush? I wasn't even altogether sure where I was going to live—although I did know with one hundred percent certainty that it wouldn't be at my parents' home. No way, no how, on any day of the year. I had also made the decision not to let even my mom know I was back in Piedmont. My family was dead to me.

Rolling into Piedmont after twenty-three hours and forty-two minutes of official time behind the wheel, I had successfully formulated a plan. The consensus between me, myself, and I was really quite simple. I would:

1. Visit Joey and Holly, although I was none too happy to see Alex or Sloan. I still felt like they blamed me somehow for Claire's death.
2. Find a place to live, preferably on the other side of town from my so-called parents, aka the ogres.
3. Get some kind of job to tide me over until I split town for good.
4. Make it a point to avoid my parents at all costs.
5. Arrange some therapy sessions with Dr. Hawthorne.
6. Get better from the PTSD and the other symptoms that came out of nowhere.
7. Stay away from alcohol and its temptations.

Reading the sign on the side of the road proudly welcoming me to Piedmont instantly gave me anxiety. I heard a strange, crazed, strangled screech, surprising me when I realized the cry had escaped my own lips. It was half-sob, half-laugh but spoke of pure desperation. My life in the Army seemed like a lifetime ago. Funny how everything can change on a dime. The anxiety I was feeling wasn't the PTSD talking, although that was always present. This was different. It was the kind of panic that leaves you in a cold sweat, with heart palpitations, unable to breathe, on the cusp of passing out.

Starting to second-guess my decision to return to Piedmont, I pulled over, taking deep breaths and commenced to talk myself down. When I had been away from the reminders of my childhood that left scars etched in my heart, I felt coming back was my only option, but, clearly, there were others. I had a feeling that my time back here would be short unless a miraculous turn of events were to take place.

First things first: after my mind was clear of the ongoing anxiety, I veered to the left, into the parking lot of a local beer joint. I was exhausted, but I knew I wouldn't be able to sleep. I had been having sleep disturbances for some time, along with difficulty concentrating and forgetfulness. I was wired from the driving and needed a beer. Just one. Knowing it wasn't a good idea, I was hoping it would ease some of the fierce headaches that had been blinding my vision lately. As I stretched, my joints cried out in pain. *Too much time behind the wheel*, I told myself, but even I wasn't convinced that was the whole truth.

Hops and Harmony sat on the corner of the interstate and Main St. I had seen it a number of times, never venturing in, but tonight it was beckoning me. Shining brightly, a string of Edison lights

CHAPTER 31 ... THE LIST

were strung under the eaves. A colorful, flashing "Welcome" sign and a giant frothy mug of beer made out of neon lights rotated on top of the roof, completing the look. It looked tacky as hell but enough off the beaten path that I wasn't likely to know anyone. I wasn't in the mood for small talk. I chuckled under my breath, thinking, *Was I ever?*

The parking lot was sparsely littered with cars, mostly pickup trucks, lifted with gigantic off-road tires. Some would say this was narrow-minded thinking, but, to me, it spoke volumes to the clientele, leaning toward a bunch of rednecks looking for trouble. Knowing I would keep to myself, I opened the massive solid wood doors, noticing they had seen better days. Chunks of wood were missing, and a knife had used the door as its easel. A waft of stale beer with notes of piss and vomit accosted me as I made my way up to the bar. It took my eyes a second to adjust to the dim lighting, nearly tripping over a chair pushed into the middle of the floor. Honky-tonk country music filtered through the air, and I made out a couple slow dancing as Patsy Cline belted out, *"I fall to pieces/ each time I see you again."*

Bellying up to the bar, I was cognizant that all eyes were on me. I hadn't taken this for a local hangout, but, then again, I hadn't had my wits about me in a while now. I was a misfit at the best of times, but, tonight, it felt like I was a green alien who had just landed the mothership right smack dab in the middle of the room. The first to speak was the bartender. He was tall and spindly, with tattoos covering his arms and knuckles. A green John Deere tractor hat sat perched backwards on his head, covering a scraggly black mullet. "What can I do you for, stranger?" He eyed me with skepticism while wiping a spill with a dirty cloth rag. A smile emerged through his clenched teeth with enough tension that I was afraid a tooth would crack and crumble, leaving a gap, which would surely produce a whistle when he spoke.

Feeling anything but at ease, I put on my best smile and jovial demeanor, and replied halfheartedly, "What's on tap tonight? I'm in dire need of a tall, cold one. It's been a week." I could feel it in my bones that this was a make-or-break moment as he eyed me up and down. Standing my ground, I wasn't about to show the angst that was running through my veins. After a couple of tense moments, he let out a hearty laugh, and all was right with the world as he poured me twenty ounces of Red Tail ale. Herbal notes mixed with passion fruit and honey permeated the air as I gulped it down, barely tasting a drop. I ordered another, sipping this one as I instigated a conversation with the bar keep, looking to gather information before I dove into my tedious task of apartment hunting.

Turns out my bold move to strike up a conversation with my new, unlikely acquaintance, Zeke Jones, was the right one. As luck would have it, he was a Vietnam veteran and the sole owner of a couple of rental properties. I couldn't help thinking this was the universe working behind the scenes again in this serendipitous way. A guy could get used to the universe looking out for him, since it was apparent that I was doing a feeble job of it by myself.

"I kinda pegged you for a military guy," he said as he slid my fourth beer across the counter. "What's your story? On leave?" I wasn't keen on spilling the goods, so I kept it on a need-to-know basis as I answered him. "I was in the Gulf War, and let me just say, it wasn't kind to me, so I've decided to part ways amicably. That's what brought me into town. I'm starting fresh and looking to set up some roots while I get my sea legs back." Luckily this was

CHAPTER 31 ... THE LIST

good enough for him, and he didn't ask for any explanations of my vague comments.

Two hours, five beers, and too many tequila shots later, I staggered out into the night air. What was I thinking—drinking this much? I was slightly disappointed with my actions but justified it by telling myself I was celebrating my discharge. A breeze had picked up, and the air felt cool as it swirled around my head, causing me to question if it was the beer or the wind that was making my head feel like it was floating like a cloud. I knew I was in no position to drive in my inebriated state, but I didn't give a damn, either. Alcohol had a way of making me feel indestructible, as I threw all doubts out the window and proceeded to climb behind the wheel and truck down the interstate, going ninety miles per hour.

Weaving from one side to the other, I was feeling no pain as I reached over to switch the channel on the radio. Taking my eyes off the road for only a split second almost spelled disaster; when I looked up, I was inches from crashing head-first into a telephone pole at the road's edge. Wiping the sweat off my brow, singing Bon Jovi in my own little world, I was assaulted with red lights and sirens. My mind went blank as I tried to formulate a plan, knowing that they had me dead to rights. There was no possible way I would pass a field sobriety test or a breathalyzer. Crap.

Pulling over, I ended up in a ditch, as dust and dirt flew up, encasing my truck. Just minutes before, I had solidified a time with Zeke to meet up at 10 a.m. tomorrow at one of his rental properties. Positive I would be thrown in the slammer to sleep off my bender, I would miss the appointment and the possibility of an apartment, left with having to explain why I was a no-show. Telling lies wasn't my thing, but I also wasn't proud of the truth in this instance. I certainly didn't want to get off on the wrong foot with Zeke, but I saw no other way to escape the reality of the situation. He had to have known I was wasted when I practically crawled out of the bar just moments before.

The officer sauntered up to my side of the truck with an attitude. You didn't have to be a rocket scientist to see that I was drunk. If my bloodshot eyes weren't a dead giveaway, the moment I opened my mouth would have done it. Shining a flashlight directly in my eyes, an officer asked me to produce my driver's license.

"Shir, why da yous need to seeth dat?"

He looked at me with a mixture of disgust and contempt as he angrily replied, "OK, wise guy, get out with your hands up."

I needed to pick my battles, and it wasn't going to put me in his good graces to resist, so I carefully opened my door and tried my damndest to get out without falling over. I wasn't successful, as I tumbled to the ground, face-planting on the gravel road. The ground welcomed me as one of its own, as I curled in a fetal position and started to snore, until a steel-toed shoe kicked me in the ribs.

The officer wanted no part of my drunken shenanigans as he slapped cuffs around my wrists and threw me in the back of his police cruiser while I was still picking gravel out of my hair. As we rode in silence, I had no way of knowing at the time this was the start of a cycle of alcohol abuse. I might as well have a permanent bed at the local jail—I would spend so much time sleeping off my drunken stupors in the months to come. This was something I wasn't proud of. Addiction is a horrible thing, taking over your life with total disregard for what's right and wrong. Years later, I had plenty of time to reflect on the toll it took on me and others.

CHAPTER 31 ... THE LIST

Pulling up to the police station, it looked as if time had stood still. It still had the drab-brown paint exterior with missing bricks on the façade. The memories I conjured up regarding my last stay here were anything but pleasant. And this time was proving to be no different. I was of legal age this time around, with no mom to come bail me out, leaving me a bit depressed. It was a slap in the face that I was all alone in the world, with no one to call in times of need. No shoulder to cry on. No one to lift me up out of the depths of despair. The funny thing about alcohol, for me, anyway, was that, once I started to sober up, I turned sappy and melancholy. Reality had a way of showing me my faults—and, trust me, there were many. Too many to count, in fact.

There was a weird energy in the air, vacillating between abhorrence and detestation. Grabbed by the scruff of my neck, I was herded off to my cell to sleep it off, as they say. I got the distinct impression that one wayward look or word on my part, and I would be pummeled within an inch of my life. The disgust was evident on every face I saw as I took my walk of shame to my detention cell. It was more commonly known as a drunk tank or a holding cell, where I was placed with others who had been foolish enough to drive while intoxicated.

I was mortified. The smells of human excrement and pee were overpowering. All I wanted was to crawl in a corner and lick my wounds, but there was no place that even allowed me to think straight. Not that I could have anyway, because my head was groggy, and dizziness was consuming me. So, I did the next best thing and sat my sorry ass down on a wooden bench, careful to avoid splinters this time. I fell into a fitful sleep and dreamt I was covered in sores, crying for help, but no one came.

Having time for self-reflection can be counterproductive at times. Many hours later, I was released, with a promise to appear in court. I stood alone once again, contemplating my life. I was better than this. I knew right from wrong. I was smart. I had determination and was resilient, but there I was, standing in the parking lot of the police station. My clothes were torn and dirty. Thankfully I had sense not to look into a mirror, because I knew what would have stared back would have been a shell of who I wanted to be. A mere image of what I knew I could be.

CHAPTER 32
THE MEETING
JANE

My life has been a whirlwind of uncertainties since I returned home from Lucas' graduation. Watching him walk across the stage was a moment I'll never forget. But now I'm home, living a lie bigger than me. Not only the Lucas lie, but the lie that I secretly despised my pathetic tyrant loser of a husband. I daydreamed about leaving him once and for all. If only I could ride off into the sunset and never look back—it would be heaven on earth. But once reality set in it I was faced with fear—fear that I would die. I wasn't necessarily afraid to die, because, honestly, I was dead inside already. What I was afraid of was dying without being given the chance to make it right with Lucas. To tell him the truth and beg for forgiveness. To fold him into my arms in a warm embrace and tell him how much I loved him.

My new obsession is trying my damndest to get information on Lucas' whereabouts. After receiving the letter that he was being deployed, I'd been a fright. I'd bitten my nails down to their nubs and acquired a set of bags under my eyes that could rival a hundred-year-old cancer patient. My hair had been falling out in handfuls. What I do have left is a dull shade of gray. Going through the motions as a doting wife and mother to the twins was taking its toll, and I was at my breaking point, once and for all.

Basking in the sunshine on the patio, I was trying to breathe some life back into my hollow shell, when I came to the realization that I needed help. Not just help with my mental state but help getting information on my Lucas. I was sick with worry that he had met his demise and was left lying in a sandy ditch, bleeding out in the middle of Saudi Arabia, all alone. Most nights I woke from a nightmare drenched in sweat, my nightgown knotted and hiked up around my neck threatening to strangle me, having visions of death. Any outsider looking into my life would surely understand the angst that plagued me daily. Most would be left scratching their head wondering how I had lived in silence my whole life. But then, most would not understand Stockholm Syndrome and how it worked unless they could swap places with me. It was something I wouldn't wish on my worst, most-hated enemy.

My new plan was dangerous. I would have to be sly to avoid any confrontation from Peter. I could tell he was at his tipping point as well. When he did look at me, it was a leer that shot daggers through my heart. He clearly despised me as much as I did him, but he would never walk away, due to the sheer fact that he would have to admit defeat. That word didn't exist in his vocabulary.

CHAPTER 32 ... THE MEETING

First things first: I booked a much-needed spa date. I hope those poor women possessed a magic wand because they had their work cut out for them—getting my haggard state into something that could pass for semi-attractive. I missed the days when I would look in the mirror and see what Mr. Stanford saw. A self-confident woman with beauty more than just skin deep. That was a thing of the past. Not only did I not look great, but, most importantly, I wasn't a good person. How could I be, to turn my back on my son?

While I was lying in a mud bath, my mind wandered to a tropical beach. Donning a two-piece on my svelte body, I parted my lips as Mr. Stanford plopped a strawberry into my waiting mouth. I stretched my long legs, letting out a cooing sound as he snuggled in close, planting a seductive kiss on my lips, sucking the strawberry juice… "Mrs. Travers, hello. Mrs. Travers, are you all right?" I jerked as I was brought back to the present. What a wonderful dream in my nightmare of a life.

Hours later I emerged a new woman. The gray was gone out of my hair and replaced with a shiny auburn cut into a stylish bob. My pampering had done the intended job, and all that was left was to pick out the perfect outfit for my impromptu rendezvous. With my limited resources, I was pulling out all the stops to find my Lucas. I was prepared to stop at nothing.

Peter was out of town on business, so he said, but I didn't believe anything that came out of his nasty mouth. I have to admit I did a little dance around the living room when he told me he would be gone a whole week. A week of freedom to come and go as I pleased, without having to explain myself and make up lies! With as many lies as I've told over the past years, one would think I would resemble Pinocchio by now. I still had more than a suspicion that Peter was having an affair—but ask me if I cared. Not two shits. In fact, I welcomed it.

As I pulled into the parking garage at Stanford, Bridges and Howe, I was a ball of nervous energy. I had made an appointment under a fictitious name with a bogus problem to discuss. I wasn't sure why I was being so secretive, but I wanted Mr. Stanford to be caught off guard. What I really needed was Mr. Stanford's help. I remembered from my days of working here that private investigators were used on a regular basis. I needed a recommendation for the best of the best to find Lucas.

Running a brush through my hair and reapplying my red lipstick, I parked, taking my time to calm my nerves. I looked good—I knew I did. My spa day had tuned a toad into a princess, and I was ready to make him regret the day he fired me. Lately, I had toyed with the idea of coming clean with him. Peter's threat was still a looming black cloud over my head, but the older Lucas got, the more I felt he was going to be safe from any harm Peter could cause him. I, on the other hand, would be a sitting duck, but it really had never been about me. The reason I signed the contract in the first place was only to keep Lucas safe and alive. I laughed out loud, knowing Peter wasn't a physical threat. Lucas towered over him and weighed twice as much. I would pay big money to watch Lucas crush Peter. But I still had doubts if it was the right thing to do—more like if it was the right time to do what I knew was the right thing to do.

Running a hand over my navy-blue mid-length pencil skirt, I smoothed a crease or two that had formed on the drive over. I could feel my face was flushed with anticipation, giving the perfect amount of color to my cheeks. My slingback heels click-clacked on

CHAPTER 32 ... THE MEETING

the pristine, white marble floor as I made my way to his office, while my heart stopped in my chest. I was a nervous wreck.

Clickety-clack.

Clickety-clack.

Clickety-clack.

I didn't recognize a soul, and, for that, I was thankful. It wasn't the time to take a stroll down memory lane and dredge up old memories. The interior of the law firm still left me in awe. Rich walnut paneling adorned the walls, and it smelled like power and money. I was greeted pleasantly as I approached his office. His secretary was a young stylish girl with long blond hair pulled back, woven smartly into a French braid. Her smile showed a perfect set of pearly white teeth. "Good afternoon, ma'am. Do you have an appointment with Mr. Stanford today?" she asked in a chipper, friendly tone.

Just as I opened my mouth to answer, his office door swung open, and he appeared like the Greek god that he was. He had his head down, looking at a file folder he was holding in his hand. "Miss Rothfield, will you please get me the file for..." He stopped dead in his tracks and gawked at me standing there. "Jane, what are you doing here?" he questioned, while trying to collect his composure, which had disappeared the minute our eyes locked.

He looked like an older, more sophisticated version of the man I had fallen deeply in love with and still pined for, decades later. He still had a full head of hair, but it had turned salt-and-pepper, only adding to his sexiness. There were laugh lines creased around his mouth and a faint scar on his forehead that could easily be mistaken for a wrinkle. I had to suppress the urge to gingerly run my fingers over it before planting a kiss upon it. And his voice. Lord, the rasp was beyond sexy and made my heart beat double time.

Trying to explain the clandestine meeting was more awkward than I had anticipated. It seemed like a good idea at the time I made the appointment, but now it seemed childish and unnecessary. Ushering me into his office, he instructed Miss Rothfield to hold all calls and to bring us lattes. I stood in awe of his memory as he told her *exactly—verbatim—*how I took my coffee. I guess our love hadn't been one-sided, after all.

"What an extremely pleasant surprise to see you here today," he said, adding a wink that made my heart melt on the spot. I lost track of time as we caught up on each other's lives. I didn't have much to contribute to the conversation, since my life was anything *but* pleasant, but I was all ears when he told me about his. Especially the part where I discovered he was single again.

"I unfortunately lost my wife last year to a long illness." He paused and wiped a tear from the corner of his eye. "We never had any children, a regret I have to this day."

Oh, holy crap. This was news to me and made me immediately want to blurt out, *Oh, yes, you do!* Now more than ever, I knew it was the right thing to tell him, but after all the time that had passed, I'm not sure how. Or what his reaction would be. Would he be pissed at me? Not want to meet Lucas? Want to kill Peter? Or me? This is something that can't just be blurted out casually on a whim. Nope, I needed a plan on how, when, and where this was going to happen. The only thing I knew for certain was that it *was going to happen*. I was euphoric, with a newfound purpose.

"Not that I haven't enjoyed our catch-up session, but I must ask. What really brought you here today?" He inquisitively looked at me with raised eyebrows. All this reminiscing had put my real reason

CHAPTER 32 ... THE MEETING

out of my mind, but now I needed to come up with a reason on why I needed some recommendations. So I lied. Again.

"It's kind of a touchy subject, but I think my husband has a hidden life and is cheating on me." I didn't bat an eye as the lies rolled off my tongue, melding one into the other and taking on a life of their own. It seems making up things about a hidden life—clandestine bank accounts, private yachts, you name it, I created within my mind—wasn't above me. I even got caught in my own lies and started believing Peter was a real scoundrel—even worse than in real life. "I need some recommendations for some private investigators because I want to catch him red-handed and leave his sorry ass!" The last part wasn't a lie, at least. I did want to leave him.

Hours later, the sun was setting, and shadows played on his desk from the last bits of filtered light struggling to get through his shutters. I was content and happier than I'd been in years, not wanting the day to end, but knowing I couldn't remain in this joyous cocoon forever. He was everything good I remembered him to be and more, making walking out the door painful. Was I wrong to wish for a life with him? One I had dreamt about for decades only to be awakened by my *real-life* horror show.

Quoting *Romeo and Juliet* in my head, I couldn't have said it better myself: *Parting is such sweet sorrow.* He reached up, grabbing my hand as he enveloped me into a warm embrace. I inhaled his musky scent and clung to him as if my life depended on his very existence. Had I imagined him whispering in my ear that he missed me?

Promising to keep in touch, I left feeling dirty and remorseful but on-top-of-the-world happier than a kid celebrating their birthday. I sat in my car, trying to bring my head out of the clouds and decipher why I had the feelings I did. It's not like I hadn't cheated on Peter before, so why did my meeting with Mr. Stanford feel dirty? And why was I feeling remorseful? Had I grown a conscience? Highly unlikely, but, in my life, nothing surprises me anymore.

Putting the thoughts aside, I looked over the list of five private investigators and called the first one on the list, woozy with excitement on what I might find out about Lucas. I needed to know he was safe. And happy. I needed to clear my conscience of all the torturous things I had put him through. These new feelings of guilt had me questioning my sanity. Had they always been there, or did it take seeing the father of my child to shed a much-needed light on them?

I needed a change, and there was no better time than the present to put Operation Tell-All in motion. I pinky swore with myself that telling Lucas and Mr. Stanford the truth was my main priority. Good things were on the horizon and within my grasp. I could feel it in the air. As I envisioned the reunion, a warmth filled my body as I brushed the tears off my cheeks. I'm coming for you, my son.

CHAPTER 33
THE STRUGGLE

Being on the outside felt like new beginnings. I was in dire need of a shower, a cup of coffee, a new attitude, and a toothbrush, not necessarily in that order. My head had a dull ache behind my bloodshot, droopy-bagged eyes. Six words could sum up my current state… I looked and felt like hell.

Fumbling in my pocket for some change to call Zeke, I came up empty-handed. My watch told me it was 10:30 a.m., which meant I was already late for my scheduled meeting. I despised being late, but not nearly as much as I despised my behavior last night. I had already violated one of the bullet points on my list. Number seven had clearly stated to stay away from alcohol and its temptations. Before when I dabbled in alcohol consumption, it was out of boredom or means to an end, but last night was intentional, and it hit altogether differently. I didn't want to stop enjoying the buzz, although it had me questioning if I had a problem—one that could derail my life if I didn't get it under control.

My head hung low as I took off on foot to find a phone booth. I was feeling sorry for myself, partially because I had no one else to blame but me. Claire would be mortified at my behavior, almost, if not more, than I was. Clouds had rolled in, bringing a nip to the air, making me miss the times we cuddled on the couch wrapped in each other's arms. The memories of our life together flashed before my eyes, leaving me in tears, grabbling for some normalcy again. I think it was being back in Piedmont that was doing it to me. Either that or my pitiful state. Probably both.

I had foolishly left my jacket behind in the truck, I shivered, rubbing my arms with my hands. I sped up my walk to a brisk pace. Before I knew it, I was back at the truck, still sitting sideways in the ditch, covered in a layer of fine dirt. Revving the engine and cranking the heat, I sat contemplating my next move. Had it been wise to come back to Piedmont, where my life had been nothing but one heartache after another? Was a new start in a new place the answer to my happiness? Or was I ever going to be happy again?

The call to Zeke wasn't as troublesome as I had anticipated. I decided on telling the truth, because lies always come back to bite you in the ass. I was over trying to make a good impression. That ship had sailed when he saw me last night, sloppy and stinking drunk. But then again, he was a bartender, after all, making me one on a very long list of people whom he'd seen making a fool of themselves.

My head was pounding, and I was nauseous, on the verge of hurling, while I stood on the doorstep of what I hoped would be my new apartment. This time, *Zeke* was the one who was late, and

CHAPTER 33 ... THE STRUGGLE

I couldn't help thinking it was payback. Turnabout is fair play, after all. I just wanted a place to call my own so I could lick my wounds and drown my sorrows.

Lost in my own pathetic world, I jumped a foot in the air when Zeke came up behind me yelling, "Earth to Luke!" So much for looking cool and collected. Two things I'd never been proficient at, anyway. Luckily, he took it all in stride and laughed it off, clearing the air. It felt good to laugh. I had missed it.

The apartment was small. And depressing. And dark. But I loved it, thinking it was an inanimate object that had my exact personality, minus the small part. Signing on the dotted line, I arranged a move-in time for later in the day. I was about to put some roots down in Piedmont, even though I didn't know what the next day had in store for me.

It turned out that not only my next day was crap but months to follow as well. The days held little promise that I would shake whatever had followed me home from Saudi. It remained like a hovering, black, dismal nightmare. I was sick the majority of the time. The headaches, fatigue, and sleep disturbances I had suffered from while stationed at Fort Leonard Wood had not only continued, but I had added shortness of breath, forgetfulness, and severe joint pains to my growing list of maladies.

I was so miserable I contemplated calling my mom on the off chance I would catch her on a good day. Maybe, just maybe, she would find it in her black heart to bring me some chicken soup. Or, at the very least, an encouraging word. But I thought better of it and struggled through in silence. I had since gotten a job at a construction company. It was a tough pill to swallow, since last time I was here, I had owned Golden Ray, my own construction company, which, by the way, was flourishing under its new ownership. I suffered through the pain on most days, showing up to work, only to come home and collapse. What I did do though, which I was abundantly proud of, was stay away from alcohol. I wish I could take full credit, but, honestly, I was too exhausted to even eat, let alone drink. I was bound and determined to keep it out of my life and turn over that new leaf I had heard so much about.

Having no desire to make my apartment a cozy place to live, I moved my meager belongings into my place on Downward Lane. The irony wasn't lost on me that even the street name described my life to a "t." The walls were painted the color of clay, adding an earth-like appearance that smelt like moldy vegetables. There was one window in the living room that looked out across the street over carbon-copy apartments with landscaping that would give Edward Scissorhands a severe migraine. I owned two prized possessions—and they were sitting on my coffee table front and center. Claire's and my wedding picture sat next to Marmalade's ashes in her wooden box—a reminder of better times, long since gone, taking with them a huge chunk of my heart.

My visits to see Joey and Holly were the only thing that was adding joy to my life, overshadowed by the contempt Alex and Sloan bestowed on me. I was a painful reminder of their only child, and they made it abundantly clear I was tolerated, at best. I contemplated not going anymore. I wasn't big on being where I wasn't wanted, but I put my feelings aside and sucked it up, reveling in the licks and tail wags. I had lived a life of being where I wasn't wanted, and one thing that I would never want to do is to replicate my childhood—now that I had finally escaped that hell on earth as an adult.

CHAPTER 33 ... THE STRUGGLE

I began spending my off-time volunteering at the local animal shelter, where I showered the pets with love. It made my heart happy knowing I was making a small difference. I was humbled by their eagerness to please and the sheer happiness these dogs showed, even after they had been abused and discarded like week-old trash. Their resiliency was nothing short of a miracle, and, once again, I thought to myself, *Dogs are too good for us.*

When I wasn't being plagued by earth-shattering nightmares that often left me in a fetal position on the ground, dripping in sweat and with a frighteningly high heart rate, I was working through the pain, adding funds to my nest egg. When I was younger, I used to refer to all my days as "Groundhog Day," where I would live the same day, day in and day out—like Bill Murray in the movie. Now, I was doing the same thing as an adult. Stuck in a rut and going nowhere quick. It was like I was stuck in quicksand, trying to inch forward, but being swallowed up a little more every second of every day. Until the day that changed everything.

CHAPTER 34
THE VISIT

Clouds had dumped buckets of rain, leaving everything slick to the touch. If it hadn't been for a deadline, I would have been called to take the day off. Days off were my nemesis. I often spent them living in the past, reliving my memories, desperately wanting a drink to escape the pain. It was getting harder to avoid the temptations of alcohol, but I knew what a slippery slope that was. I had finally come to accept that I had an addictive personality. Like it or not, the struggle would be mine to deal with for life.

Rain-soaked, slippery roofs and sleep deprivation were not a good combination any day of the week, but, when you add in dizziness, it's a recipe for disaster. And that's precisely what happened. "Hey, Luke—can you come here and lend me a hand?" Wiping my eyes, I carelessly took two rungs of the ladder at a time, jumping off where my fellow laborer was hammering composite shingles onto the roof. "What's up, Liv?" I said, nonchalantly oblivious to the

CHAPTER 34 ... THE VISIT

dangers surrounding me. As I approached her, my boot slipped on a drenched spot, and I spiraled through the air and over the side of the house, landing at the base of an old oak tree. Time froze as sharp pains shot through my body, and an agonizing scream pierced the air as I lay motionless, broken, and battered. The pain was unbearable as I tried to sit.

Do you know the expression, *Life can turn on a dime?* I was living proof of that. There was a reason I was in excruciating pain. I'd broken my femur, and now I was looking at a minimum of twelve weeks' recovery. Talk about shit luck, but, then again, that's the only kind I ever had. After being rushed to the hospital, I now lay recuperating from surgery, feeling more alone than ever.

My days blurred into one. I survived in a haze of constant pain but drugged out of my mind. I wasn't sure how that would fare with my addiction issues, but, honestly, that was a bridge I would hobble over later, after I was out of the weeds. Right now, they were a necessary evil, keeping me from clawing my eyes out from pain. Thankfully, I slept the majority of my days, or else I would have been forced to face the reality that I had no visitors. Well, no family, anyway, but, then again, that was partially my doing. I had been adamant that no next of kin be notified. I wasn't even sure if my mom would come, so I was trying to spare myself the dagger to my heart if she shunned my request. Better to err on the side of caution.

It turns out feeling indestructible was just a feeling. I proved that shit wrong. One of the dangers of youth. You never think it could be you. But it was, and now I was left to pick up the pieces and try to formulate a plan. I silently chuckled to myself, thinking how many times through the years I had tried to formulate a plan. I obviously sucked at it. Even though I was an adult, I was no closer to having a plan for my future. All I could say for certain was that I needed to leave this place as soon as I was able. OK, two things. I needed to stay away from the temptations of alcohol that loomed in the forefront of my mind 24/7. This latest fiasco would set me back a bunch of time, but I tried to see the silver lining in which I could have a vision and a goal for my future once I hit the open road once again. The plans would have to wait until I was released, though, because planning was not an easy process for someone who was living in a foggy, drug-induced state.

Day in and day out, I lay listening to the heartbeat of the hospital. It never changed, no matter the time of day. The nurses were fanatical about waking me up at all hours. It was cruel, actually, and I think they enjoyed it. The sounds of hurried footsteps down the corridor, the clatter of carts with dishes stacked from meals, machines beeping, and the dreaded *Code Blue* blaring over the intercom system. And, of course, the ever-present sirens wailing all day and night. The smells were something I would never get used to. Antiseptic mixed with bodily fluids was enough to make me want to vomit. And don't get me started on the bland, generic interior of my room. Off-white walls with ivory-colored curtains left little to the imagination. I did have a room to myself, which allowed me some modesty, anyway.

As soon as I was able, I maneuvered my bruised and battered body to my wheelchair and would spend my afternoons looking out the window. My room was facing the front of the hospital, so there was always a flurry of activity, with visitors coming and going, giving me plenty of opportunity to play Claire's and my game of guessing occupations. It helped pass the time and kept me from going stir-crazy. I wouldn't go so far as to say I was ready to run a

CHAPTER 34 ... THE VISIT

marathon, but I was making steps, literally and figuratively, in the right direction. My pain meds were scaled back a tad, but I wished I could have them back to the point where I didn't remember what day it was. I missed the joys of inebriation—when you don't know what end is up so you don't have to face reality.

"Luke, you have visitors," said the chipper nurse with the flaming red hair tied neatly in a bun at the nape of her neck. She busied herself plumping my pillows and raising my bed to a semi-sitting position. I cautiously opened an eye, grunting in discomfort, hoping they would go away. I wasn't in the mood for small talk or pity. My mind was still a tad foggy, and I slurred my words while searching for the right ones. Not a great recipe for meaningful conversation. "Oh, come on, Luke. Put a smile on that handsome face. It'll be just what the doctor ordered," she pleaded, while I continued to grimace and curse under my breath.

Just as I was about to beg her to send them away, my mom and dad peeked their heads around the curtain that hung from the ceiling, separating my bed from the room. The nurse patted me on my good leg while whispering "Be nice" under her breath. And then she was gone, leaving me se to face with the two people I never wanted to see again.

My mom looked better than I had seen her in the past. Her hair was dyed and cut in a smart bob. She meekly smiled at me as she took a chair by my side. "We read about your accident in the *Daily Gazette*. We wanted to give you a chance to start feeling better before we came to visit." I immediately noticed a twitch in the corner of her eye, as she turned pale right before my eyes. I didn't respond but cautiously turned my head to look at my dad. He hadn't aged well and, if possible, looked smaller than usual. His ever-present sneer was prominent on his ugly face. I couldn't remember the last time I saw him smile.

"So I imagine you were drunk on the job, leading to your careless fall. I'm shocked anyone would hire you in the first place with your despicable track record. Who would want someone like you working for them, giving them a bad name?" His face was contorted and red, as if he were unhinged and on the verge of a stroke. One could only hope.

I lay speechless. I wasn't about to get into a shouting match with the likes of him. But, surprisingly enough, my mom came to my defense and said, "Peter, how dare you accuse Lucas of such a thing? You have no proof to make such outlandish accusations." It was like I was watching a ping-pong match, with my head swiveling back and forth as they sparred about me like I wasn't even in the room. Their voices got elevated, which caused the nurse to scurry into the room. With a look of abhorrence and her eyes as big as saucers, she calmly said, "I'm afraid you'll have to leave. My patient needs his rest." She was my new hero.

My mom collected her purse from the end of my bed, smoothed her wrinkled dress, and apologized before patting me on the cheek and wishing me well. My dad, on the other hand, huffed out without another word, but his eyes spoke volumes. He yanked my mom's arm, causing her to squeal in pain. I couldn't help but yell, "Don't let the door hit you on the ass on your way out!" That, my friends, was my dysfunctional family in a nutshell, and, if I never saw them again, it would be too soon.

After eight days in the hospital, countless pills, and an assortment of disgusting meals, I was discharged with a bag of medication, a stack of prescriptions, and a referral to physical therapy. I was never

CHAPTER 34 ... THE VISIT

so happy to smell fresh air, as I sat in my wheelchair, waiting for the medical transport to come give me a lift back to my apartment. Life as I knew it was on the verge of changing.

Finding it almost impossible to maneuver around my apartment, I was determined to make it work without help. I didn't want to be a burden on my fellow workers or on Alex and Sloan, so I spent countless hours racked out on the couch. I continued to take my meds even when I started to feel better, loving the hazy state of oblivion they left me in. All was right with the world when I didn't have to be part of it. Traveling down this path was dangerous, but I'd given up caring weeks ago.

I managed to go to physical therapy only because I deemed it a necessary evil. It was painful, which led me to medicate more. I was living in a vicious circle of despair, with no way out. I put my wedding picture in the drawer, so I couldn't be judged by Claire's face. I hated disappointing her, but I didn't know how to stop. I was still suffering from the multitude of issues I had prior to the accident, which sent me in search of answers to the vet hospital. I was finally diagnosed with Gulf War Syndrome on top of my PTSD. I fell into a state of depression and began to drink again, thinking I was a lost cause.

And I was a lost cause. I lived in squalor and filth. My days and nights morphed into each other, not remembering one thing that had happened. The pharmacy cut me off of the pain pills, only causing me to drink more. I ended up in the vet hospital trying to detox. *Trying* was the operative word here. An addict has to want to change to make a change. And I didn't want to.

Every now and again in my drunken, wasted haze, I thought I heard a knock at the door and my mom's voice reaching out to me. Getting myself off the couch to answer was more than I could be bothered with, no matter how many times she tried. I didn't care, so I didn't respond. I continued my descent into the desperate world of darkness until one night another intervention was held. I was livid. Well, at least as livid as I could be while stumbling over my own two feet.

My mom, dad, brothers, Alex, and Sloan all stared at me, shaking their heads with the same look of repugnance as I tried to articulate why I didn't need help. It wasn't very effective when every other word was slurred and unrecognizable. Why had my dad even bothered to come when I knew he despised me? The others tolerated me on a good day. Today wasn't one of those.

Leaving them standing in the kitchen to talk behind my back, I went into the bathroom to throw water on my face and caught a glimpse of myself in the mirror. I *think* it was me, anyway. It was the face attached to my body, but I was unrecognizable. Days-old stubble, swollen eyelids covering red-rimmed, inflamed vacant eyes, a ruddy redness to my puffy cheeks, and hair that was standing on end, filthy with grease. I stunk to high heaven. I couldn't remember the last time I had showered or brushed my teeth. A layer of film covered them, making the inside of my mouth taste like a rancid, stale bottom of a rubbish bin. My T-shirt that was once white had crusted-up remnants of barf and spilled food on it, camouflaging the color. I sat on the toilet seat, bent over, with my head between my hands, rubbing the sand out of my eyes, fighting off the urge to vomit.

"Lucas, it's your mother. Can I come in, please?"

"Leave me alone!" I shouted with a voice that was raspy and crackled. Moments passed as I listened intently for footsteps leading away from the bathroom, but none came.

CHAPTER 34 ... THE VISIT

"Luke, please. I'm begging you," she cried, choking back tears. *Oh, hell—no good could come out of this.* With just enough alcohol coursing through my bloodstream, I knew I would have no filter, which would result only in hurt feelings. Once again, I questioned why I cared. No matter how horrible of a drunk I was, I still had morals and feelings. So, I remained silent until I heard the front door slam, knocking Marmalade's collar and leash off the coat rack I kept by the front door.

I peered around the door, making sure the coast was clear. How had I allowed my life to become a person I barely even knew—or would *want* to, for that matter? Opening up the fridge, expecting a stale loaf of bread and a twelve pack of Coors, I saw it fully stocked with fresh eggs, a wedge of manchego cheese, salami, veggies, strawberries, and milk. A loaf of freshly baked sourdough bread lay next to a tub of butter and a jar of peanut butter on the tile countertop. Tears sprang from my eyes. The only person who could have done this was my mom. Maybe she had paid attention through the years, and knew my favorites. Maybe this was the olive branch I had prayed for my whole life. Maybe she loved me after all. Maybe it wasn't too late for us, knowing in my heart I was wishing for something that was never to be.

The food tasted better than I could have imagined, as I sat like a scavenger demolishing the whole loaf of bread and half of the other groceries in record time. I hadn't realized how famished I was. I let out a huge belch and wiped my mouth on my T-shirt before remembering how disgusting it was. I padded to the shower and stood under the hot steam, while going over some of the awful things my dad had said to me during the intervention. Showers always cleared my cobwebs and made me think clearer, with a focus.

He wasn't wrong. I was acting irresponsibly and out of control, with no consideration to anyone other than myself. I was wallowing in self-pity, and, yes, I did indeed have a problem, but I honestly didn't think I was trying to get attention, like he accused me of. He was especially harsh when he said I was a big disappointment and was dead to them, but, then again, I would have expected nothing less. I cringed when I remembered him calling me a *no-good loser* and the *black sheep* of the family. Visions of myself sitting on the stairs as a twelve-year-old came flooding back. It had hurt then, and it hurt now. The only difference between now and then was that I no longer gave a shit what he thought.

Alex and Sloan had stayed silent, with their heads bowed, unable to look me in the eyes. I couldn't say that I blamed them much. I was a bit of a disappointment. A small piece of me felt like they understood my dilemma because they missed Claire as much as I did. It wasn't just about the loneliness I felt but more the need *to not feel*. Plain and simple, I was an alcoholic, and it was about time I realized I had a problem. A problem I needed to face head-on if I wanted to make myself proud again.

Not wanting to admit that the intervention was a bit of a wake-up call, I couldn't help but see it for what it was. It made me take a step back and re-evaluate my life, seeing myself as others did. It wasn't a pretty picture, although, deep inside, I knew I was still the same me. The one who was resilient, determined, and kind. And smart. Smart enough to know coming back to Piedmont had been a monumental mistake—and one I was about to rectify. Broken, beaten, with a limp—*and* a new addiction—it was time to start over, someplace the demons and ghosts didn't come visit me every day and night. But I had one thing to do before it was time to leave.

CHAPTER 35

THE SHELTER

Hopping out of bed with new determination, I jumped into my truck, doing my best to ignore the achy joints and headache that was ever-present. The Gulf War Syndrome maladies were brutal. Coupled with my new limp and PTSD, I had to laugh at my misfortune. If I couldn't laugh at myself, I might as well crawl into a hole and cover myself with dirt.

The last time I had done volunteer work at the local shelter, I had my eye on a yellow labrador retriever named "Cali." I felt like this was an omen, since I was about to make my trek to the west coast. I would have gladly taken Joey and Holly with me, but I knew their life was with Alex and Sloan now. They were living the life of Riley and loved Rowdy. It would be cruel to uproot them. They'd always hold a special part in my heart that was reserved for my animals. I had done some research in the past about therapy dogs and how beneficial they were with people suffering from

PTSD. I was sure Cali was the missing puzzle piece to complete my transformation.

It was like old home week as I walked through the doors. "Luke—oh, my goodness! How are you?" I was asked by everyone I came in contact with. I mustered up a smile bigger than I felt in my soul and lied telling everyone I hadn't been better. If I were as proficient at quitting alcohol as I was at telling little white lies, I'd be golden. Even so, I felt like royalty, even though I knew I looked like death warmed over. I beelined to Cali's pen, and, lo and behold! She was still there, curled in a ball sleeping on an old threadbare blanket. "Hey, girl—it's me, Luke," I whispered so as not to scare her. The excitement on her face and the tail wags were enough to make my whole month. I knew right then and there that it was a match made in heaven. Not only was *I* rescuing *her*, but *she* was rescuing *me*.

As we said our goodbyes, I felt like my heart had grown wings. The excitement a shelter dog has when getting adopted is unmatched by any other type of joy. I rolled the windows down, and a warm blast of wind blew through as she held her head out the window, ears flopping and slobber flying. I hadn't been this happy in months.

Making plans to move away for good took a bit of planning. When I wasn't at the park with Cali, I was making my list, so as not to leave any stones unturned. I had recently contacted the Veterans Affairs office to see what, if any, compensation I could collect due to my unfortunate PTSD and Gulf War Syndrome.

It was getting increasingly more difficult every day not to give into the temptations of alcohol, but I procrastinated and told myself that, once I got out west, I would join AA and find a sponsor to keep me on the straight and narrow. I desperately needed help, as I caught myself drooling over the thought of being lost in the haze of

CHAPTER 35 ... THE SHELTER

inebriation. The pull was stronger than I imagined, begging me to take *just one sip*. But I kept with the plan, not knowing how much longer I could hold out.

Cali was a godsend. She had an innate ability to know when I needed her the most, which, honestly, was most of the time. I had healed as much as I was going to by now, but I still had a dull ache and a limp as reminders of my accident. I doubted that would ever change, making the desire to drink even stronger—if that was even possible. I was in a pitiful state both mentally and physically, making the impending move more important than ever. I was hoping to be able to make a fresh start, with different scenery and projects to focus on; it would be the magic pill I was searching for.

I wish I could say my days were full of optimism, but it was anything but rainbows and unicorns. If anything, it was more like monsoons and centaurs. The seasons had changed once again, and recent bouts of thunderstorms had soaked the ground, leaving beautiful wildflowers in their wake. Summer was always a welcome change after the brutal winters and dismal, dark days that only intensified my depression. There was something about the sun high in the sky that gave me a newfound optimism, which had been woefully lacking recently. Even as a young boy, I had loved to feel the sun on my shoulders, warming my soul, and having a smile appear out of nowhere.

After a day of chores and planning, Cali and I were pooped. That girl was full of energy, but she knew when it was time to settle down as well. We stretched out on the couch; while she rested her head in my lap, I stroked her fur, instantly feeling a calm wash over me. I contemplated the letters I wanted to write prior to my departure. I had always been a bit of a loner, but now, more than ever, I couldn't care less about people in my life. I felt I owed an explanation of my absence and future plans to a small handful of people who had been placed in my path to show me much-needed guidance and love.

The list was small, including Aiden, Paige, and Harry. As I searched through my memories, Ivy popped up, with her lopsided smile and chopped copper hair. I said a silent prayer that she was safe and well, wherever life had taken her. I saw Theo sitting on his veranda, laughing his contagious belly laugh as he held his stomach. What a tragedy his death was. I guess leaving Piedmont once and for all had made reminiscing come easier.

Leaving me in a melancholy mood I pulled out my stationery and began to pen the letter I would send to the three people who had made an impact on me. I was still on the fence about writing one to Alex and Sloan. As for my mom, she didn't deserve one, but I couldn't shake a voice whispering in my ear that she cared more than she let on. I wasn't altogether sure I believed it, but I sure wanted it to be true. There was no denying she had done some snooping around to find me, so I guess she deserved a couple of brownie points for the effort.

Dear (Aiden, Paige, and Harry)

I've been negligent in my attempt at keeping in contact as promised. My sincere apologies for being a slacker. I'm back in Piedmont after being honorably discharged due to medical reasons. I won't bore you with the details, but, suffice to say, I've been messed up. I recently recovered from a nasty fall that broke my femur, but I've since healed as well as expected. After hours of reflection, I've realized coming back here was a mistake. So, I'm taking the bull by the horns and taking a road trip to beat all road trips and heading out

CHAPTER 35 ... THE SHELTER

west. Ever since I was young, I've had a strong pull to the Pacific Northwest. The idea of living among the trees and feeling one with nature appeals to me. I won't promise I'll be better at corresponding once I plant roots, but I'll try my damndest to let you know where I end up. You are in my thoughts, and I want you to know how much your friendship means to me.

Your friend,
Luke

Feeling a little pissed at myself for being lazy and taking the easy way out by writing one letter and adding their names, I knew that was all I was capable of in that moment. I had deliberately left out the alcoholism part. I was ashamed to admit I had a problem. I decided I owed it to the pups to say goodbye in person, so, no letter for Alex and Sloan, since I could tell them in person. I half expected them to jump for joy at the thought of never having to cross paths with me again.

Now the hardest one. I paced back and forth, running my hand through my hair, trying to pull out the right words. I wanted things to be different. I *always* had, but, clearly, it was what I was, so I poured my unfiltered thoughts and feelings out onto paper.

Dear Mom,

I'm leaving Piedmont for good. Not sure why I feel the need to tell you, but something in my heart hopes that you'll do an about-face and love me. My whole life, all I've ever wanted was your love. But all my life, all I've ever gotten was your pity and disgust. It hurts more than you know. I've tried to act like I didn't care, but I'm tired of pretending. You need to know what you've done to me and, hopefully, suffer a little of the pain I've endured for years. My whole life, actually. It's been a meager existence—trying to muddle through as best as I can without wearing the scars I feel in my heart on my sleeve. Do I blame you and my sorry excuse for a dad for my alcoholism? Yes, I do. I've tried a variety of coping mechanisms through the years to block out the pain, and alcohol is the one that allows me to erase the memories for a short period of time. When I'm drunk, I don't have to face the reality that my own mother hates me. I'm trying to do better and take some of the responsibility on myself, because, ultimately, I haven't been force-fed.

Have a good rest of your life, mother. I hope I cross your mind once in a blue moon. When you see a golden retriever, think of me and Marmalade. That is the one good thing you did for me in my whole life.

I love you,

Luke (the son you never wanted)

Wiping tears from my eyes, I was drained, physically, mentally, and, most definitely, emotionally. I felt sorry for myself. Sorry for what should have been. I wasn't sure I wanted to write that I loved her, but I needed her to know, and maybe she would feel a sense of sorrow for what she had done—or, more appropriately, what she *hadn't* done. I could rinse my hands of her and Piedmont forever now. And never look back.

I shoved the four letters into their corresponding envelopes and placed stamps in the corner, except for my mom's, and breathed a sigh of relief. I put it all out there for her to read in black and white. I wasn't expecting a reply. Even if she found it in her black heart to reach out, I would be long gone. An inexplicable sadness

CHAPTER 35 ... THE SHELTER

washed over me, making my desire for alcohol stronger than usual. I grabbed Cali's leash, my mom's letter, and made a mad dash out the door so I wasn't tempted any longer. A ride in the summer air was just what I needed.

Planning to drive by my mom's house to drop off the letter, I was hoping she wouldn't recognize my Ford F-150 truck I'd purchased upon arriving back home. Turning down the street hit me like a ton of bricks. It hadn't changed one bit, but I had. A couple houses down the street from my old house, I pulled over and stared, lost in a sea of memories. I saw a silhouette of myself and Marmalade sprawled out on the front yard under the big willow tree that still stood strong and tall, with its wispy leaves blowing gently in the twilight. Memory after memory came flooding back, colliding into one another. My head felt like it was about to explode, and a blood-curdling scream emerged out of nowhere, bringing me back to reality. I didn't realize it had come from *me* until Cali was sitting, whimpering and licking my free-flowing tears. I was wrecked from taking a walk down my nightmare childhood lane.

Looking both ways, I ran across the street, dodging between trees so as not to be seen until I reached the front porch. I placed the letter under the same sunflower welcome mat she'd had for years, wondering what she'd think when she found it in the morning. I wasn't concerned that it would fall into the wrong hands, because the front door was used by my mom only to grab the paper off the lawn in the morning. As I started my truck to drive off, a feeling of profound sadness engulfed me. Was I running away from my problems? Should I stay and confront them? Was there life away from here?

My mental state was in the depths of hell. I needed a drink, so I took off toward the *Hops and Harmony* to drown my sorrows. I hated the fact that I had let my memories take control of me like this. Not thinking clearly, I pulled into the parking lot and looked around. I witnessed couples stumbling out of the bar, drunk on their ass, making complete fools of themselves. I was envious that they were cocooned in a mist of obscurity. I wanted that feeling for myself, so that I didn't hurt so bad, but when I made a move to open my door, Cali barked and pawed at my arm. "It's OK, girl. I won't be long. Daddy just needs to drown his demons right now so we can start fresh out west."

I swear she understood, because the more I made a move to leave, the more she barked and grabbed at my shirt. I waited till she calmed down, trying to reassure her and make her understand, but she wasn't having it, so I did the responsible thing and drove away. It took all my willpower to listen to her and leave from the one place that could make me forget. Chalk this up as one more day I dodged a bullet and remained sober.

One week remained for me to tie up loose ends in Piedmont and confirm the moving van. I didn't have much, but what I had was mine. It offered me a sense of security in a world that was spinning in another orbit faster than I could keep up. My days were filled with struggles and wondering what my mom thought when she read my letter. I was filled with doubts and questions, too many to answer. Why had she not even made an attempt to say goodbye?

CHAPTER 36

THE BRUSH WITH DEATH
JANE

Talk about an impetuous time since my visit with Mr. Stanford. My rendezvous was everything I could have dreamed it would be and a million times more. Was I wrong to daydream of a life with the man I had pined my whole life for? Or would he even want me all these years later? I wasn't the beauty I used to be, that's for sure. That's what living a horrendous nightmare will do to you.

After I left him looking hot as hell in his office, my feet still have not touched the ground. I was as euphoric as a sixteen-year-old school girl with her first crush. Keeping the smile off my face has been near-impossible, but I can't let Peter see how happy I am. This would surely alarm him that something was out of the ordinary. Not that I really care what he thinks, but it was more the hassle of having to make up more lies. One would think I had a list a mile long ready to pull from at a moment's notice, with as much lying as

I had done in the past, but this was different. Now that I've made the agonizing decision to come clean and spill the truth to Lucas and Mr. Stanford, I didn't want anything to stand in my way. When I was a woman on a mission, watch out!

Busy wouldn't begin to explain how I was spending my days and nights. Busy *scheming,* that is. I took it to heart when Mr. Stanford said to keep in touch. I wasn't about to let that invitation slip through the cracks wondering whether he meant it or not. I saw a golden opportunity to sweep the man of my dreams off his feet, and I'll be damned if I didn't try to get my fairytale ending after all. I deserved it after spending my life under the watchful eye of an ogre. The best part was, he wouldn't even see it coming.

First things first—and most important—was finding my Lucas and praying he was safe. The private investigator I hired eagerly accepted the job. I waited, not at all patiently, until I heard back, all the while making steps to set my plan in motion. Assuming Luke was safe, that is. If the unthinkable had happened and he hadn't made it back from Saudi, I don't know what I'd do. Would I still fess up to Mr. Stanford? I don't think he'd forgive me. And then what? My life would be over. No Luke. No Mr. Stanford. No life.

Wait. Wait. Wait. I was getting way ahead of myself. *One thing at a time*, I told myself. While I waited for word, I took every opportunity, even creating my own, to talk to or see Mr. Stanford. I needed to get him to the place where we were before—before I screwed everything up by acting like a lovesick puppy, getting myself fired for my indiscretions.

I showed up at his office, under the pretense that I was in the neighborhood, each time making sure I looked perfect from head to toe. I was shameless, hiking up my dress on my thigh and caressing

CHAPTER 36 ... THE BRUSH WITH DEATH

my leg seductively, while casually licking my lips. I had a bouquet of his favorite peonies sent with a note attached that read "Let our dreams blossom. XO J" I called a few times just to let him know he was in my thoughts. Then I waited a couple of days to see if he would make the next move. Lo and behold, he did. He was as smitten as I was, so it was time to step it up.

One evening, as I was relaxing and dreaming about a life away from here, I got a phone call from Mr. Baldwin, the private investigator. He had found Lucas safe and sound, back from Saudi Arabia, in one piece. Faring well was another story. He seemed to be having a tough time adjusting with life away from the front lines. *A tortured soul* is how he was described to me. It broke my heart knowing he was alone. In all actuality, he had been alone most of his life, thanks to my stupidity. I don't think I'll ever forgive myself for doing what I'd done. If only I could turn the clock back and muster up the balls to leave Peter years ago. But the fact remains that I was scared half out of my mind for my son. I still got a tingle down my spine reliving the nightmare of the night I was forced to sign the harrowing contract.

Peter, thank God, had been traveling a great deal lately. Or so he said. It didn't matter what the truth was, as long as he was out of my way. The twins had their own lives and were seldom home for long, so I was left to come and go as I pleased with no explanations or convoluted lies to concoct. Mr. Stanford and I stepped it up a notch and went out to dinners off the beaten path, always acting discreetly in public, but, once inside, we were like horny teenagers unable to keep our hands off each other. Secret rendezvous to hotels where he always spoiled me with trinkets and seductive kisses. I never knew sex could be this good, and I was addicted to him in every way possible.

Happiness hadn't been part of my life for so many years that I found it hard to embrace it to its full potential. It was as if I were waiting for my bubble of joy to burst; I would be left with a broken heart, a shattered ego, and a shitty life. Being true to his awesome self, Mr. Stanford did his best at making me feel wanted, appreciated, and loved. Yep, I said *love*. We were in love once again. For me, I'd never stopped loving him, but he had enjoyed a good marriage with a tragic ending. I couldn't help internally celebrating even though I knew it was wrong to find joy in someone else's misfortune. I seriously questioned my morals sometimes.

I kept Mr. Baldwin on the payroll and was sporadically given updates. None seemed positive, as Lucas continued to struggle in silence. Knowing this reassured me I was making the right decision by telling Lucas the truth. Once everything was out in the open, he would never have to be alone again. I often let my mind wander, imagining one big reunion and a happy-ever-after for us all. Was I delusional, or was this finally within my grasp?

As much as my head was floating in the clouds, most days I had to use a level head as I walked a tightrope on the days Peter was at home. I said it before, but it bears repeating… he was no dummy. He had a keen sense for knowing if things were amiss. Age had only intensified his surly disposition. I honestly felt nauseous in his presence and found it taxing on my mental state to pretend I enjoyed his company. But I mentally counted the days until I could serve him with divorce papers and walk out for good.

Time escaped me as it flew by in the blink of an eye. Recent news on the Lucas front was that he was being medically discharged and

CHAPTER 36 ... THE BRUSH WITH DEATH

supposedly heading home. I did a happy dance in the closet when I heard this. Peter was still none the wiser, or so I hoped. Knowing him, if he was on to something, he wouldn't be able to keep it to himself. He would most certainly blow his stack, sending all the animals in the neighborhood running for cover. His tirades came often, and my self-esteem took a beating—along with my face—every time. I contemplated letting Mr. Stanford see the physical damage Peter inflicted on me, not wanting pity but, ultimately, decided it could only work in my favor. Chivalry was not dead with him, always the gentleman.

Peter came home one night, stinking drunk, out of his mind with rage, looking for a fight. I cowered in the corner, knowing full well where this was headed, although that made him angrier for some reason.

"What the hell's wrong with you, Jane, and why do you look so smug all the time? It's apparent you haven't looked in the mirror lately, or you would have probably committed suicide already, you stank whore!" he shouted while grabbing my hair and jerking me out of the corner.

Inward, I screamed in pain, but there was no way I was about to let him see the anguish he was causing. This only made him madder, lashing out and connecting with my right eye. Doubled over in pain, I struck back. This was something new, because I had always been submissive to a fault. No more of the old Jane anymore.

He stood confused while spitting in my face. "What has gotten into you? Don't you know your place after all these miserable years together?"

I was livid, as a sort of animalistic scream came out of me, yelling, "Fuck off, Peter, you sorry excuse for a man. Does hitting me make you feel like a big man? Is it your Little Man Syndrome rearing its ugly head?" The more I yelled, the madder he got, but I couldn't control myself any longer. And then I said the unthinkable: "I want a divorce immediately!" It wasn't planned. I was planning to wait and serve him, but it came tumbling out. He stopped dead in his tracks and spat out, "Over my dead body!" All I could think was, *Don't tempt me, Peter. Don't tempt me.*

Not giving him an opportunity to respond further, I grabbed my purse and flew out the door. As I peeled out of the driveway, I looked back and saw him standing at the living room window with a look of utter confusion and his tail tucked firmly in between his ball-less crotch. My hands were shaking as I tried to calm myself. I took a peek in the rearview mirror, assessing the damage to my face. My eye was already beginning to bruise and was closed, leaving only a slit to stare back at me. Needing to contain my rage, I pulled over and sobbed. Why had I let it come to this? Or was I less tolerant because I knew what true love felt like?

Making a rash decision, I drove in a blur to Mr. Stanford's house, wanting the protection I knew he would offer. Knocking hastily at the door, I heard his all-too-familiar sexy rasp yell, "Just a second. I'm coming." And then he was a vision as he opened the door and collected me in his strong embrace before questioning me on what the hell had happened. To say he was beyond irate was an understatement. It took everything in my power to calm him enough so that he wouldn't go flying out the door in a rage, ready to pulverize Peter. Not that I wouldn't have paid to see that, but I didn't want him caught in the middle of my dysfunctional marriage.

Gently pressing ice against my eye, he listened intently as I outlined the series of events that had led to Peter's outrage. I wondered

CHAPTER 36 ... THE BRUSH WITH DEATH

how it had escalated so quickly. Clearly, Peter was unhappy, but I refused to be his punching bag. Been there, done that. Trust me when I say it's not ever OK—under *any* circumstances. As I lay sprawled on Mr. Stanford's rich maroon-colored velvet chaise, I couldn't help but reminisce. Had it always been this bad, and had I turned a blind eye? Was I going to get into a fight for my life pursuing this divorce?

I yawned as Mr. Stanford rubbed my feet. A girl could get used to this. "Please tell me you'll stay with me tonight," he begged, batting his heavy-lidded dark-chocolate eyes. "I need to know you're going to be OK." Who was I to protest? Besides, I wasn't about to show up at home. There was nothing left for me there, besides the twins, of course, but they'd understand.

Stretching, I let out a little purr as he collected me in his arms and carried me up his grand staircase. The coolness of his silk sheets wrapped me in a seductive caress as I rolled over, putting my head on his manly, chiseled chest. His heartbeat escalated as he rubbed my back, his touch igniting something in me that had been extinguished years ago.

"Good morning, my love," he whispered as he nibbled my earlobe. Today was going to be a great day. Despite the dark clouds looming overhead, threatening to ruin my day, I was feeling on top of the world. We had talked well into the night, making plans for our future together. I pinched myself thinking I would wake up any second and come face to face with my demon seed of a husband. My future was looking bright, and even *Peter* couldn't put a damper on that. Or could he? I knew he'd try his damndest, because he wasn't happy unless I was miserable. I had to dig deep to remember the last time I heard him laugh. What a pitiful life he lived.

Making plans to meet up later, I finally worked up the courage to return home. Peter was nowhere in sight, so I quickly packed an overnight bag in case he had planned a rerun of last night. Something inside of me had snapped. I didn't recognize who I was last night, but I liked it. *Jane the badass* had a nice ring to it. Emotionally, I was still a tad fragile, and, physically, I was a wreck, but, mentally, I was getting stronger by the day.

Lucas is here! Lucas is here! Lucas is here! Mr. Watkins called this afternoon with an address where Lucas was now residing. Whooping with joy, I rushed out of the house to do a drive-by. I was going to have to choose my time to approach him wisely, since he obviously wasn't keen on getting in touch with me. Can't say that I blamed him.

Hiding behind a trash can across the street, I peered through some binoculars, hoping to get a look at my handsome son. The neighborhood he'd picked left a lot to be desired. It was a dump. Overgrown shrubbery and dead grass struggling to survive lined the outside of his apartment on Downward Lane. What a depressing name for an equally depressing place.

Hours passed before I was rewarded. Hearing a honk, I was jerked out of my trance. A taxi was sitting in front of his house, and he was coming toward it, jumping in the back. I gasped. He was so thin and pale-looking. *My poor baby*. What had he been through? I stood as I watched the taxi round the corner. *I'll be back, Lucas—don't you worry.*

I daresay, my life was boring on the home front. Peter returned days later, but nothing was mentioned of the dreaded night. He stayed clear of me, and I of him. I was biding my time until the time was right to make my move. Mr. Stanford remained patient. And perfect. The man had no flaws. Not only was he handsome beyond

CHAPTER 36 ... THE BRUSH WITH DEATH

words, but he was perfection in every way. I was so over the moon in love I couldn't see straight. We spent every minute we could with each other. Every minute was a slice of heaven.

One dreary morning as I was sitting, towel-drying my hair from the rainstorm that had soaked me while searching for the morning paper, I did a double take. An article tucked in the local news section read *Local Man Falls from the Rooftop, Lucky to Be Alive*. My hand went to my mouth as I screamed. My Lucas was lucky to be alive. I needed to see him ASAP. Dropping the paper onto the table, I ran upstairs to change, not knowing Peter had been lurking.

"Where do you think you're going?"

I ignored him, pulling clothes out of my closet.

"I asked you a question, Jane. There's no need to be rude."

"Uh, I'm going to the grocery store. I just realized we're out of milk."

Before I knew it, he flew across the room and grabbed my chin. His face was contorted as he yelled, *"Don't lie to me. I saw the article in the paper, and if you think you're going to the hospital to see that albatross without me, you're sadly mistaken!"*

The moment of truth was upon me: Fess up, or lie, again. I knew he would follow me, as mad as he was, so I confessed, choosing to pick the battles I had a chance at winning.

We drove in silence, the tension in the car unbearable. The rain had continued with a swift breeze blowing sideways, turning my umbrella inside out. Running to the entrance, Peter was on my heels; he grabbed my arm, mumbling, "No funny business, Jane."

I yanked away, scowling at him. *How dare he?*

Putting a smile on my face, I peeked around the curtain shrouding my son in privacy. He looked like he'd been through the wringer. His coloring was ashy, and a grimace was noticeable, even though he was trying hard to camouflage how he felt. I took a seat by his bedside, explaining how we had learned of his unfortunate accident.

I knew the fact that Peter had come along with me was a bad idea, because he immediately went ballistic, accusing Lucas of hurtful things. It turned ugly. And we were ultimately kicked out, when all I wanted to do was wish Lucas well.

Pissed didn't begin to explain how I was feeling, especially when he had the audacity to grab my arm and belittle me for showing Lucas a bit of compassion, for once in his life. I had already known he was going to find an issue with it prior to going into the room, but I didn't care. I felt like a rebel, finally taking matters into my own hands. Did the man not have any compassionate genes in his body at all?

From the minute I saw the pain Lucas was in, I was scared for him and his addictive personality. Would the pain medication cause withdrawals, leading him to turn to alcohol again? I became obsessed with driving by his apartment regularly. Numerous times, I knocked and pleaded for him to let me in, but he never answered. I must have looked like either a crazy woman or a stalker as I put my ear to the door, listening for signs of life. Knowing he was in there and ignoring me sent a dagger through my heart. *Well, what I was expecting? I would have ignored me, too.*

My heart broke all over again when Mr. Watkins called, telling me Lucas had been drinking again. Damn it—I *knew* it was going to be hell weaning off those pain pills. He explained in vivid detail the problems Lucas was having, and I shuddered, remembering the last time he hadn't been able to control himself. I knew another intervention was imminent, so I rounded up the troops. I decided to keep Peter in the dark, but that asshole was everywhere, listening

CHAPTER 36 ... THE BRUSH WITH DEATH

in. He despised Lucas more now than ever, if that was possible, so I braced myself for the onslaught of hatred he'd spew.

Knowing it wouldn't be pretty, I couldn't have visualized what a mess Lucas would actually be. His T-shirt was crusted with vomit, and he smelled to high heaven. His apartment reeked like it hadn't been cleaned in months, with a layer of mold in the kitchen sink. The bathroom hadn't fared even *that* well and turned my stomach. The whole place needed to be bombed and burned to the ground.

As expected, it didn't go well. Actually, that was being generous. It was more like a disaster. One needn't be a psychic to know Peter would lose his shit. He came out swinging, and Lucas tried to defend himself against Peter's unfounded allegations, but he slurred his words, not able to form a coherent sentence. I wanted to give him a hug and tell him I loved him. That I would be there for him, no matter what. That his real father was a successful attorney who would love him unconditionally. But I bit my tongue and painstakingly watched him suffer.

"Lucas, please let me in," I pleaded after he had holed himself up in the bathroom. Peter came to see where I was, pulling my arm to leave. I escaped his grasp and flipped him off. I knew I would pay for that later, but all that mattered right now was Lucas. I got no response. He had shut me and everyone else in his life out for good. Jiggling the door handle, I found it locked. "Please, Lucas," I begged, but all I got in response was silence.

Everyone was still gathered in the living room, staring blindly at nothing. I had managed to sneak a bag of groceries by putting it in the oversized tote I often carried. Peter was none the wiser until I started unloading it. He gave me a death stare but maintained a level of sanity, only because Alex and Sloan were there. He was always big on keeping up appearances. I didn't plan on hanging around the house long enough for Peter to use me as his punching bag, so I continued to arrange all of Lucas's favorites. I hoped that, when he ventured out of the bathroom, he would be pleasantly surprised. That's the least I could do.

Impressed with myself for thinking in advance, I had brought my own car. I hopped in, blowing a kiss towards Lucas's apartment. *It's not going to be that much longer, son,* I whispered. *Hold on. I love you.*

And I sped away to a location Mr. Stanford and I had set up last night. I couldn't risk Peter following me to Mr. Stanford's house. If he were to find out what I'd been up to, I was positive he'd kill me. Now that I had something to look forward to, I couldn't and wouldn't let that happen.

My time with Mr. Stanford was pure, unadulterated bliss. He was everything a decent human being should be. Impeccable manners, chivalrous, attentive, romantic, and totally swoon-worthy. To think I had wasted all my years on the likes of Peter made me question my judgment. But then again, I hadn't really had much of a choice during Lucas' formative years. I cursed myself again for allowing myself to get into this awful predicament.

Unfortunately, I couldn't avoid Peter forever, so I came home later the next day. I found him sitting at the kitchen table, staring at the back door we used when parking in the garage. He looked like he hadn't slept, with bags under his eyes and the same clothes he had on yesterday. I tried to avoid him and walk by, but he moved like a jaguar and cut me off at the pass. That's when I noticed the Smith & Wesson revolver sitting on the table. I was hoping he was going to use it to end his miserable existence, but I was no fool. He loved himself much too much for that.

CHAPTER 36 ... THE BRUSH WITH DEATH

"Where have you been, Jane? Huh? Out whoring around?"

I gave him the silent treatment, which only egged him on.

"What do you think your punishment should be?" he asked as he nonchalantly picked up the gun. The sunlight streaming through the bright-yellow curtains caught the metal, giving it a sinister gleam. "Did you actually think I'd let you disrespect me like that and renege on the contract? After all these years, I thought you'd learned your lesson." He rubbed the nozzle along my cheek before forcefully prying open my mouth through gritted teeth. It was cold against my tongue, with a metallic taste.

It's true what they say about when you see your life flash before your eyes. Visions of Lucas as a baby. His military graduation. Mr. Stanford lying on silk sheets, with dried whipped cream on his naked body. The way he whispered, *I love you, my little blue J.* The twins' football games.

But not one memory of Peter. Not a single solitary one. I zoned out trying to find a happy place for my final moments when the most glorious sound pierced the air.

"Mom, dad? You guys home?" Christopher shouted from the entryway as he burst through the door. Peter scrambled and yanked the gun clumsily from my mouth knocking a molar loose in the process. He quickly tucked it under his belt, placing his shirt carefully over it. "In here," he yelled, putting a fake smile on his face as he placed his arm around my shoulders, drawing me close. *"Don't breathe a word if you know what's good for you,"* he whispered with his rancid breath.

CHAPTER 37
THE LETTER
JANE

Everyone has an expiration date, and I thank my lucky stars mine wasn't up today. Needless to say, I hightailed it out of there. Peter had taken his threats to a whole new level, and I wasn't about to find out what he was actually capable of. Things are pretty bad when you have to stalk your own house and watch for when Peter would leave. In the meantime, I parked my car in a downtown parking garage, and Mr. Stanford picked me up and took me to his house. One could never be too careful.

One morning I watched from afar as Peter loaded up some suitcases into the trunk of his car. Thank goodness he was going on a business trip! At least for a couple of nights. The twins were away at a baseball camp, so I was free to come and go as I pleased. A slight-but-welcome reprieve to give me a chance to go in and pack up some stuff. I breathed a huge sigh of relief. I looked down at my

CHAPTER 37 ... THE LETTER

hands; they were shaking uncontrollably, and sweat was running down my neck despite the cool morning air. My nerves were shot.

I tiptoed to the back door only to find my key wouldn't work. Damn it! That asshole had changed the locks. I sat on the patio and cried. Tears hadn't come freely lately, but someone had turned a faucet on, and, now, they wouldn't stop. I'd always heard tears were therapeutic and cleansing, so I let them flow, hoping they would give me clarity. They didn't work and left me looking a fright, with black mascara streaming down my cheeks. Somehow my life had taken a one-eighty while I hadn't been paying attention.

Not thinking there was a chance in hell my key would unlock the *front* door, I cautiously tiptoed like a ninja to the front. As I fumbled with the door, I heard a click before it popped open. I should have known he wouldn't be smart enough to think of changing the locks on *both* doors. Swinging it open, I noticed an envelope peeking out from underneath the welcome mat. My heart skipped a beat when I saw "Mom," written in Luke's handwriting. Barely able to contain my excitement, I skipped over to the olive-plaid wingback chair in the living room and opened it up.

Reading in silence, I couldn't believe the words. Just when I thought the tears had subsided, they erupted again, this time turning into sobs of regret and sadness. Moving away was bad enough, but to read how he thinks I hate him and never wanted him. It crushes me. All my maternal instincts that I've buried away for years came flooding back. I wanted to go to him immediately and tell him the truth. Tell him I loved him and that I'd *always* loved him with my whole heart. I loved him so much I had done what I did to save him. Would he understand? Would he see me as a horrible, emotionless monster? It was a risk I was going to have to take. And the sooner, the better.

Immediately running to the study, I grabbed my sunflower stationery and poured my heart out to Lucas. It was time.

Dear Lucas,

Please keep an open mind when reading this, and try to understand why I had to do what I did. First, and, most importantly, I LOVE YOU. I've always loved you. In fact, I adore everything about you, and I'm so incredibly proud of the man you have become. I won't bore you with the details, but, suffice to say, living with your dad hasn't been a bed of roses. So much so that I broke our wedding vows and had an affair. I fell in love with someone else, but it got messy. An affair that ended much too soon but not before I got pregnant. I ran back to your dad, crushed but determined to make it work. And it did—until it didn't.

For four glorious years, we showered you with the love you deserved. I was on top of the world, ecstatic to be a mother to such a perfect angel. All was right with the world, until your brothers came. They didn't look like you. Or act like you. They looked like your dad, and you most definitely didn't. Your dad is no dummy and started putting two and two together. One fateful night, he confronted me. It turned ugly and violent. I seriously was scared for your life—and mine, for that matter. I confessed and begged forgiveness, but that wasn't enough for him.

He drew up a contract that I was forced to sign, stating that I was to have no contact with you. I was forbidden to love you or show any type of affection, or he would kill you and then me. I didn't care about myself, but I would do anything for you. It's been pure torture throughout the years watching you struggle, begging for a hug. There were times I would have found death a better option than having to turn my back on you. I'm sure by now you're asking yourself why I didn't pack up and leave. That's a good question—I've asked myself numerous times throughout

CHAPTER 37 ... THE LETTER

my life, but hindsight is always 20-20. I was suffering from Stockholm Syndrome and half scared out of my mind. I know your father would have made good on his threat.

Not that this is any consolation now, but I have stayed in your life. I was at the airport to see you off to boot camp. I watched you graduate from boot camp as my heart swelled bigger than I thought imaginable. I hired a private investigator to make sure you made it back from Saudi Arabia in one piece. I couldn't sleep at night not knowing if you were safe or lying in a ditch somewhere, bleeding out.

I've done this for you so that you could grow up into adulthood. The only reason I'm telling you now is that you're an adult, and I don't think your dad is a threat to you any longer. You can hold your own and honestly topple him with one uppercut. Something I would love to be present for, cheering you on every step of the way.

I'm sure you're wondering who your biological father is and why he never came to your rescue, or mine. I never told him about you. He was married and loved his wife. I knew it would destroy what he had, and I had already ruined too many lives at that point. I was in too deep with the contract and your dad's devious schemes. You've actually met him. His name is Gregory Stanford, one of the partners at Stanford, Bridges and Howe law firm. He was the attorney that handled your grandparents' trust. I recently became reacquainted with him, and we've fallen in love. His wife has since passed, and he had no children with her, a regret he recently shared with me. There is nothing for me with your dad, and, now that you have a life of your own, it's time we both move on. I am going to tell Mr. Stanford about you tonight, but I already know he will love you. He's a good man, and the funny thing is, you look just like him. Even your raspy voice sounds like him.

My one wish is we can finally be a family—the type of family I've wanted my whole life—filled with love, respect, and affection. I'm truly sorry, my son, but please know I did this out of the tremendous love I have always had for you.

With all my love and admiration,
Your loving mom

Wiping the splattered tears off the desk, I had poured my heart out, hoping with everything I had that Lucas would find it in his heart to understand and forgive me. It was a big ask. But he had a huge heart and enough love to share. I prayed that he would choose me to share it with.

No matter how great my relationship with Mr. Stanford was, the gravity of my secret weighed heavily on my mind. Now that I knew Lucas was moving, my day of reckoning had come. I had been waiting for the perfect time, but, up to this point, none had presented itself. Now the luxury to pick and choose has vanished.

I had been extra quiet, mulling over the letter I had discovered on my front porch this morning. "Penny for your thoughts, my beautiful blue J," he cooed as he tenderly kissed my cheek. I loved it when he called me that. It was a little pet name he had started months ago, and I couldn't get enough.

"Um, err, um, I have something very important to talk to you about," I said as I nervously chewed my fingernail. I was having more trouble starting than I thought I would, so I decided to dive right in and spill it all. "Promise me you'll hear me out before you ask questions. Then and only then can we discuss it."

His eyes opened as big as saucers as he nervously said, "You're scaring me a little bit. What's wrong? I'll listen intently. Whatever you want."

CHAPTER 37 ... THE LETTER

I love how supportive he was and how much love shone through his eyes. "I know I don't need to remind you of the affair we had twenty-five years ago, although, I will add, it was some of the best times of my life. I thought I loved you then, but that is nothing like the love I have for you today," I gushed.

He smiled and took my hand in his, gently rubbing his thumb over mine in a calming motion.

"Well, what I never told you was, when you fired me, I was pregnant. You have a son. His name is Lucas." The color drained from his face as he stuttered, "I, I have a, a, a son, you say?" I nodded, soaking in the joy that was immediately apparent. He started to ask a question, but I silenced him with a finger to his mouth. He couldn't help himself and blurted out, "Tell me more. I want every single detail from the beginning until today."

Before I could answer, he jumped up and ran out of the room. I heard banging coming from the kitchen and inaudible mumblings. I held my breath. Was he pissed? Had I blown my one shot at happiness? I was totally in tears and in my head when he scooped me off the couch and twirled me in the air. "Oh, my precious blue J, you've given me the best news a man could ask for," as he popped champagne and poured me some bubbly into crystal flutes.

Talking well into the night, I explained it all. Every last gory detail of the contract, the abuse, the shame. I cried. He paced. His emotions ran the gamut, from joy, to sorrow, to hate, to bewilderment. My anxiety was through the roof, wondering if I would be forgiven for withholding Lucas from his dad for twenty-five years. Was our love strong enough to withstand the lies and deceit?

After his initial reaction of joy, he had gone silent. A myriad of emotions showed on his face as I spoke, but I had no inkling of what he was thinking. Or feeling. I decided to give him some space to sort through the nonsense—plus *I* needed some fresh air. Glancing back before I walked through the door, I saw him sitting with his head bowed, resting within his hands perched on his knees.

"I'm going for a walk to clear my head."

A grunt was all I got as a response.

What had I done? I tried to put myself in his shoes. I could understand why he'd be confused and definitely angry with Peter—but me? Even though I had loved Lucas, I had never shown it. My mind was in turmoil; I wondered if the happiness that had been within my grasp had now been swept away like the ocean tide.

The tree-lined streets blurred into one another as I walked mile after mile. I found a bench at a nearby park and watched the sun come up. Mother Nature had painted the sky in a pinkish hue, waking the birds, who happily chirped around me. I was envious of their happiness, without a care in the world. The world was cruel, and I had been dealt a devastating hand.

"Please, God, give me a chance to make it right," I pleaded as I bowed my head in prayer.

The only clarity my walk had given me was that I needed to do what should have been done years ago. Lucas needed the letter to read and hopefully allow me to repair the damage that had been done. If I could only get the two most important people in my life to understand my hand had been forced, or Lucas wouldn't be alive today. If it was the last thing I did, I would somehow make him understand—or die trying.

"Excuse me, miss. Is this seat taken?"

I jerked my head up to see Mr. Stanford standing over me. He looked wiped out. Almost as bad as I felt. His hair was poking up in

CHAPTER 37 ... THE LETTER

a million different directions, and a pained look in his eyes I couldn't describe had formed overnight. Even with his slight imperfections, he was still the most handsome man ever to grace the planet. He held his hand out, which I hesitantly took.

"Are you OK, blue J? I've been combing the streets for hours, looking for you."

I gulped down my nerves and meekly asked, "Does that mean I'm forgiven?"

He stared at me for what seemed like an eternity before a smile emerged, and he pulled me into his arms. "How could I ever stay mad at you? After all, you've given me a son. Now let's go get to know that boy of ours!"

My plans got derailed, but I couldn't tell Mr. Stanford "No." After all, I owed him so much, and it was time to make up for the last twenty-five years. We were going over tonight to give Lucas the good news. I compromised by agreeing that I would give Lucas the letter to read prior to him meeting his dad. If my calculations were correct, he was set to drive out in the morning. The happiness I had was nothing like I ever knew was possible. My two men were going to meet, and I was about to get my happily ever after. *I'm finally coming, Lucas.*

CHAPTER 38

THE ACCIDENT

Packing up my apartment was more laborious than I remembered. But here I was, ready to leave after the moving van came this morning to take away my stuff. I stretched and gave Cali a scratch under her chin, as she let out a contented sigh. I was wrong about my mom. She hadn't made an effort to see me off. *Had she not found my letter?* I wondered. Or was I delusional to even *think* she cared at all?

Walking to the corner to grab a coffee and give Cali a quick walk, I saw caution tape strung from stop sign to stop sign and a tremendous amount of broken glass and rubble in the street. Workers were diligently sweeping in an attempt to clean it up.

"What happened out there?" I asked the barista as she prepared my latte with a double shot of espresso. She looked puzzled as she scratched her head. "I'm not altogether sure, but I heard there was a fatal car accident last night. Supposedly a couple was killed by

CHAPTER 38 ... THE ACCIDENT

someone running a red light." Thanking her, I grabbed my coffee, and Cali, as I tucked the *Daily Gazette* under my arm, thinking about what a tragedy that was and how some people have shit luck.

Whistling all the way home, my mood was optimistic. I was about to embark on yet another adventure, one I knew was the right move. I had a spring in my step, and I hadn't felt this sure about anything ever before. "Ready to go on a road trip, girl?" I asked as I spread the paper out on the table. Passing the time, I read about farmers markets, local band competitions, and other meaningless articles until I came across a picture of the accident from last night. The headline read "Two Killed in Fatal Accident." I picked it up, looking closer. I gasped and dropped my coffee, scalding my hand. *Why was my dad standing there looking at a mangled-up car? And, furthermore, what was the paper he was intently reading?*

Scanning the article for names, my heart stopped when I read my mom's name as one of the deceased. Wait. What? She was right down the street last night? Was she coming to see me? And who was this "Mr. Gregory Stanford," whose car she'd been in? Why had my dad not notified me, especially when he was in my neighborhood? Questions swirled around, begging for answers.

I grabbed a magnifying glass out of my box labeled "Junk Drawer," scanning the picture for clues. My dad looked pissed, but, then again, that was his norm. But why would he look pissed after being notified that his wife had just perished? Shouldn't he look sad and distraught? I zoomed in on the paper he was transfixed on, but I couldn't make anything out. Digging through the same box, I pulled out a flashlight and shone it directly on the paper in my dad's hands. Wait, did I see a faint name at the top that looked like it said "Lucas," or was I imagining things?

My mind was all over the place. I felt overwhelming sadness for the loss of my mom. Not just for her passing but also for the passing of any opportunity we may have had to make it right. Tears sprang from my eyes, and I screamed out of pure frustration. Oh, how I hated dilemmas! Not only did I *want* answers—I *needed* them, but that meant confronting the person I hated the most. Time was a huge issue, since the truck was due to arrive within the hour. But didn't I owe it to myself and my poor mom to find out all I could? Making a rash decision, I beelined down to the corner again to use a pay phone. Out of breath and feeling overwhelmed, I called the moving company to postpone for a couple of days. I was in desperate need of a drink to take the edge off prior to my confrontation with my dad. I had a sinking feeling that it wouldn't go well, but I had to try.

Cali jumped in, riding shotgun, as I sped off toward the place I never wanted to see again. Summer was upon us, and the temperatures had already reached a crispy eighty-five degrees, giving the sensation that I was taking a trip to hell. Actually, I would have preferred *that* over having to see my dad again. As I pulled up in front of the house, the willow tree was weeping. There was a profound sadness covering the house, making it appear as it were mourning the loss of its matriarch. The curtains were pulled tightly closed, and an eerie vibe oozed out from the windows.

As I collected Cali for moral support, I walked slowly to the front door, feeling like a dead man walking. The all-too-familiar doormat sat happy, welcoming me in, but I felt anything but happy or welcome. Taking some deep breaths, I patted Cali for luck and rang the bell. I counted to twenty, thinking no one was home, when my dad threw the door open. He'd never been a handsome man, but I wasn't prepared for what stood in front of me. He was in his

CHAPTER 38 ... THE ACCIDENT

bathrobe, which was stained and ripped. Used tissues were spilling out of the pocket. I don't remember ever seeing him cry, but it was apparent that he had been consumed with tears for the better part of the night. Bloodshot eyes and a runny nose looked up at me like they had seen the devil himself.

"Hi, dad. I read about mom in the paper this morning and wanted to offer my condolences and ask you a couple of questions."

The silence was like "crickets," like he'd not even heard me. "Did you hear me, dad?" I inquired.

"Yeah, I heard you. I was just wondering what made you think it was all right to come over here and bother me. Last time I saw you, I made it abundantly clear that you were dead to me. Are you too dense to understand that? Now get off my property before I call the cops!"

I wasn't even sure I had heard him correctly. He was cruel and harsh, without an ounce of compassion in his voice as he sneered at me. Although I shouldn't have been surprised, I was, especially under the circumstances.

He started to slam the door in my face, but I stuck my foot in the entryway to block it. "I just have a couple of questions. Can't you find it in your heart to humor me for once and show me the respect I deserve?"

More stares and silence before he spoke again. "First of all, get your foot out of my house," and then he burst out laughing, like I was George Carlin at a comedy show. He then spat at my feet and mimicked me with mockery and contempt before he slammed the door.

What just happened? I wondered, as I stood dumbfounded, at a loss for words. That went over like a turd in a punchbowl. I guess I was never going to find out what was in the letter or why my mom was with Gregory Stanford. But I could still find out who he was. Maybe that could shed even the smallest amount of light on what the reality was. Getting in my car, Cali and I drove off as I gave my dad one last middle-finger salute. What a dick he was—and a huge disappointment!

The library was located in the middle of town, so, instead of taking Cali all the way home and back again, *plus* the fact that I desperately needed her for moral support, I packed her along with me. Once I got to the door, I saw that guide dogs and therapy dogs were welcome, so we entered, on a mission. There was no way I would leave her unattended in my car with temps as hot as they were today. Cozying up in a corner, I fired up the computer. I wasn't the most efficient at navigating around the Internet, but having done research on PTSD, I was familiar enough. I typed "Gregory Stanford" in the search engine, and a multitude of articles and an assortment of information popped up before my eyes.

I knew his name had a familiar ring to it, but I hadn't been able to place it as the attorney who'd helped with my grandparents' will, until now. Article after article praised him and the many accolades he had received. I sat in awe of the successful man he'd once been. What a waste of a wonderful life. As I opened an article, a picture appeared, and I caught my breath. It's like I was looking into a mirror. The same chiseled jaw. The same color of eyes. The shape of our noses was strikingly similar. I wracked my brain to the meeting Claire and I had had with him at his law firm. I remember finding something familiar about him, and it was clear that my mom knew him. She had been like a schoolgirl—euphoric, crushing on the star athlete. *Didn't she used to work for that law firm before I was born?*

CHAPTER 38 ... THE ACCIDENT

My mind was reeling with possibilities. Could *he* be my dad, instead of the despicable one I had? That would explain a lot of things, especially the way my dad treated me like I had the plague. But why had my mom been so distant and almost ashamed of me? Was she feeling guilty about having an affair? I couldn't stop speculating and devouring every morsel of information I could find on him. The more I read, the more convinced I became and lost all track of time until I felt Cali nuzzle up to my leg. A light tap on my shoulder brought me back to reality. "I'm sorry, sir. You're going to have to leave, because we're closing for the night." *Damn—just when I felt like I was making progress.*

Driving home in silence, I marveled at the sunset. Bright oranges and reds joined together to paint the sky a spectacle of vibrant colors. I couldn't help feeling as if it were celebrating my mom's life. Honestly, I was getting a little tired of tears lately, but, once again, I found myself consumed with grief, and tears streamed down my cheeks, choking me with emotion. Was I sad for what could have been? And then it hit me. *I was responsible for my mom's death.*

My apartment was off the beaten path, miles from home, so she must have been coming to see me. Why else would she be in this neighborhood? Maybe she'd read my letter and wanted to explain? Maybe the two of them, my mom and biological dad, were coming to tell me the truth? Now all I could think about was that, if it hadn't been for me, she wouldn't have been at the wrong place at the wrong time, and she'd still be alive.

Spinning out of control with every possible scenario under the sun, I combed through all the articles that I had printed out from the library. My head was so far down the rabbit hole that I was suffocating, but I couldn't stop. Cali sat by my side, lending a helping paw when I was on the verge of losing my shit. I didn't want to think about what could have been. What I wanted was a drink so I could forget and drown my sorrows by getting rip-roaring, stinking drunk.

Feeling utter remorse for the accident was eating me alive. It was apparent my so-called dad wasn't going to be any help, so I drove myself down to the police station seeking answers. The hustle and bustle of everyday life at the station was irritating me. I needed answers *yesterday*. Waiting for my turn, I picked at a thread on my T-shirt, watching in amazement as it unraveled; was it mimicking my life? An hour later, with frazzled nerves and no patience, my number was called. Digging deep, I tried to put a smile on my face and be polite, when, in actuality, I wanted to rip someone a new one.

"My name is Lucas Travers; I'm the son of Jane Travers, who lost her life in a tragic automobile accident the night before last on the corner of Downward Lane and Prospect Avenue. I would very much appreciate it if I could talk to the officers who were first on the scene." I pleaded my case, looking as pitiful as possible, which wasn't much of a stretch because I was further down in the dumps than I'd been in years. Holding my breath, I eagerly watched him rifle through some paperwork and check the computer before picking up the phone.

"Hey, Terrance—Patrick here. I've got a kid down here at the desk who says he's the son of a fatality from an accident you responded to the other night. Do you have a second to come talk to him?" The man, named Patrick Donahue, winked at me and gave me a thumbs-up before saying, "He'll be down in a bit, son. Take a seat."

Perspiration was dripping down my back, soaking my shirt, despite the air conditioning blowing at full speed. I waited on pins and needles. I wished Cali were by my side to give me support, but,

CHAPTER 38 ... THE ACCIDENT

instead, I sat alone, counting the seconds down as I stared at the analog clock that hung clumsily at a slight tilt against the gray wall.

Tick, tock.

Tick, tock.

Tick, tock.

At my wit's end, I was about to hurl when a man about my height came barreling through the door in a rush. He had a crew cut and a gnarly scar that ran the length of his cheek. But his smile was friendly as he held out his hand to shake mine. "Officer Terrance Chesham here. Pleased to meet you. 'Lucas,' is it?" After all pleasantries were over, he escorted me into a room that was used for interrogations. Inside was a metal table and two metal chairs sitting across from each other, with a camera mounted on the wall. I felt like a criminal.

Even though I was not religious, I said a silent prayer that the answers I was desperately seeking would be forthcoming. He spoke first. "First of all, my condolences. I was told you have questions regarding the traffic accident."

I nodded, explaining how I'd found out and my eagerness to know more about the letter my dad was holding.

"Just curious, but why don't you ask your dad?" he asked while raising an eyebrow. I wasn't in the mood to spill my dirty laundry. It was embarrassing, and I'd rather forget my dad ever existed, so I told a little white lie.

I tried to look convincing as I said, "Honestly, he's so distraught over my mom that I don't want to add more to his plate right now." That seemed to pacify him. *Whew!* I thought as I wiped my brow.

He looked at me with a sympathetic smile and said, "I don't know the specifics of the letter, as I didn't read it. It was clutched tightly in your mom's hand, resting upon her heart when I arrived at the scene. I'm sorry to say she was in bad shape, but she managed to whisper your name, saying that it was important that you got the letter. Shortly after that, she passed before the paramedics arrived. Your dad was called as next of kin, and he told me he would give you the letter. All I saw was the name 'Lucas' written on the outside of the envelope. Does that help?"

Having trouble speaking, I managed to eke out a "Thank you" and stood up on my wobbly legs. They felt like jello, making it difficult to walk, but I managed to get into my truck before I collapsed, distraught. How could he keep the letter from me? Knowing him as well as I did, I was positive he had destroyed it by now and would even deny its existence. His ego was much too big to accept that my mom was with another man—or even the fact that I might find out the truth and live a happy life. I had hit a brick wall at a thousand miles an hour and was shattered. The one thing I was convinced of that brought a much-needed smile was that my dad really wasn't my dad. I couldn't think of any news that could have made me happier.

Somehow managing to make it home without a pit stop at the *Hops and Harmony*, I collapsed onto my bed, with Cali spooning me and licking my hand. So many unanswered questions and no possible way to get answers was going to eat at me for a long time. I was also going to have a hard time not blaming myself. Too many people in my life had died. Was I the common denominator? A bad seed, like the Grim Reaper? Just one more reason to remain a loner.

CHAPTER 39

THE MOVE

After a restless night of feeling sorry for myself, I woke to the sound of a woodpecker outside my window. I lay in a sleepy daze, being lulled back into sleep by the rhythmic pecking, until an urgent pounding on my door sent me scrambling. Throwing on my jeans and a polo shirt, I threw open the door to see the movers, waiting with their dollies. I had been so wrapped up in the letter drama I had totally forgotten that I had rescheduled moving out for today.

Moving was never a walk in the park, but I was actually looking forward to this one. I had overstayed my welcome in Piedmont. Wanting to put as much distance between me and my imposter dad was on top of my list of things to do. I still had questions, plenty of them, but I knew getting answers from Peter was a dead end. I had decided I wasn't going to refer to him as "my dad" anymore, because, in my heart, I knew he wasn't. Plus, he'd never once acted like it, mentally abusing me every chance he got. Rifling through the memory of my childhood paid some big dividends, as it helped to put many things in perspective. I remember numerous times my mom would be lost in thought, daydreaming with a smile across her face. I often wondered what she was reminiscing about. It saddened me beyond words knowing I would never know why my mom treated me the way she did and why I never got a chance to meet my biological dad.

As far as I could tell, he had no family to contact—a sad ending to an otherwise stellar professional life. When I was younger, I had contemplated becoming an attorney. I wondered if it was a "Like father, like son" kinda thing. I'd never know. For my own sanity, I needed to let it go. The truth had died with them.

Deciding to leave before my mom's funeral was another thing weighing on my mind. I couldn't stand the thought of having to see Peter ever again. I was afraid, if I ever came face to face with him, I wouldn't be able to control my anger. No good could come out of that. As for my brothers, we were never close. It was clear they cared for me about as much as I cared about them, since they hadn't even come to say "Hi" when I was there the other day. My whole life, they had stuck together, and I was always the odd man out, constantly being subjected to their relentless ridiculing. They were the spawn of the devil himself, a carbon copy of Peter. They could all have each other. I knew it was petty, but I couldn't help hoping they would all have a miserable rest of their pitiful lives.

The packing went quicker than I expected, and I was left standing in an empty apartment with only Cali and my steadfast demons. I felt more alone than ever. I kept telling myself over and over again that I needed to let it go, but I was having trouble. I had the

CHAPTER 39 ... THE MOVE

strongest gut feeling that I was very close to finding out the truth. The only problem was, as it stood now, it was pure speculation on my part; all the definitive answers had evaporated like a puff of smoke. Although it all made perfect sense, the missing puzzle piece was still gone—maybe forever.

Cali and I took a walk down to the corner. I don't know why I was torturing myself, but I felt an irresistible urge to go. It was as if my mom was summoning me. Standing there, looking out into the abyss, I closed my eyes. I could see my mom and "dad" in love. They were holding hands, laughing and happy that they were going to share the secret of my whole life. I heard the crash, and I jumped, scaring Cali as she let out a yelp.

Lost in my own world, something caught my eye in the gutter. A sparkle glinted in the sunlight, and, as I bent down, I saw a Rolex watch. Picking it up, I instantly recognized it as the one my "dad" was wearing in one of his pictures. I held it close, thanking the gods who had intervened, giving me something to hang on to. I might not have the letter, but, in my heart and soul, I knew the truth. Not only did I know the truth, but, now, I had something of his to cherish. Securing it on my wrist, it was a perfect fit. I would treasure it forever.

Saying my final goodbyes, I could have sworn I heard my mom say, "Be well, my son. I've loved you from the moment I set eyes on you. Your dad loves you, too." I looked around, expecting to see her standing there, hand in hand with him, but all I saw were people frantically racing about, living their lives without a second thought about anyone else.

In a weird way, I could feel them here with me. A warm sensation passed over me, as a tingle ran from my head to my toes. No matter how foolish I looked to others, talking to the air, I was positive they had been waiting here to see me and have one last reunion before floating off to heaven. And that's when I had my eureka moment. I put my hands out, immediately feeling warmth within them. They needed to know I was going to be all right. "Mom, dad, I swear from this day forward, I will make you proud. I will lead with my heart and show compassion and kindness. I'll be a son you will be overjoyed to call your own." I was choking on the tears streaming down my face when I felt a wind pick up and a swirl vanish into the air in a circular motion. Right then and there, I knew they were gone but smiling down from above.

Cali started turning in circles, whimpering as if she had felt a presence unlike anything else. "It's OK, girl. We can go now. I've said my proper goodbyes. It's you and me against the world, with a couple of guardian angels to lead the way." A calm washed over me, and a feeling I'd never felt before touched my soul. I was at peace. My demons could be put to rest. I had the rest of my life to make them proud, and that's precisely what I planned to do.

Walking back to my apartment, I felt a weight lifted off my shoulders. By no means does that mean I'll forget about the abusive childhood I'd had. How could I? It has shaped me into the man I am today. It taught me to be tough and resilient, traits I admire. Besides, forgetting and forgiving would be giving my mom and Peter a get-out-of-jail-free card, which they hadn't earned or deserved.

Taking one last look around, I loaded up my remaining boxes, a suitcase, and Cali's bed. The open road was calling my name. The moving van was going to unload my belongings into a storage unit until I could settle in to some place to call my own. The possibilities

CHAPTER 39 ... THE MOVE

were endless. For the first time in a long time, I had something to look forward to.

One last pit stop to say goodbye to the pups before I made my adventure out west. This would be the last time I would ever see them, and that thought made me misty and reflective. I couldn't help thinking I'd failed them somehow. If only Claire was still around, my life would be so different. Not only would I still have the pups, but I'd have a child of my own, and, most importantly, I'd still have her. Me, a dad? It had a nice ring to it. Although I never picture myself with anyone but Claire, one never knows what the future holds. I'm living proof of that. Maybe I'll be lucky enough to become a dad someday. One thing I could swear on, if I'm fortunate enough to have that happen, I will give them the world. The love and acceptance I had craved my whole life would be theirs, tenfold. No questions asked.

I was feeling a tad apprehensive about seeing Alex and Sloan, since the last time had been at the intervention, where they stood quietly off to the side; their disgust and disappointment evident in their body language.

"Luke, what brings you here today?" questioned Alex as he ushered me into the living room. "I assume you've come to see the pups, who are grabbing some sun rays after a swim. Sloan and I want to offer sincere apologies for the loss of your mother. Such a tragedy for everyone involved." As Sloan breezed around the corner, I did a double take. I hadn't noticed the similarities between her and Claire as much as I did today.

"Hey, Luke. I heard my name," she said as she gave Alex a sideways glance. I couldn't stop staring, tuning out my surroundings until I realized they were talking to me. I must have looked like a lecherous pervert, but when I apologized, she took it in stride, telling me she'd heard that millions of times before. It was awkward to say the least. I never had gotten the impression I was on their list of favorites to start with—they simply humored me for Claire's sake. Now, with my latest bout with alcohol, they barely tolerated me. But, then again, I wasn't there for them.

Was there anything better than the exuberance of a dog? I'll wait while you try to think of something, because, honestly, there's not. As I peeked around the door leading into the backyard, Joey perked his head up at the sound and sprinted toward me, ears floppy and tongue out. Holly and Rowdy weren't far behind, and, pretty soon, it was a huge dogpile, with me on the bottom, having the time of my life. As grumpy as Alex and Sloan were around me, they couldn't help but laugh. After an hour of dog licks and kisses, I explained to them that I was leaving town and moving out west. After everything that had happened in Piedmont, there were too many ghosts and bad memories to keep my head in the right place. They nodded and said they totally understood. I doubt I'll ever hear from them again, but that was fine. They were a sad reminder of what I had lost. Kissing the pups and telling them I loved them, I left to pick up Cali and hit the road.

CHAPTER 40

THE CABIN

I had been a tad concerned about how I would handle all the time in the truck with just my thoughts and the highway, but I was pleasantly surprised. As I drove mile after mile, with my box with Marmalade's ashes in it and my picture of Claire tucked tightly next to me, with Cali riding shotgun, I was guided by my two guardian angels.

In a weird way, I found driving therapeutic. I never thought it would be something I was proficient at, but I had the whole process down to an art. Having traveled from Fort Jackson to Fort Leonard Wood and then from Fort Leonard Wood back to Piedmont, that time with my body and ego bruised and beaten. My poor body had taken a beating for its mere twenty-six years. My Gulf War ailments were insufferable, at times causing debilitating symptoms. Coupled with my limp from my fall, I was in constant pain. Luckily, I wasn't on a tight time schedule, so Cali and I pulled over every couple of hours or so to stretch our legs.

After almost three thousand miles and six days, driving through countless states, we crossed the Oregon border, feeling exhausted, sore, and thankful. I fell immediately in love. The air was fresh, smelling of Christmas. It must have been the huge pine trees that dotted the landscape for as far as I could see. I pulled over at the first state park I saw. As I was sitting under the canopy of branches, a slight breeze blew them in cadence with my thoughts. I was enveloped in silence. It was golden. Whoever had been the observant person who had said that, had nailed it. I watched in bewilderment as Cali ran among the trees, weaving in and out, chasing butterflies, with her tail in full whirlybird fashion. Project happiness in progress, activation launched.

The smells, the sights, the people were perfect. I immediately felt like I had found my home—someplace where nobody knew me and my pathetic past. Free to make a life for myself and Cali from scratch, no expectations. No eyes of judgment boring into my back. No painful memories staring back at me through tears of sorrow. No random chances of running into Peter and the twins. I felt free as a bird to fly with abandon, making decisions as I went.

As a child, I had always dreamt of living in a log cabin with some land for animals, so when I was scouring the real-estate section of the paper, I stopped and did a double take. The description sounded too good to be true, causing me to question my good fortune. I wasn't accustomed to having luck on my side. Laughing to myself, the exact opposite had been true. It was more like the

CHAPTER 40 ... THE CABIN

Grim Reaper had taken up residence in the spare room, waiting to strike at a moment's notice.

"Rustic cabin in Mount Sierra, sitting on ten acres of land available for immediate occupancy. Adjacent to the forest, the possibilities are endless. Don't miss this once-in-a-lifetime opportunity. Price: Negotiable. Please call Ponderosa Realty at (971) See-Home or (971) 733-4663. There was a small picture attached that caused my heart rate to elevate with excitement. It was made out of ginormous logs with a stone chimney jutting out of the middle of the roof. Surrounded by trees, it looked perfect and secluded. I had never heard of Mount Sierra, but, then again, it wasn't like I was an authority on the towns in Oregon. Cali and I had been staying at the edge of the Tillamook State Forest, getting the lay of the land for the past week, but I was itching to plant some roots.

Doing a little happy dance, I called the number immediately and arranged to meet up tomorrow. Keeping an open mind with my fingers crossed, I was hoping this would be an answer to my numerous prayers. I had been kicked in the teeth too many times to count, and I started to get ahead of myself, dreading the disappointment I was sure would follow. I took a deep breath to bring myself back to reality. I was getting my hopes up, and, truthfully, things very rarely worked out in my favor, although I had a good feeling about this one.

Sleep didn't come easily that night, and I woke the next morning with a splitting headache and negative thoughts. I hated that about myself and had been told in the past that I tended to shoot myself in the foot before I ran the race. It was easier that way—not trying so that I wouldn't fail.

I had been working on the negativity that consumed my thoughts, but old habits were nearly impossible to break—yet another product of my environment growing up. I rarely was good enough or worthy of good things happening. But this time was different. I was different. A metamorphosis had begun, and I was going to embrace all it entailed. The dawn of a new me. You know what they say: *There's no time like the present.*

Grabbing a cup of coffee and an attitude adjustment, we drove east, toward Portland. Mount Sierra was a small town slightly southeast of the big city and supposedly a quaint, old gold-mining town. It sounded perfect. I wasn't a fan of big cities, preferring the solitude off-the-beaten path places offered.

Caught up in thoughts of red barns and weathervanes, Cali and I, with her head nestled in my lap, drove the hour it took in silence. I was in awe of the beauty this state had to offer. From backwoods deep, dark forests to big metropolitan cities within an hour's time. Pulling into Mount Sierra, I was immediately smitten. The charm it exuded took my breath away. From mom-and-pop shops lining Main St, all brightly painted and offering their wares, to the majestic mountains and babbling brooks running through the middle of town, it was everything magical rolled into one.

Having made arrangements to meet Ms. Elkins at *Frosty Trails*, the local ice-cream parlor, I sat patiently waiting under a bright pink-and-red polka-dot awning, soaking in the charm surrounding me. The chocolate mint ice cream was delicious, adding to the already perfect setting. A feeling of contentment washed over me, making it impossible to keep my happiness inside. Uncharacteristically, I greeted people with a smile and a jovial "Beautiful day today" or

CHAPTER 40 ... THE CABIN

"Enjoy your day!" I don't know what had gotten into me, but I was bursting with joy at the possibilities.

"Luke Travers?" Before me stood a stunningly beautiful woman about my age, extending her hand while she scratched Cali behind the ear. "I'm Ms. Elkins, but let's not be so formal. Please call me 'Abby.'" With all the pleasantries aside, we loaded into my truck to go check out what I hoped would be my property.

My excitement had reached a whole new level by the time we pulled up in front of the most perfect log cabin I had ever laid eyes on. Cali jumped out, excitedly running here and there, sniffing as she took in all the new smells. At the end of a dirt path, I walked up the steps leading to the porch, where I could visualize myself rocking for hours while soaking in the clean pine air and gazing toward the misty, rugged, enchanting forest that lined the edge of the land to the east. Although summer was upon us, sending temperatures blazing throughout the country, in Mount Sierra, it was a pleasant seventy-degree day. Full sun shone as a breeze rustled the treetops, causing them to sway in what looked like a welcoming wave. I could hardly wait to explore. The hidden secrets under the pine needles on the damp ground were calling my name.

Touching my arm ever so gently, Abby brought me out of my trance. "Would you like to see the inside, Luke? It looks like the outside has more than met your approval."

Would I? I almost screamed with anticipation, but I casually murmured, "Yes, please," so she wouldn't think I'd lost my marbles. Opening the solid pine front door into the massive great room made me weak in the knees. I drew in a breath as I took in the room and all its possibilities. A ginormous stone fireplace with a welcoming hearth and mantel stood proud, taking up the whole wall. Exposed wooden beams adorned the vast, soaring twenty-foot ceilings. There were warm hardwood floors covering every square inch of the ground. It was cavernous, and everything about it spoke to me. I felt like I was floating through each room, having an out-of-body experience as I fell more and more in love with all it had to offer.

There was one bedroom downstairs that was being used as a study, with built-in bookcases and a sliding ladder. The upstairs bedroom was a spacious loft with an adjoining bath. The only hiccup in the whole place was the downstairs bathroom. It was spacious, but it had wasted space. Visions of the remodel danced in my head. I almost forgot to ask about the kitchen as Abby guided me through an opening on the other side of the great room.

"Luke, I'm not sure if you like to cook, but I think you'll find the kitchen a chef's dream," she said enthusiastically. I audibly gasped when I walked in, taking in the farmhouse sink that sat under a paned window that looked out onto the vast wilderness. A wolf stove and every gadget a cook could dream about were visible, blinking in the sunlight that streamed through the window. The whole place was magical and almost too perfect. Dare I say a *chef's kiss*?

It made me wonder why it was for sale. *Had there been a murder here*, I wondered? I didn't care what the reason was—I wanted it. I couldn't contain my excitement any longer and blurted out, "When can I move in?" She laughed, but little did she know I was going to do anything to make this place mine. I felt *found*, and that feeling was priceless.

Driving back into town, I was a never-ending talking machine, asking question after question, never waiting for a reply. I was on a high like no other—before she burst my bubble with the price.

CHAPTER 40 ... THE CABIN

"I read that it's 'negotiable,' correct?" I questioned with fingers crossed behind my back.

"Well, yes it is, but I'm reasonably sure the owners are pretty set on the price or thereabouts."

I hung my head and bid her farewell, telling her I'd be in touch.

My exuberant feeling from earlier had turned cautiously optimistic. I had all my inheritance and my nest egg, so it was probably doable—but barely, not leaving me with much in my bank account. But did I really need much as long as I had a roof over my head? Taking some of the land to grow my own vegetables and fruit would help. I needed time to think, so, after saying my goodbyes to Abby, Cali and I took a drive to the property again.

Standing in front with Cali by my side, it just felt right. It already felt like home as we walked the perimeter, mapping out where I would plant the vegetable garden and build the big red barn. Ever since I was little, I'd wanted animals around me. They were better for my mental state than any therapy session could offer. I was big on omens, and the fact that this property's address was on "Redemption Lane" spoke volumes. It was meant to be, but to make one hundred percent sure, I decided to sleep on it—knowing I wouldn't change my mind.

Tossing and turning, I woke up with a start, disoriented and confused. Claire had come to visit me in my dream, looking like the goddess she was, to tell me to go for it. *Take the leap of faith. Live your dream, Luke*, she had whispered, gently kissing me on the lips before she vanished into thin air. She was right. She'd *always* been right, and who was I to argue with an angel?

Glancing at the clock, I saw it was only 5 a.m. Cali was snoring at the foot of the bed, and, as I peeked through the blackout curtains, I saw the sun just starting to make an appearance over the mountaintops. I wanted to go back to sleep, into my dream, so I could see Claire again. God, I missed that woman. Her smile. Her touch. Her wit. Her smell. Her love. Her everything.

Sleep wouldn't come, so I padded to the bathroom and stood under a steamy shower to clear the cobwebs. I not only wanted Claire back, but I wanted a drink, too. Just one shot of Jameson in my coffee wouldn't hurt, would it? I knew that was a rhetorical question, knowing the answer, but the pull was strong. Almost too much to withstand. Yet another reason to plant roots. I needed something to occupy my time, and I had a feeling the cabin would keep me plenty busy, making it the perfect place to call home. I also desperately needed to join an AA group. Baby steps.

I snuggled into Cali's neck, and she yawned, stretching her legs. "Rise and shine, girl. It's time to take a drive."

You didn't have to tell her twice. That pup loved a car ride. After my dream with Claire, I needed to go back and take a walk in the forest. Feeling like the trees would hold the answer, I was eager to dive in. I wasn't sure what my reluctance was to call Abby first thing this morning and put in an offer. I needed my magic eight ball, from when I was a kid. I was sure it would say, "My sources say 'Yes'" when asked if I should flip the switch.

Arriving in Mount Sierra, I was once again struck by the magical, charming quaintness engulfing me. A feeling of contentment came over me—an odd feeling for me to experience when my entire previous existence had been nothing but turmoil. I felt like I belonged—almost as if I were one with nature here, overwhelming me, embracing me in a warm hug.

CHAPTER 40 ... THE CABIN

The cabin sat proud and stately, welcoming me with its imposing monumental beauty. It seemed to be calling out to me, welcoming me with open arms. I sat on the steps of the porch and visualized my life here. Yep, I could see it in vivid colors. The only time I'd been more positive about anything was when I met Claire. I knew from the second I gazed into her eyes that I was done for. Now, staring at the logs and stone, I had the same feeling. To me it was a done deal. Now I needed to convince Abby to make it work.

Since the forest was the main reason for coming back this morning, Cali and I ventured in. I was instantly caught off guard by the chill and dampness in the air—plus the darkness. Slivers of light could be seen through the thickness of the trees casting shadows. It had a peaceful, eerie feeling the deeper I went in, cocooning me in silence from the outside world. The whispers of the trees as they swayed, birds chirping nearby, and an occasional rodent scurrying added to the charm. It took on a vibe all its own as I breathed deeply, enjoying the mossy, pungent smell.

The calm that had washed over me, morphing me into someone I didn't even know, was profound. And intoxicating. "Relaxed" and "happy" were two words I usually didn't use to describe myself, but they were fitting right now, and I wanted more of it.

"Come on, girl—it's time to buy a house," I ecstatically exclaimed while holding the door open for her to ride next to me. Abby was putting a sandwich board out front of the realty office when we drove up. I tooted my horn, causing her to jump a foot in the air. I laughed. She didn't, but, upon seeing me, she enthusiastically waved, inviting me in. The office had eastern exposure, allowing sunshine to flood through the windows, casting a warm glow over the rich oak desks that inhabited the space. She ushered us to a desk in the back that was neat and tidy, with numerous contracts stacked in an outbox tray.

"Well, have you had time to mull over your decision?" She raised her eyebrows, questioning my decision.

"Matter of fact, I have, and I've decided it needs to be mine ASAP, so I'm ready to make an offer!" *Boy, that felt good to say.* I was going to be a homeowner again, with any luck.

The morning was spent drawing up a proposal that she drove off to present to the owners, while Cali and I hung out at the local hamburger joint. My appetite rarely took a back seat, but I was more nervous than a whore in church, causing my stomach to be on the verge of cramping. Having been warned that it may take days for a counter-offer, I was overjoyed when, an hour later, she peeked around the corner, grinning like a Cheshire Cat.

She pulled up a chair and proceeded to make small talk. I never took her as the torturous type, but she was killing me with suspense. If ever there was a time I wished I was clairvoyant, it was now. Whatever she had to say, she was in no hurry to share, which made me anxious as hell. Not being a fan of small talk, I was even less a fan of secrets, so manners be damned. I blurted out, "Well, what did you find out?" I couldn't contain myself, looking with sad, puppy-dog eyes as I fidgeted with a wayward fry that had kamikazed out of the bag.

Time stood still as I watched scores of emotions play across her face, looking for one of jubilation but seeing one of refusal instead. Or was I imagining it because I had already set myself up for rejection? She picked up her satchel and rifled through it for what seemed like hours, before she pulled out a file with my name printed on the front. A smile that could have lit up the cloudiest of days spread

CHAPTER 40 ... THE CABIN

from ear to ear as she stood and started clapping before cheering, "Congratulations, Luke. Your offer has been accepted!"

Acting on impulse before thinking, I jumped up, grabbed her in my arms, and twirled her around! Cali got caught up in the moment and turned in circles while barking her approval. Turns out the tipping point in my favor was that I was a Gulf War veteran. The owners loved the idea of selling to what they referred to as *a stand-up guy*. I guess it was a good thing they didn't have a key to the closet that housed my numerous skeletons.

About a month later, having signed the final paperwork, escrow closed, and I was handed the keys to my new home. I waited till I exited the office to let out a whoop and do a little dance! *Officially a homeowner again* was music to my ears. I was ecstatic that the tides had turned in my favor. Or had they?

CHAPTER 41

THE ILLUSION

Days turned into months, as I watched the seasons change right in front of my eyes. As quick as the days turned into months, the months turned into years in record time. As time sprouted wings and flew by, one thing never changed—the love I had for my little cabin in my corner of the world was growing exponentially. It was my slice of heaven in a cruel world.

My days were long but fulfilling, for the most part. If I wasn't making improvements, adding structures, or working as a local handyman, I could be found in the forest, with Cali by my side. She was slowing down, and I knew the inevitable was approaching, but the thought sent me into fits of despair, wiping a wayward tear off my cheek. My newly adopted slow, mundane lifestyle allowed me to savor every second of every day with her, for which I couldn't have been more thankful. Still, the time I had left with her would never be enough.

CHAPTER 41 ... THE ILLUSION

Memories of saying goodbye to Marmalade invaded my thoughts. That was such a rough time in my life. In many ways, I still had the same struggles as back then—just a different time with different scenery. I would like to be able to say *a different me*, but I would be deluding myself. I was alone and lonely back then, and that hadn't changed. Most of the time, I didn't mind not having friends, but on nights like tonight, I craved human interaction. Damn it, why did you leave me, Claire?

The cabin has shaped up nicely into a home for me. Furnishing it with mine and Claire's style had been therapeutic. Remembering her turning our house into a home, I worked hard to mimic and emulate what she had done, clear down to the claw-footed bathtub in the newly renovated bathroom. She came to visit often, encouraging me to move on, settle down with someone else, and start a family, but I couldn't. My heart belonged to her and only her—a once-in-a-lifetime love for a once-in-a-lifetime woman.

On the nights I got lost deep in my memories, craving a drink, I would wander into the forest. The mossy, pungent ground, with its cushion of fallen pine needles welcomed me, wrapping me up in its embrace, making me one with nature. There was something about the earthiness that grounded me and got my head screwed back on correctly—at least until the next time my demons would come knocking again. Loud, incessant, and annoying.

I spent hours in my chef's dream of a kitchen, honing my culinary skills. Claire had been a great teacher. I still wear the apron she had surprised me with remembering how we would spend hours concocting recipes, laughing, and ending with a food fight. Those were the good old days—the days when I walked around with a lighthearted step and a smile plastered on my face, the days when I had finally found the love and acceptance I had craved my whole life.

Knowing that it wasn't healthy for me to live in the past, I couldn't help it, because the present missed her touch too much. I purposely kept our framed photographs tucked safely in a drawer so as not to have those painful reminders staring at me on a daily basis. I often pulled them out when I felt the urge to feel the love I missed so much now. My heart ached, along with the rest of my body, making me wonder if it was all worth it. But then I would be brought out of those soul-crushing memories by a nuzzle in my hand by Cali, giving me a reason to go on.

Just as I suspected, I never heard from Peter or my brothers again. I was one million percent OK with that. Good riddance, losers. As for Alex and Sloan, they, too, were out of sight, out of mind. I would have loved to know how Joey and Holly were, but I had never given Claire's parents my new address. They were painful reminders of what should have been. I think they both breathed a sigh of relief not having me around, having to pretend they were happy to see me. I never felt welcome there, so it was just as well.

Cutting ties with my past home life was cathartic. Releasing the anger, heartache, and confusion is the only way I knew how to move on. And, even at that, I wasn't being very successful. Yes, I had a cabin and land to call my own, but I also had memories of the cacodemon that haunted me. I tried my damndest to keep them buried, but they appeared at the most inopportune time, causing havoc and invading my thoughts. I accepted the fact that I was messed up, but I didn't want it to define me. I was more than a screwed-up loser. I was a proud war veteran. A keeper of secrets. Loyal as the day was

CHAPTER 41 ... THE ILLUSION

long. Honest to a fault. Great with my hands. Lover of all things furry. And still head over heels in love with an angel.

Since being good with my hands had always been something I was proud of, it seemed only right that I would become the local handyman. I was good and in demand, which erased some of the money angst I felt after buying the cabin—besides the fact that it made me feel wanted, not a feeling I was accustomed to. There wasn't much I couldn't fix, build, or assemble with precision. Living proof was on my own property. I had taken a portion of my ten acres and built a big red barn that housed all my farm equipment and bales of hay for my horses, who stood corralled in their own carefully constructed structure. I added a chicken coop and some alpacas just for the hell of it. My childhood dream of being surrounded by animals was finally a reality, and, even on my darkest days, they brought a glimmer of hope and light that better days would lie ahead.

Even though an outsider looking in would have thought my life was in order and running smoothly, it was all an illusion I had crafted perfectly so others wouldn't feel sorry for me. But the exact opposite was true. I was discombobulated and lonely. Without my Claire, I was a sailboat without a sail. Peanut butter without jam. An angel without wings. A life without a purpose. This was the loneliness talking, which I worked at daily. Unfortunately, when thoughts like these reared their ugly head, it quickly turned into a snowball gaining momentum and taking on a life of its own. I found myself at a loss, craving alcohol to escape.

In all fairness, though, not all my days were spent with my head in the past, living a life of regret. The animals, my cabin, the forest, and, of course, Cali, all gave me a purpose and reason to move on. I was always searching for the elusive dream that would erase my past once and for all and give me peace. Maybe I just needed a mulligan in my life.

One night, while I was sitting in front of a roaring fire, listening to the gale-force winds blow the trees and the weathervane on my red barn squeaking with every turn, Claire came to visit, encouraging me to seek help from a therapist again. "Remember how helpful Dr. Hawthorne was when you were struggling to come to terms with your childhood?" she whispered while caressing my cheek. I couldn't deny that she had helped me with my suicidal thoughts and given me a outlet to air my childhood trauma, although it still haunted me. It was no fault of hers, though, because, seriously, there weren't enough doctors in the world or time, for that matter, to get me to accept and understand my wretched childhood. Cali sensed her in the room, getting up from where she was lying at my feet. Sniffing the air and pawing at my arm, she spun around a couple of times before collapsing on the floor with a groan. She could feel the air in the cabin change. Reassuring Cali everything was more than fine, I kissed Claire sweetly before she departed, promising I would seek help.

A promise is a promise, and that's how I found Dr. Wesley. The poor guy hadn't a clue as to what was in store for him when he agreed to see me. Making a special point to go bi-monthly, I owed it to myself and Claire to seek help, although the forest and my animals were just as helpful. It was kinda nice having a non-judgmental human to confide in, but I always had an eerie feeling that I was being judged. As much as I trusted Dr. Wesley to keep our meetings confidential, half of me expected a knock on my door from the local looney bin, to take me away. Great—now I can add *paranoia* to my list of issues.

CHAPTER 41 ... THE ILLUSION

Fall was in full swing, causing the trees to turn their lush green leaves to vibrant shades of reds, oranges, and yellows, looking like fire. Dropping to the ground, a flurry of colors danced as a crisp breeze swirled them in the air. The ground was littered with acorns that had tumbled to their death. I wondered if it's true that if you plant one, it will eventually turn into an oak tree? I was curious enough to put one in my pocket to plant later.

Mount Sierra was huge on celebrating holidays and the turn of the seasons, especially fall. Corn mazes were set up alongside pumpkin patches. Apple picking was at its prime, and Halloween decorations of witches, bats, and spiders adorned every store window along Main Street. Even I got caught up in the hullabaloo, decorating my porch with hay bales from the barn and setting a scarecrow on top. I worked feverishly in the kitchen, perfecting my apple-pie recipe and gifting some to my therapist and the teller at my local bank. All was right with the world. Until it wasn't.

CHAPTER 42

THE SCREAM

My peaceful forest had taken on a creepy, ominous vibe lately. Out of nowhere, I heard blood-curdling screams pierce the night silence. My arm hair stood on end, and my heart beat out of control, while Cali barked incessantly. "What was that, girl?" Scratching her behind the ears, I tried to settle her down. There was no way in hell I was investigating in the dead of night. The forest was dark even during the day, casting sinister shadows. The nighttime made it impossible to make out much of anything, giving it a mysterious, spine-chilling, petrifying aura.

Getting sleep that night was like asking a dog to give up a bone. It wasn't going to happen, so I grabbed *The Grapes of Wrath* and made myself a bowl of popcorn to pass the night until I could investigate in the morning. Finding it hard to concentrate, even with Cali curled by my side, my mind wandered to the war. The last time I had heard screams like that was when assault rifles were

CHAPTER 42 ... THE SCREAM

taking down soldiers left and right around me. I was nowhere near ever wanting to relive that nightmare again.

A sliver of sunlight filtered through the break in the curtains, settling on my face. Jerking my eyes open, I strained to get my bearings, fogginess clouding my brain. Cali yawned and planted a big slobbery kiss on my lips. "Good morning, girl, my bright little ball of sunshine," I gushed while wrapping her in a bear hug. Sitting up, I noticed the book on the floor next to the couch and a half-eaten bowl of popcorn. And then it all came flooding back to me: The scream, the erratic sleepless night, the panic in the air.

"Do you want to go on an adventure this morning?" I questioned as doubt clouded over my judgment, gripping me with fear. Always ready for an adventure, she jumped up and ran for the door. Although the sun was out, a bitterly cold wind whipped through the door when I peeked out. I could see the trees swaying erratically, calling out with secrets. Donning my warm winter Carhartt jacket and a beanie, I grabbed some courage and a flashlight. The unknown scared the bejeebers out of me, but I had an irresistible urge to explore.

The opening of the forest was a lot like walking into a fairytale, expecting to see insects having tea parties and a parade of bunnies wearing their Sunday finest. There was nothing whimsical about it today, though. It was dark, ominous, and frightening. My jaw was clenched so tight I was afraid I would break a tooth if I didn't take a second to regroup. I was much too tense, which was something I'd never felt among the trees before. They usually offered me a peaceful aura, but, today, they were pissed. The trees were bending and shaking with every wind gust that I thought they might snap. It was as if they'd watched a horror movie and were begging for answers. Either that or warning me to stay away.

I got out my flashlight and wandered further in, dodging the sharp branches. Cali stayed glued to my side, frightened in a sixth-sense kind of way. I'm not sure what made me think I was being watched, but the hair stood up on the back of my neck, and an eerie feeling washed over me. Jerking my head around, I was thankful that I was alone. Only steps away, I came across a clearing of sorts where a campfire had been built, with various rocks forming a ring and a collection of pine needles and broken branches arranged inside. There was an odd smell I hadn't noticed before. Usually the forest smelled earthy and pungent, but, today, the air had a metallic tinge to it.

Looking around with my flashlight darting from tree to tree, I came upon an area where the ground was mussy. All I could think was that there had been a tussle there, because the pine needles were shoved to one side and the earth exposed, showing parts where something had been dragged. My heart froze as I bent down, picking up a pink ribbon. *What had happened?* I wondered, as a flash of lightning burst through the trees, making me jump a foot. The light cast gruesome shadows of death and torture, and a loud clap of thunder rang through the air. I knew it was close, and I needed to run home before I was immersed in a mud bog.

Cali and I reached the cabin drenched and muddy. Grabbing some towels, I dried her soaked fur. I leaned over to inhale her fur; she smelled like rain and wet dog. I wanted to remember her like this forever. I knew in my heart that her time on this Earth was ticking away, second by second. Time is an hourglass with a collection of sand on the bottom with a small amount remaining on the top, filtering down grain by grain. How could I get it to stop and freeze my time with her forever?

CHAPTER 42 ... THE SCREAM

In the two short months that followed, visions of the scuffle in the forest took a back seat. Thankfully it had remained quiet, because all my time was devoted to taking care of Cali. Her days were spent in her bed, nestled in front of the fireplace. Arthritis and old age riddled her body, leaving her unable to move most days. On a good day, which were few and far between, she and I would slowly make our way around the property.

Temperatures plummeted when winter showed up in all its wonderland glory. I pulled Cali around in the red wagon I had built for her, leaving wheel marks in the snow-laden fields. Wrapped tightly in a red tartan wool blanket and a collection of dandelions I had preserved just for her, she stared in wonderment, taking in the crisp, fresh mountain air. I knew she felt the end coming the same way I did, as she snuggled close to me, resting her head in my lap.

My heart shattered as she took her last breath, wrapped in my arms. I whispered to her how much I loved her. A presence filled the room, and I saw a superimposed vision of Marmalade over her body, gently lifting her as they floated over the rainbow bridge, off to heaven. I was wrecked, unable to catch my breath. A tsunami of emotions flooded over me, leaving me an unconsolable, blubbering disaster curled in a fetal position in the corner of the couch. I needed a drink.

The only thing that kept me from drinking away my sorrows was that I was unable to move, frozen with crippling grief. Memories of losing Marmalade came back like a gut punch. The sadness I felt then, never thinking I could love another dog as much as her, made me realize how many animals were out there waiting to share their love. If I could eventually get over Marmalade, there must be life after Cali, too.

BLACK SHEEP

Not knowing how or when it happened, I slowly found myself moving on. Still missing her terribly, I dreamed about getting another pup. I was reminded of a quote by Dr. Seuss that said *"Don't cry because it's over, smile because it happened."* I couldn't have said it better myself. I needed not only the companionship of a dog but also the calm they brought as my therapy dog.

The local shelter was nestled in the middle of tall pine trees, with a babbling brook taking center stage. The building was painted a sunshine yellow, with a beautiful hand-painted mural depicting happy puppies and kittens frolicking in a meadow, surrounded by bright flowers. A giant paw print, encased in a big red heart, was painted on the door, with a slogan that read, *'A house is not a home without an animal to share it with!'* The outside aesthetic did an amazing job at camouflaging the horrors that were housed within their walls—stories of cruelty, neglect, and abandonment too horrific to fathom. Still the animals wagged their tails, straining at the bars for someone to give them a second chance at happiness. Shelters always tugged at my heartstrings, wanting to take every single animal and give them their forever after. I was barely afloat myself. In constant pain, struggling with addiction, and living a life of regret, I knew it wasn't the right time, but I wouldn't give up my dream.

Cali and Marmalade were by my side as I walked down the aisles, my heart breaking with every step. And then I saw her. She was huddled in the corner, shaking and scared, grasping a pink stuffed bunny between her paws. Her information read, "Sydney. Stray female. Approximately one year old. Gentle, scared and withdrawn. Loves attention and pets." She sounded perfect for me. Like we were one and the same, since I also was gentle, scared, and withdrawn.

CHAPTER 42 ... THE SCREAM

"Hi, Sydney. Do you want to come and share your life with me?" I optimistically whispered. She picked her head up and looked me in the eye. It was love at first sight. When you know, you know. And, trust me, I knew she needed me as much as I needed her. Filling out her adoption paperwork, I could hardly believe my good fortune. She reminded me of Marm, with fur the color of a golden ray of sunshine.

I'd never been so happy to hear the sound of toenails clickety-clacking against the hardwood floor. It was music to my ears. Her first night home was exactly like I expected. She was confused and skeptical, but happy nonetheless. I doubted she'd ever had a home, or, if she did, it was one that had never allowed her in the house as part of the family. She paced, barely sleeping. I knew this would pass when she settled in and realized I wouldn't fail her like she'd clearly been failed before.

From pure exhaustion, she finally closed her eyes. I tiptoed out of the room to whip up a home-cooked meal fit for the queen she was. This is where she found me, in the kitchen, as she nonchalantly walked into the room like she owned the place. "Good morning, sleepy head. Are you hungry, girl?" I said as I dished up a heaping serving of vegetables, grains, and chicken ground to perfection, into her brand-new stainless-steel bowl. She greeted me with a quizzical look of skepticism as she dug in, devouring it in record time.

From days of working at the shelter, I had learned there was a process a newly adopted rescue pet would go through. Called the Rule of Three, it simply meant that it took three days for them to decompress, at least three weeks to start to learn, train, and feel comfortable, and about three months to fully adapt to a new home. I would gladly wait.

Never leaving her side, we went everywhere together, trying to build trust. I had never had to do this with Joey and Holly, partially because they had been an owner-surrender, and they had the companionship of each other. I was much too young to remember the transition Marm had made into the family, but I assumed it was much like I was dealing with now. I broke my heart visualizing what awful, horrendous things she had endured.

But slowly she came out of her wounded shell and started to love. The young pup in her was apparent in all that she did. From having her head hang out of the truck window with her tongue lolling, slobber flying, to chasing the ball nonstop, until I was the one worn out. She was smart and learned commands quickly, already having an innate ability to retrieve. Her fur grew from raspy to velvet smooth to the touch. Sleeping peacefully now, either by my side or in her fluffy bed with her name stitched on the front, I knew she felt at home.

We were inseparable, leaving me wondering how I ever had survived a moment without her by my side. The chores around the farm were her favorite. I had quite a collection of animals now, which she loved. I had cordoned sections off for a flower garden and a vegetable garden, growing all my own vegetables. My life was nearly perfect in every way—now, if I could only find a way to ease the pain I suffered and get over the desire to drink. It came out of nowhere when I craved a beer or a bottle of wine. Would I ever lose the urge?

There was no way I was going down that path again, so I bit the bullet and joined a local AA group. I brought Sydney with me for moral support. Needless to say, everyone fell immediately in love, but how could they not? She was gentle and patient, lending a paw to those in need when they broke down in tears. It was abundantly clear she was going to be a great therapy dog.

CHAPTER 43

THE FOREST

Life as we knew it was peaceful and, I daresay, boring, but we were living life to its fullest nonetheless. It fit our lifestyle perfectly, because I was an introvert. Not necessarily by choice—more by necessity. Not having a traditional nine-to-five, five-day-a-week job, I worked steadily re-growing my nest egg—for what I wasn't sure. I had everything I ever wanted right at my fingertips. If I wasn't on a job, I could be found in the gardens, tending to the animals or soaking up all nature had to offer. It was a rewarding life.

Until the screams erupted one fall night out of nowhere, startling Sydney and me. Thinking back to the last time, I realized a year had flown by. You know what they say, *Time flies when you're having fun.* Sydney was agitated, putting her nose in the air like she smelled trouble. Or death. Even worse.

"It's OK, girl. We'll investigate tomorrow, when it's light outside." She wasn't having it, though. She was pacing and whining like she'd lost her best friend.

The last thing I wanted to do was go into the forest at night, but to pacify her and my own curiosity, I threw on my boots, gloves, and a warm jacket. Fall was upon us again, chilling the night air to almost freezing. I grabbed a lantern, and we cautiously walked to the perimeter. The screams had subsided a good hour ago, but I couldn't help thinking danger was still looming around every tree. The air was thick and acrid with the pungent metallic smell—stronger than last time.

Even though the forest was dark during the day, it was a different kind of dark, allowing sunbeams to sporadically peek through. At night, it took on a whole different vibe. It was almost sinister and definitely spine-chilling. I strained to get my bearings, lost within the pines as branches snapped beneath my feet and pine needles lodged in my beard and hair, scraping my face. The sounds of silence were intimidating, causing me to hear things that weren't there. Or were they? The night air was bitter cold. Raising the lantern up, I could make out a cloud of breath escaping between my chattering teeth.

Sydney stayed by my side, quietly weaving in and out on our way toward the campfire spot. A high-pitched scream that would have rivaled a high-school cheerleader's escaped my mouth as a varmint scurried up my pant leg. I was on edge, feeling and hearing things I hoped were a figment of my imagination. A couple hundred feet ahead, I could see what looked like the outline of the boulders surrounding the fire pit.

CHAPTER 43 ... THE FOREST

Arriving there, I bent over to check for heat or a burning ember. It was cold and untouched, which was more than I could say for the ground. Pine needles were scattered about, and claw-like indentations were visible in the dirt. Reaching down to get a better look, I saw that it looked like fingernails had dragged against the damp earth in a feeble attempt at escape. My mind saw visions of torture and death, when a white earbud caught my eye, lying wedged next to a stone. I shuddered as a cold breeze blew by, making the trees whistle untold secrets. "Let's get the hell out of here, Sydney. This place is giving me the creeps!"

The next morning, I woke up bathed in sweat, fighting for air. The roosters had startled me out of a restless night filled with nightmares and moral dilemmas. I was not a fan of the law, having had my brush with them in the past still fresh in my mind. I had also heard snippets of town gossip that the Sheriff's Department was a tad on the shady side, turning a blind eye when it was convenient for them. Although, before leaving Piedmont, I had made a promise to my mom and dad to make them proud, so what was I to do? Weighing my options, I ultimately decided to let things be. I really didn't have much to go on, and who's to say they wouldn't turn the tables on me?

Trying to forget what I had witnessed was no easy task—it invaded my thoughts at all times of the day, with images of mayhem running on repeat through my mind; I imagined the worst but hoped and prayed I was wrong. I placed the earbud with the pink ribbon in a velvet-lined box thinking it was a final resting place for their unfortunate owners. I tried to reel in my visions, not knowing if, indeed, a murder had taken place. There had been nothing in the paper, so maybe it was just my imagination working overtime. If I could just get the frightening, eerie scenes out of my mind, I might be able to get some quality sleep.

Life has a way of moving on, and Sydney and I returned to our normal humdrum, although peaceful, existence. I spent my off time reading and building my library to a masterpiece a librarian would be envious of. Continuing my AA meetings was giving me a new purpose. The urge to drink hadn't diminished, but I was finding ways to address the daily temptations. My culinary skills were top-notch, having followed in Claire's footsteps. I knew she would be happy I had expanded on what she had taught me.

Fast forward, and another year had flown by without incidents. I was more than OK with that. I had finally taken the time to sit down and write to Aiden, Paige, and Harry, letting them know my address and giving them updates on my life. I found it sad that those were the only three people I wanted in my life, although at a distance. I'm not entirely sure what that said about me as a person, but it couldn't be good. I didn't give a boat full of shits, though, because I had all I wanted and needed in my private little corner of the world.

They all wrote back, thanking me for reaching out. Paige had graduated from university and gotten married. Aiden had finally retired from the Army after serving more than twenty years. He was a grandpa now. A twinge of jealousy coursed through me upon reading that, catching me off guard. It sent me into a spiral, wondering how different my life would be if Claire was still alive and I had a child or two to call my own—and I was the one answering to "Grandpa."

I wasn't "old"—by any stretch of the imagination—but I was feeling my years. My hank of hair was still thick but was now tinged

CHAPTER 43 ... THE FOREST

with gray. My face looked weathered from years of manual labor. And my gait had a noticeable limp, causing me to look a lot like Quasimodo. All part of living and aging. I often thought of my mom. They were horrible memories, but I tried to focus on the bits and pieces of hope she'd sprinkled throughout my life. Something that still weighed heavily on my mind was the night of the accident. My thoughts were like dominoes. Once one question started, the rest fell. What was she coming to tell me? To shed some light on why my childhood was filled with hatred, disrespect, and loneliness?

While life flowed like a meandering river, the one thing causing unrest in my life were the spine-tingling screams from the forest. They were coming more frequently, but when I got up the nerve to venture in, I saw much the same I'd seen every other time: Pine needles scattered about and remnants of a scuffle. Sometimes I found articles left behind—but not always—making me wonder if I was imagining the whole thing. My moral compass was tipping slightly to the left, until my voice of reason came calling, so I remained quiet and stoic, hoping and praying it had been a wild-animal fight.

One afternoon in particular, I was restless. Not that this was anything out of the norm, but it *was* different. I was pacing, tugging on my beard, and mumbling to myself. As I reached down to pick up a book, Aiden's letter tumbled to the floor. I opened it, rereading every word, wishing my life could have ended up like his. "Why?" I screamed. "Why did you leave me, Claire? Why did my child die with you? Why did my mom keep my dad's identity from me? Why was I the *black sheep* my whole life?"

The questions kept coming, but no answers followed. Reaching down to pet Sydney did little to calm my restlessness. My nerves were shot. I was about to lose my shit as I jumped into my truck and headed to a bar. Fearing I might know someone there, I drove to the next town over, while tears flowed like a dam had collapsed against the constant strain of pressure pushing against it. I knew this wasn't the answer, but I needed to stop the voices in my head from wailing their high-pitched *"Loser!"*

The parking lot was sparsely populated. Sitting in my truck, I was having an internal battle with myself. It was like I had an angel on one shoulder telling me how great I'd done for years and not to bow to temptation. On the other shoulder sat the devil, yelling in my ear not to be a pussy and do what I wanted. The devil won out as I told my voice of reason to shut the fuck up, and I bailed out of the cab. The cold air blasted me in the face, reminding me that, in my haste, I had left my jacket behind, hanging in the hall closet.

Opening the door, I was greeted with the most wonderful smell of beer. God, how I had missed that smell and taste. As I sidled up to the bar, I forgot about everything but losing myself in alcohol. And plenty of it. The more, the better, actually. "What's your pleasure?" yelled the bartender over the blaring music. He was a burly guy with a shaved head and a variety of tattoos fighting for space. "Thor" was embroidered on his white apron, which, clearly, had missed laundry day. I ordered a beer and two tequila shot chasers. The music was so loud the floor was vibrating under me; the bass thumped, causing pain behind my eyes.

I glanced around; everyone was whooping it up, having a grand ol' time. That's one of the things I missed about alcohol. All your inhibitions flew out the window, and a false sense of security flooded over your body. Problems, worries, and sorrows took a back seat to happiness. I needed this in the worst way right now. Downing my drinks, I let out a huge belch. *Oh, my lord—that was better than sex,* I

CHAPTER 43 ... THE FOREST

thought. The coolness ran down my throat as I gulped it, telling the bartender to keep them coming. The floodgates had been opened, and there was no stopping me now.

Stumbling off my stool, having lost count of my drink consumption, I cautiously made my way to the bathroom, tripping over a chair or two along the way. I had always been a sloppy drunk, and time had not changed that. Catching sight of myself in the mirror, I gasped. I looked like I had been caught in the middle of a stampede. It wasn't a good look. A ruddy complexion with humongous bags under red-rimmed, moist eyes stared back. Something that appeared to be barf chunks were caught in my beard, but I didn't remember throwing up. Hah! Who was I kidding? I didn't remember *anything* about today except that I hadn't thought about Claire for three whole hours. A record for me.

Knowing I was way too wasted to get behind the wheel, I struck up a conversation with a guy sitting alone in the corner, nursing a double shot of what appeared to be bourbon floating amongst an ice cube or two. We spent the next hour shooting the shit. It was mindless talk, about nothing in particular; I enjoyed it as long as it allowed me to escape within myself. The guy was a wounded soul, like myself, so we fed off each other's insecurities. That sounds like a recipe for disaster, but it passed the time until it was time to leave. He offered me a ride home, which I gladly accepted.

That was about the tenth mistake I'd made that day, starting with getting my happy ass into the truck in the first place. Second was walking into the bar, and it never got better from there. I was so inebriated, I wasn't even coherent enough to see that he was in an equally wasted state. Driving down the road, singing at the top of our lungs, totally oblivious. I had achieved everything I'd set out to do when I left earlier in the day. I had not a care in the world until I looked up, and he was swerving through the center divider, taking out a row of beautifully colored oleander bushes.

Thwack! He plowed head first into an unsuspecting car. The next hour was a blur of screams, blood, and mayhem. A woman died. I cried, standing mortified, watching the horror unfold. And it wasn't just a woman but a young mother with her son witnessing the whole thing. Holding her in his arms while sobbing, he begged her to wake up. It was soul crushing watching him pleading with everything he had. I stood in horror on the side of the road, physically not hurt but broken-hearted for the poor boy. I reached out to comfort him, but he brushed me away, consumed in his worst nightmare. Little did I know that this young man and I would cross paths in a year and that my life would be changed.

CHAPTER 44

THE DISCOVERY

What had I done? I was a pathetic fool, acting out of stupidity in a weak moment. The worst part was that I knew better. Not only was I inadvertently responsible for that poor woman's death, but I had wrecked her son's life in the process, too. I was consumed with guilt day in and day out. When I closed my eyes at night, I heard the crash. I saw the pain and anguish as sobs ravaged him. Sydney stayed close, helping however she could, but I knew time was the only healer. The only good that came out of that night was that it sobered me up once and for all. I started going to my AA meetings again and swore off alcohol forever.

The cravings remained, but all I had to do was imagine that poor boy's face, and a queasy feeling would come over me. I'd made promises to myself before, but, from this day forward, I swore I would do better. I scanned the paper for information on the boy, but, being a minor, his name was being withheld, so I lit a candle and said a silent prayer that he would forgive me.

Ashamed, embarrassed, and *afraid* don't come close to explaining what I was feeling. Ashamed of my weak moment. Embarrassed at my actions. Afraid of what temptations lay ahead. I'm pretty sure if anyone was asked, they would have described me as a bit of a recluse or *a loner,* if you will. I made a habit of keeping to myself but did enjoy an afternoon stroll through town to grab a burger at *Here's the Beef* and a coffee-chocolate-chip ice-cream cone at *Lickity Split.* The ice-cream parlor's name made me laugh every time I saw it. If it weren't for the pink-and-white polka-dot awning, the name could have easily been mistaken for a porn shop.

Since that dreaded night, I had given new meaning to the word *recluse*. I was pretty sure nobody knew about it, but I did, and that was enough for me. That last thing I wanted was to become the brunt of all the town gossip. Once again, I threw myself into my animals and gardens with my weekly visit into the forest for my zen moments. Even though so much had gone on in there, I still felt a peacefulness wash over me. It was almost like the trees were accepting me as one of their own, no questions asked. I read once that the reason the forest makes you feel at peace is because breathing in the oils that are produced from the trees—called phytoncides—lowers your cortisol levels, which are your primary stress hormones, causing you to feel calm and less stressed when walking among the pine trees. Made total sense to me. I loved little bits of trivia that stuck in my mind.

Claire and I used to spend hours lying in each other's arms, quoting movies, songs, and meaningless trivia facts. I miss those times almost as much as I miss her touch. I reached over to give Sydney a scratch on her back, as she lay intertwined in my legs. Suddenly,

CHAPTER 44 ... THE DISCOVERY

Sydney's head shot up with her ears at full attention. "What do you hear, girl?" I questioned, not yet hearing the scream that followed seconds later. It pierced the night and made the hair on my neck stand up. I glanced at the clock on my nightside table. It was 3:20 in the morning. Lying still, I strained to hear more. Sydney was up, nervously pacing and howling, with her head raised, sniffing the air. Before I could throw my overalls on, she was down the stairs at the door, pawing to get out.

It was bitterly cold outside, making my breath form in puffs of smoke like I had lit up a doobie. Sydney was in such a state—I had left in such a hurry, foolishly forgetting my coat and beanie. I wrapped my arms around myself for warmth as I entered the forest, listening for trouble. It was quiet except for the pine trees. They were vexed tonight, swaying and bending as if they were trying to escape the horror they had just witnessed. I forged my way through to the campfire spot with ease this time, following the path I had stored in my memory.

There were embers still glowing within the snubbed-out fire, offering much-needed warmth. Rubbing my hands together, something caught my eye. Cautiously walking toward the other side of the fire pit, I saw what appeared to be a red-and-black ASICS running shoe. Bending down to get a better look, I gasped. To my horror, there was a leg attached. I froze in my tracks as my breath caught in my throat. It was gnarled, with a bone sticking out, lying within a fresh pool of blood. I'm not positive, but I think I screamed like a little girl who just got dumped by her first crush.

Anxiety started to take hold as my heartbeat accelerated, fighting off the urge to hurl when I heard a branch snap, followed by a squeal coming from behind me. Jerking my head up, I saw an outline of a person standing within the pines. Not sure what came over me, I shrewdly moved with precision toward the sound, hoping I wasn't walking into a trap.

As I limped closer, I could make out that it was a boy, standing perfectly still like his life depended on it. We locked eyes. I gazed into two frightened, petrified, hollow eyes. I reached out my arm, and he took off like a bolt of lightning. What was he doing there in the middle of the night when he should have been tucked in safe and sound, dreaming of high-school proms and his first kiss?

Then it hit me. He looked terrified because he thought I was a killer. I have to admit, I looked a bit scary with my unruly hair after being woken from a deep sleep. I had thrown on the first thing I found, which happened to be my old rat-tatty overalls with dried-up red paint the color of the barn. I didn't try to chase after him, knowing I would only frighten him more. Not only did I not know what to do with the leg, but how could I explain being in the wrong place and the wrong time to a boy I might not ever see again?

I was in a real conundrum. I took a couple of minutes to scan the area for further clues, but all I saw was upturned dirt and littered pine needles where a scuffle had taken place. Whoever she was had given 'em hell trying to escape to freedom. Dousing the fire with more dirt, I decided to return when I had my wits about me. I was spooked and not thinking clearly.

In a daze, I stumbled home in shock; I threw some kindling on to start a fire and ground some beans for a fresh pot of coffee. All the while my mind was turning somersaults with sickening scenarios. Was there a serial killer out there, using the forest as his own personal playground?

CHAPTER 44 ... THE DISCOVERY

I was afraid to sleep, knowing nightmares would surely come knocking. In the flesh, I had already witnessed a horrifying nightmare in my very own backyard. As fragrant notes of chocolate and caramelized nuts filtered through the air, I curled up on the couch next to Sydney, massaging her haunches. Whereas before I had strong suspicions there had been foul play in the forest, I now had proof. There was no way I could idly sit back and pretend any longer. But what to do?

CHAPTER 45

THE ADVENTURE

Pulling Claire's and my wedding picture out of the bedside-table drawer, I lovingly ran my finger over her face. "I miss you, my love," I whispered as I kissed her cheek. In times of turmoil, I often found solace just by staring at her beauty. If only she were here, so I could bounce ideas off her on what my next step should be. I knew with 100% certainty I would get justice for the poor woman who had been hacked up like a rabid wild animal, but I was still reluctant to seek help from the local Sheriff's Department.

Not finding answers by staring blindly at Claire, I gathered Sydney and went to the back side of the barn to finish the painting I had started weeks ago. With each stroke, I heard pleas for help. The paint reminded me of blood, and, after an hour, I called it a day. Needing some comfort in the worst way, I busied myself with whipping up a batch of Claire's infamous chicken soup. It was sure to be just what the doctor ordered.

CHAPTER 45 ... THE ADVENTURE

Sydney let out a bark and pawed at the door to go out. The air was chilly as I opened the door for her to run out to do her business. I busied myself with building a fire and starting the day, but when Sydney didn't return as usual, I started to panic. The sun was struggling to make an appearance, turning the sky a grayish-orange hue as I stood on the porch, starting to hyperventilate. Right then, out of nowhere, she appeared with the boy from the other night by her side.

"Sydney, come here, girl. What have you been up to this time?" She was clearly as happy to see me as I was her, as she licked me from head to toe. Looking up, I saw the boy slowly, unsteadily, and unsure, walking toward the cabin before he did an about-face and took off in a full sprint toward the forest.

"Stop, son! Please don't be scared of me. Come back," I yelled to deaf ears, as he was long gone. It pained me to think he was scared of me. I was gentle as a lamb, but, obviously, he felt differently.

The next two nights were eerily quiet, urging me to explore. I was afraid of what I might find lurking. I had never been one to shy away from danger but not one to go in search of it, either. So, when I threw my coat on and set out in the middle of the night to explore, I surprised myself. The voices in my head couldn't be quieted any longer.

As usual, the temperature plummeted to what seemed like twenty degrees once I was covered within the canopy of branches. I shivered, pulling my coat tighter around me. Standing still, I listened intently, but all that greeted me were hooting owls and rustling trees. I was on edge, worried there could be a repeat of the other night when the gnarled leg, dripping in blood, lay by the campfire, but, to my surprise, I saw the boy hovering over a pile of dirt, digging with a small shovel.

My presence must have startled him. He jerked and looked at me with unblinking eyes, flummoxed and bewildered. Visibly in fear, he stood with his arms in the air, like he was a criminal caught in the act. The poor kid was petrified, and I started to laugh. It was a chuckle at first, but as I increasingly found the situation hilarious, it soon turned into a guffaw, shaking my robust belly. Sydney wanted to play but sat by my side, watching and waiting for a command. The boy eased up a bit and cracked a smile. Before long, he, too, was laughing as tears ran down our cheeks. Laughter did that to you.

Extending my hand, I said, "I'm Luke. Pleased to meet you finally. Why did you run the other day?" I saw confusion play through his eyes before he shook my hand, introducing himself as Jonathan. Just as I had suspected, he had been horrified of me after seeing me hovering over the severed leg. I couldn't say that I blamed him one little bit. The sight had startled and terrified me as well.

Out of nowhere, the trees began to bend and shake, and a freezing-cold rain fell down in sheets. It was as if our conversation had accidentally woken the dead, and they were angry. Now, more than ever, I felt the presence of others watching, listening, and begging for answers and justice.

I shuddered and wrapped my coat around me, trying to shield myself from the rain. Sydney was most definitely on edge, with her tail tucked under her and her ears pinned close to her face. She began to bark and turn in circles. That's all we needed to see, and we took off running toward my cabin and shelter.

And to a wonderful friendship.

After that night when we talked until the wee hours of the night, we've been inseparable, except for the times Jonathan was away at university. Have you ever met someone that you can't imagine how

CHAPTER 45 ... THE ADVENTURE

you survived without them? Jonathan was an extension of myself. *Two peas in a pod*, so they say, suffering, looking for guidance and acceptance. We spent hours pouring out our souls to one another, which was therapeutic and frightening all at once. I had kept my past buried for so long, I was unsure of what to share. I had experienced horrors never to be revisited again, so I kept much of my life to myself. Not that I didn't think he wouldn't be a good sounding board. It was more like the older I got, the more I wanted to forget.

Jonathan had an adventurous spirit a mile long, and I was happy to oblige. It kept me young and agile. Well, as young and agile as I could get for an aging old man. Oh, the trouble we got into. I couldn't help but laugh at some of the off-the-charts escapades we shared. But one thing was for certain: We always succeeded in the end.

And the rest, as they say, is history. Who knew Jonathan was the missing puzzle piece to make my last years complete? As someone who had always been a square peg trying my damndest to fit into a round world, it was a pleasant and satisfying surprise. I couldn't help thinking that he was yet another person placed delicately in my path to help me survive. But not only did I survive, I flourished. I found new meaning to life.

My guardian angel of a mom had intervened and worked her magic, pulling strings from afar, making sure my path intersected with Jonathan's when we both needed each other the most. Our two souls together finding their sanity on the heels of loss would be paramount in our healing process. Honestly, it was the least she could do for me after years of turmoil. I would make it a point to thank her someday when we united once again.

As the days melded into weeks and the months turned into years with lightning speed, I knew more than ever that getting to know Jonathan had been the best blessing anyone could ask for. All my life, all I wanted was a family to call my own. A child to spoil, protect, and love unconditionally. He brought out in me a person I didn't know I could be—a person who thought of others before myself and cherished the ground they walked on. A person with a heart of pure gold, as Jonathan liked to say about my personality. I'm not sure I was worthy of such high praise, but I was flattered.

EPILOGUE

I'm sick. I'm old. I'm tired. I'm grateful.

I spend my days daydreaming of the past and the adventures Jonathan and I shared. I reach down to pet "Nutmeg"—"Meg" for short—Jonathan's golden retriever. She never leaves my side these days—she's always close. She knows my time is near. We have that in common.

Unable to walk most days, I sit in my wheelchair, covered with a soft, fluffy blanket Quinn knitted for me. Staring out at the trees, I know I can leave this Earth knowing Jonathan and I have done good. We brought justice to the women who'd lost their lives at the hands of a serial killer running amok in my beloved forest. What a great team we made, and, for that, I was more than eternally grateful. I was a proud papa. Through the years since I met Jonathan as a young boy of thirteen, I've been fortunate to call him my son and witness him grow into a respectable pillar of the community.

The thoughts of losing my own child aren't as painful as they once were, with Jonathan to share my life with. I've been blessed beyond words, and I pinch myself daily over having gotten to share so many wonderful years with him. Now that he's married, I have a "daughter" in his beautiful wife, Quinn. And the best part is that I don't have to be jealous of Aiden anymore, because I have amazing grandkids of my own that live a stone's throw away in a home Jonathan had built on an acre of my land.

Shrieks of laughter and joy brought me out of my daydream of Claire and me on our wedding day. "Grandpa, grandpa, look what I made in school for you today!" shouted Michael, my energetic, angelic grandson. He had adorable ringlets of blond curls that spilled down around his freckled face. Running toward me with a gapped-tooth smile, he was the splitting image of his dad. Climbing into my lap, he joyfully presented me with a vase made out of popsicle sticks with a bunch of dandelions poking out of the top. Wrapping him in my arms, I tickled him while he giggled. It was music to my ears.

It was perfect. He was perfect. Life had come full circle.

Turning, I saw Quinn approaching, with Emma tugging on her dress. She glowed. Pregnancy does that to you, so I've heard. It was another boy, and I was honored they were naming him after me—Lucas Gregory, to be exact. I knew this was Jonathan's doing to honor me and the dad I never had the privilege of knowing. I had shared all my deep, dark secrets with Jonathan one day, hoping I could bury it forever. It hadn't worked.

Emma reached up and planted a kiss on my cheek. "I love you, grandpa!" She smelled like strawberries and lemons, and I couldn't get enough. "Come here, sweetheart, and tell Grandpa all about your day," I mumbled. Time had gotten the best of me, and my days were slipping through my fingers faster than sand through an hourglass.

EPILOGUE ... EPILOGUE

"Can I get you anything, Dad?" Quinn affectionately asked as she bent down, wrapping the blanket tighter around my legs, rubbing my arms. "Time, Quinn—just time to see my grandchildren grow into adulthood," I answered, knowing I was asking the impossible as big, fat, hot tears collected in the corners of my eyes, threatening to spill out. After years of tears, enough to fill an ocean, I had learned to accept myself for who I was meant to be. I was proud to say I was in touch with my sensitive side, and I wasn't about to change. Nor did I want to.

My little family had turned out to be better than I could have ever dreamed of when I was struggling daily, barely surviving my childhood. Giving them the world was all I ever wanted, and seeing them successful and happy made my life complete.

Jonathan came home for lunch every afternoon from his job as an attorney to eat with me. We would sit on the porch as he shared his day. Always the doting son. And humble. I often told him what a blessing he was to me, to which he would reply, "Dad, you're making me blush. I'm nobody special. I'm just me, just Jonathan."

I was prouder of him than I was of myself for surviving all the obstacles that had been thrown in his path throughout the years. Reaching over and hugging me before planting a kiss on my wrinkled, weathered forehead, he wiped a tear from his eye. "Dad, I know I've told you before, but I can't thank you enough for being my everything. I owe you my life. I love you to Pluto and back."

My job here was done. I knew Jonathan would be fine with his loving wife and children. It was time for me to go and find my mom and dad, and finally get the answers I had craved my whole life.

THE END

ABOUT THE AUTHOR

A California native, Donna Scuvotti resides in the Bay Area with her husband of twenty-seven years, three dogs, and a dog-savvy old persnickety cat. Having always been an avid reader, she let her imagination run wild when she wrote and released her debut novel, *Just Jonathan*, in 2021. Since that release, she has also written and released *Deadly Vendetta*. *Black Sheep* is her latest and most current work of fiction. She is a huge animal lover, passionate about animal rescue, and a beach enthusiast. When not writing, reading, or spending time with her family, you can find her traveling, searching for more story ideas.

Thank you for reading *Black Sheep*. To be notified about upcoming releases, sales, and other promotions, join Donna Scuvotti's mailing list at: info@donnascuvottiauthor.com

Or follow her author profile on Amazon. You can also connect through Instagram: @donnascuvottiauthor

REQUEST FOR REVIEWS

If you enjoyed this book, please leave a review on Amazon or Goodreads or tell your friends. Reviews and word-of-mouth recommendations are the best way to help readers find great new reads and to support independently published books and the authors who write them.

Follow her at: www.donnascuvottiauthor.com

www.ingramcontent.com/pod-product-compliance
Lightning Source LLC
Chambersburg PA
CBHW060547080526
44585CB00013B/476